Imagining the Course of Life

Imagining the Course of Life

Self-Transformation in a Shan
Buddhist Community

Nancy Eberhardt

University of Hawai'i Press
Honolulu

Library of Congress Cataloging-in-Publication Data

Eberhardt, Nancy.
  Imagining the course of life : self-transformation in a Shan Buddhist community /
Nancy Eberhardt.
      p.   cm.
  Includes bibliographical references and index.
  ISBN-13: 978-0-8248-2919-3 (hardcover : alk. paper)
  ISBN-10: 0-8248-2919-0 (hardcover : alk. paper)
  ISBN-13: 978-0-8248-3017-5 (pbk. : alk. paper)
  ISBN-10: 0-8248-3017-2 (pbk. : alk. paper)
  1. Shan (Asian people)—Thailand—Religion. 2. Buddhism—Thailand—Customs
and practices. 3. Shan (Asian people)—Thailand—Social life and customs. I. Title.
  DS570.S52E34 2006
  305.895'919—dc22

                                        2005024344

Designed by University of Hawai'i Press production staff

For my parents

Contents

Acknowledgments

THIS PROJECT HAS benefited greatly from the help of more people and organizations than I could possibly acknowledge in these pages, but I would like to single out a few to mention here. First and foremost, I would like to thank the Shan villagers who welcomed me into their midst for over three years and shared their lives with me. I have tried to render their words and actions in a way that is in keeping with the generosity and trust they extended toward me; I can only ask their indulgence for any errors or misinterpretations that may have nevertheless found their way into this manuscript. My education in Shan customs and thinking is certainly not over, and I look forward to their continued tutelage in the years to come.

The fieldwork that formed the basis for this book could not have been done without the helpful cooperation of the National Research Council of Thailand and the generous support of several granting agencies. Financial support at various stages was provided by the Fulbright-Hays Program, the Social Science Research Council, and the National Science Foundation. Knox College also provided help in the form of a faculty travel grant, as well as ongoing support since then of various kinds.

My intellectual debts are many. For introducing me to the Shan and encouraging me to pursue fieldwork in a Shan village, I want to thank Paul Durrenberger. It was also my early work with Paul that first prompted me to consider how the study of cognition and worldview might be situated in a broader political and economic context. I am also deeply indebted to F. K. Lehman, who gave me my first lessons in the Shan language and supervised my first extended fieldwork among the Shan. He has taught me countless things over the years, but, most germane to this project, I thank him for encouraging me to view Buddhism as a rich and living religion, one that is open to many interpretations. I am grateful to my friend Nikki Tannenbaum for her comments on an earlier draft of this manuscript, for her amiable companionship during a portion of my first field trip, and for endless conversations, in and out of the field, about all things Shan.

Although the process of making sense of my field notes and writing this book has been, for the most part, a rather solitary endeavor, there have been moments in the process when I have enjoyed the help and stimulation of others. During an early sabbatical, I was fortunate to be able to sit in on Sherry Turkle and Mitch Resnick's graduate seminar at MIT entitled "Evolving Conceptions of Systems and Self," where I first started thinking about ritual as a kind of "technology" that affects the self. Later, during a year spent in Amherst, Massachusetts, a weekly writing group with fellow Southeast Asianists Susan Darlington and Margaret Sarkissian provided fellowship and feedback (and deadlines!) that kept me writing. In its final stages, the book profited from a close reading by Steve Collins and thoughtful comments by Julia Cassaniti. I am grateful to them both.

Two anonymous reviewers of the manuscript provided many helpful suggestions that have greatly improved the book. I regret only that I did not have the time or expertise to follow up on even more of them. I would also like to thank Pamela Kelley of the University of Hawai'i Press for her early enthusiasm about the manuscript, her good advice during the publication process, and her patience as I struggled to make production deadlines. I am thankful, as well, for Rosemary Wetherold's careful and thoughtful copyediting and for her expert guidance during the final stages of the production process.

Others have provided help of a more diffuse nature. I thank Lorraine Aragon for sustained friendship and support over the years, as well as stimulating conversation about all aspects of Southeast Asia. Clark Cunningham, Janet Keller, David Plath, and Jacquie Hill have been among the many mentors and friends too numerous to mention whose ongoing interest in this project has encouraged me to continue the work.

My family deserves a special note of thanks. My parents, Odra and Jerry, and my brothers, Dan and David, have provided support in myriad ways that extends beyond the confines of this particular project but, without which, it never would have happened. My first husband, Roland Stone, accompanied me on my initial field trip and contributed mightily to its success, not least by his eager participation in all aspects of village life. His memory lives on among our many Shan friends. My son, Maury, who cannot remember a time when his mother was not working on this book, has been an enthusiastic cheerleader for the project, urging me to do things like bring a clipboard and a pad of paper to the basketball court so that I could "work on my book" while watching him play. Finally, my debt to my husband, Steve Cohn, is simply without measure. He has shared the fieldwork experience, provided thoughtful commentary on numerous drafts, and done more than his share of domestic tasks during those crunch times when deadlines loomed. More than once I wondered about the wisdom of pursuing a project that had already taken much longer to finish than I had anticipated; I owe its completion to his gentle prodding and unwavering conviction that it was worth the wait.

Note on Transcription

THE SHAN WORDS used in this book have been transcribed according to their modern spoken form. For those words that have well-known Thai equivalents, I have tried to indicate those as well. However, I have not attempted to indicate the five tonal markers that occur in each of these languages. Vowel length is undifferentiated in Shan except for the vowel *a*, written as *a* (short vowel) and *aa* (long vowel). In Thai, all vowels have a short and a long form and are indicated accordingly. The following is intended as a simple guide to the pronunciation of the Shan and Thai words that appear in the text; it is not an exhaustive account of Shan or Thai phonetics. All frequently used Shan terms can be found in the glossary.

Vowels

		Approximately the sound in . . .
i	As it occurs in open syllables in Shan, and in the long form (*ii*) in Thai	R*i*ta
i	As it occurs in closed syllables in Shan, and in the short form (*i*) in Thai	s*i*t
u		d*u*ne
ei		r*ei*gn
o		hell*o*
e		p*e*n
a		f*a*ther
ai		Th*ai*land
ao		La*o*s

continued on next page

Vowels *continued*

		Approximately the sound in . . .
au		c*au*ght
ae	Similar to the *a* in	b*a*nd
oe	Similar to the *eu* in the French	bl*eu*
ʉ	A high, back, unrounded vowel. There is no equivalent in European languages (the tongue is positioned as it is for *u*, but the lips are spread).	
aʉ	A diphthong formed by the combination of *a* and *ʉ*. (This and *ai* and *ao* are the only diphthongs in Shan. The diphthongs in Thai are *ia*, *ua*, and *ʉ*; they correspond, respectively, to the Shan vowels *ei*, *o*, and *oe*.)	

Consonants

Aspirated stops are distinguished from their unaspirated counterparts by the addition of *h* (*ph*, *th*, and *kh*). However, to avoid confusion with the English consonant blend *sh*, the aspirated Shan sibilant (which has no unaspirated counterpart) is written simply as *s*. The initial *ts* in Shan is similar to the middle consonant sound in "flo*ts*am"; it corresponds to the consonant *c* in Thai, which is similar to the middle consonant sound in "ju*dg*e."

Chapter 1

Introduction

Every story that begins with original innocence and privileges the
return to wholeness imagines the dream of life to be individuation,
separation, the birth of the self, the tragedy of autonomy, the fall
into writing, alienation . . .
>   DONNA HARAWAY, *Simians, Cyborgs, and Women:*
>   *The Reinvention of Nature*

To know who you are is to be oriented in moral space, a space in
which questions arise about what is good or bad, what is worth doing
and what not, what has meaning and importance for you and what is
trivial and secondary.
>   CHARLES TAYLOR, *Sources of the Self*

WHAT DOES IT MEAN to be successful, mature, or psychologically
healthy? Who gets to decide, and by what criteria? The ideas that people
hold about the course of human development and the nature of the self are
more than idle speculation. For those of us living in Europe or North America, Western theories of human development have had a profound impact
both on the external organization of our society and on our subjective experience of ourselves as particular individuals. Almost daily, some aspect of
our lives is touched by the body of knowledge that our recognized experts
have accumulated on what constitutes the "normal" course of cognitive, social, and moral growth. Although the assumptions underlying this body of
knowledge are rarely examined, they exert a powerful influence on such diverse aspects of social life as our philosophies of child rearing, the structure
of our schools, our timetables for career advancement and retirement, and
our methods for recognizing and treating mental illness. More than that,
they orient us toward certain goals and away from others; they inform our
retrospective judgments of our past deeds. In short, they define the moral
boundaries of a life well lived.

This book is about how people come to understand and find significance in the trajectory of a human life and how, in the process, they come to understand themselves. As such, it is a rather long answer to a series of questions that arose during an earlier research project on culture acquisition and moral development in a small Shan community in northwestern Thailand. At the time, I was an earnest young graduate student, anxious to show that the moral reasoning of Shan children was every bit as sophisticated and "developed" as that of European and North American children. To do this, I felt I needed to expose the inadequacies of the then current method for assessing moral development, a method that relied on standardized story problems depicting moral dilemmas. The project was successful, I think, in demonstrating the need to consider how the content of cultural beliefs affects moral reasoning, but it raised a host of other questions that I was unable to answer fully. Many of these pointed to the cultural significance of age and one's position in the life course—themes that seemed to figure prominently, and in unexpected ways, in Shan children's thinking about moral dilemmas.

Nor was this perceived connection between morality and the life course confined to children. Adults, for example, frequently remarked that it was impossible to follow the five Buddhist precepts (injunctions against killing, thieving, lying, intoxication, and improper sexual behavior) on a daily basis until one was old. Moral behavior had to be, in some sense, postponed until later in life. Although I eventually learned to appreciate the larger rhetorical context that helped make sense of such comments,[1] I continued to be struck by the references to age and one's stage in life whenever people talked about appropriate and inappropriate behavior. Unlike the familiar image of life's standard trajectory that Donna Haraway alludes to in the opening quotation, an alternative conception of the process of human development was hinted at by the people I spoke with, one that did not begin in innocence nor end in alienation.

At the same time, I gradually began to realize that Shan talk about age and the life course—including, and especially, any evaluative talk about people's behavior—was always predicated on a particular view of what it meant to be a person or, more specifically, a "normal" person. There, as here, "crazy" behavior was not always obvious to the untrained eye. If I wanted to understand Shan talk about appropriate and inappropriate behavior throughout the life course, I would have to learn more about their views of self and personhood, about what it meant, quite literally, to be a healthy, normal human being.

Thus, ten years after the original fieldwork that raised these issues, I returned to the same village in order to take a closer look at local beliefs and practices surrounding the life course and their implications for indigenous theories of the self. This book, the result of that inquiry, explores the ways in which Shan villagers' expectations regarding the course of human development are tied to concepts of self that are rehearsed in daily conversation, enacted in religious ritual, and embedded in the very structure of community social life.

It is a book that has taken a long time to write. As a result, it has been influenced by a large and somewhat unwieldy range of literature—some of it relatively recent, some no longer fashionable. These sources include not only the obviously relevant titles on similar topics that have appeared since I began this project, but also some seemingly unrelated but (to me) inspiring items I came across while teaching or writing about other things. It would be impossible to discuss all of these sources of influence adequately, but in the interest of providing the reader with some sense of the thinking that has informed this work, I will briefly discuss three of the major research traditions that have found their way, in one form or another, into this book: the literature on ethnopsychology and the life course, studies of Buddhism and religion in Southeast Asia, and the history of modern ideas of human nature and selfhood in Europe and North America. Additional sources are discussed in a more focused way in the chapters that follow. The chapter ends with an introduction to the Shan village that is the focus of this study.

Selves and Lives

While I was struggling to reconcile moral development theory with the demands of cultural difference (Eberhardt 1984), another rapprochement between anthropology and psychology was occurring in the form of ethnopsychology (White and Kirkpatrick 1985) and a closely related strand of psychological anthropology that dealt with "mind, self, and emotion" (Shweder and LeVine 1984). In some ways, the writers who were featured in these two important collections represented a new generation of researchers in psychological anthropology.[2] Although familiar by training with the older culture-and-personality approach (which appealed to differences in cultural institutions and socialization practices to explain the observed variation in personal styles), this generation questioned the cross-cultural validity of the very notion of personality and embraced the emerging consensus within the discipline that the assumptions underlying it were fundamentally flawed.

In its place, they emphasized the need to uncover the locally relevant categories (hence, "*ethno*psychology") that people employed to describe human nature and human variation. In local terms, what are people like? And what accounts for the differences in the way people behave? In contrast to the body of research done in the 1970s under the rubric "ethnoscience," which eschewed the study of affect and focused instead on cognition and on describing native systems of knowledge, this group of researchers enthusiastically embraced the project of exploring local understandings of emotions. But unlike earlier studies of affect that were psychoanalytically oriented, this time emotions were understood to belong not in the realm of private, individual (un)consciousness but, rather, in the realm of public, culturally organized social life.[3] Instead of looking for the effect of culture (understood as something external to the individual) *on* emotions that were "inside" a person, students of ethnopsychology have been more interested in how emotions emerge between two or more social players in the course of social interaction.

Methodologically, their increasing attention to discourse—that is, to larger units of talk and naturally occurring conversation, as opposed to discrete concepts or symbols—signaled a move away from a representational view of language (in which words, independent of their speaker, are thought to represent some aspect of reality) toward a view that is more oriented to social relations and praxis. What, they ask, is the pragmatic force of a given discourse about the nature of the self? What are the behavioral and ideological consequences of constructing the self in this way as opposed to some other way? Who ends up being empowered by such a formulation, and who is restrained? And how, finally, are such discourses used and manipulated during everyday social interactions? In a volume entitled *New Directions in Psychological Anthropology*, Geoffrey White put it this way:

> Once we view local discourses of person (including talk of "personality") as having directive force in shaping psychosocial reality, the constituents of those discourses assume a more central role in theories of person, action, and society. Talk of selves and persons everywhere constitutes a moral rhetoric—a way of explaining and evaluating everyday actions and events. Investigating the conceptual and institutional forces that sustain such talk and make it socially consequential requires a more broad study of discourse than has typically been pursued in individual-centered studies of cultural psychology. (1992, 33)

This inherently dialectical approach that sees meaning as emergent in social interaction makes it much more difficult to sustain the traditional dichotomies that separated the psychological from the cultural (or the individual from society), dichotomies upon which an earlier distinction between self and person was typically based (where "person" referred to a public role or socially recognized position, while the term "self" was reserved for reference to a more private and perhaps idiosyncratic subjectivity). Indeed, one of the hallmarks of this branch of psychological anthropology has been the repeated calls to dismantle one or another invidious dichotomy, such as individual/society, thought/feeling, or mind/body.

These dichotomies, it is argued, do not reflect natural or objective aspects of the human condition but, rather, are features of a particular ethnotheory about the nature of persons, namely, that of "the West," a situation described most vividly by Clifford Geertz:

> The Western conception of the person as a bounded, unique, more or less integrated motivational and cognitive universe, a dynamic center of awareness, emotion, judgment, and action organized into a distinctive whole and set contrastively both against other such wholes and against its social and natural background, is, however incorrigible it may seem to us, a rather peculiar idea within the context of the world's cultures. ([1974] 1984, 126)

Other societies, according to this view, may cultivate a sense of self that is not necessarily opposed to society and may, in fact, entail identification with it or some subgroup (such as an extended family or lineage). Further, the degree to which people identify with their internal thoughts and/or feelings (that is, the degree to which they are willing to be defined by them and to define others by theirs) is also quite variable, according to this view. Although some have continued to argue for a more universalist understanding of the self (e.g., Spiro 1986), there seems to be broad agreement that real and significant differences do exist in how people conceptualize personhood (Shweder and Bourne 1984). Where controversy remains is in deciding where precisely to locate those differences. Many have criticized the monolithic view of Western society implied by statements such as that of Geertz quoted above (e.g., Murray 1993), suggesting instead that multiple and perhaps contradictory views of the self are at work in all societies (including those of "the West") and, further, that these differences often fall along lines drawn by class, race, and gender.

One of the leading and, to me, most helpful voices in forging a synthesis between these concerns has been that of Catherine Lutz (see, for example, Lutz 1985 and Lutz and Abu-Lughod 1990). In her pathbreaking monograph, *Unnatural Emotions: Everyday Sentiments on a Micronesian Atoll and Their Challenge to Western Theory* (1988), Lutz' finely tuned analysis of how emotions are understood to work in a small island community in Micronesia provides a model for how to link sensitive, "site-specific" ethnography with insightful analyses of larger issues, including gender theory, that have a broad impact on the discipline. I have drawn on several aspects of her approach in my work with the Shan.

One is her urging that we become more self-conscious of the tacit basis of comparison (usually some version of the writer's own cultural background) that lurks behind much ethnographic description, and that we strive to make these assumptions explicit. In her own ethnography of Ifaluk emotional life (Lutz 1988), this task becomes the centerpiece—a comparative analysis and deconstruction of the term "emotion" and its links to gender constructions in American society and on the Micronesian island of Ifaluk. In my case, it has meant an effort to interrogate the concepts of "a life" and "development" by comparing what I have learned about Shan theories of self and human development with those in several other societies, including my own. While the main thrust of this book is clearly about Shan culture and society, I have tried to insert comparative examples, where relevant, in order to highlight both our tacit assumptions about these concepts and what is distinctive about the Shan case.

A related and welcome aspect of Lutz' work is her willingness to consider how the particular understandings of self and emotion that prevail on Ifaluk are grounded in concrete aspects of the social structure, gender relations, and material conditions of life in that community. Although hers was an early voice on this, it has since been joined by others such as Kondo (1990), Mageo (1998), and Holland et al. (1998), all of whom insist upon the crucial role played by power relations in the fashioning of emotion, gender, selves, and lives. If people's understandings of themselves and their emotions are truly emergent in the process of social interaction, then it is not sufficient to explain their logical coherence as abstract conceptual systems. Rather, one must show how such understandings arise in everyday life, whose purposes they serve, and how they are maintained, deployed, contested, and revised. With this in mind, I have tried to link the particular conceptions of self and human development that currently prevail in the Shan village that is the focus of this study to an identifiable constellation of social arrangements regarding the organization of work, gender, and the household.

Finally, and most fundamentally, Lutz' work has been useful for this project because it deals explicitly with people's ideas about human development and the life course.[4] Her work demonstrates that looking at a society's indigenous theories of human development is often a particularly effective way to find out about local constructions of self and personhood, including people's ideas about the causes and effects of human behavior. Drawing on her experience in Micronesia, Lutz has suggested that one of the advantages of examining people's ideas about the life course is that, in most societies, the course of human development is explicitly conceptualized, classified, and explained (Lutz 1985, 58). She goes on to note:

> The ways in which children and adults are seen to differ will often reveal important ethno-theoretical dimensions that might otherwise go undiscovered. In addition, the process by which development is thought to occur is revealed in talk about the life course, including conceptions about which human behaviors are changeable and about how that change may be caused. Such conceptions thereby often point to the hypothesized origins of behavior. (Ibid., 59)

The suggestion that a link exists between concepts of self and concepts of human development is one I have adopted as an organizing frame for this project as well.

Other writers, who do not necessarily look at the life course as a whole but focus on particular segments of it, have also been significant influences. David Plath, for example, observing the numerous studies of childhood socialization and the dearth of work on adult development, has long urged anthropologists to stop treating human development as if it were something that ended with adolescence. His nuanced study of adult development in modern Japan (Plath 1980) inspired me to listen for "rhetorics of maturity" in Shan talk and to be alert to cultural differences in "archetypes of growth." Similarly, the engaging collection of papers in Richard Shweder's edited volume on middle age (1998) has reinforced my inclination to focus on the culturally constructed aspects of developmental stages and to think about how the Shan experience of midlife compares to others. Although I came to it much later in the project, Sarah Lamb's ethnography of aging and gender in North India (2000) has been stimulating on multiple levels. Her emphasis on the benefits of using age as a category of analysis is one I find especially congenial to the approach I have taken in this book.

The Southeast Asian Context

As the examples above suggest, while numerous studies of self and human development have been conducted in the nearby areas of East Asia, South Asia, and the Pacific, there has been an almost complete lack of research on this topic among the societies of mainland Southeast Asia.[5] This is all the more surprising, given that societies in island Southeast Asia have provided the material for some of the pioneering studies of cultural constructions of self and the life course, as well as more recent work (e.g., H. Geertz 1959; C. Geertz 1973, [1974] 1984; Rosaldo 1980; Keeler 1983, 1987; Broch 1990; Wikan 1991; and Hollan and Wellenkamp 1996). In contrast, similar topics on the mainland have not received sustained treatment, showing up only in passing or for the space of a chapter in works devoted primarily to ritual, religion, and worldview. In fact, the only book-length treatment of an eth-nopsychological topic that pertains to the culture of lowland Buddhist soci-eties on the mainland is Collins' incisive textual analysis of images and ideas about "selves" and "persons" found in Buddhist scriptures (1982), a work that does not pretend to be an empirical study of actual beliefs and practices. Indeed, Collins notes in the introduction to his book, "There is a good book waiting to be written on the relation between the psychological universe of the Buddhist Canon and the indigenous psychology of 'popular' culture in 'Buddhist' countries" (ibid., 20).

What has, however, received considerable anthropological attention on the mainland, particularly in Thai studies, is precisely the study of ritual, re-ligion, and worldview, especially among those ethnic groups (the vast major-ity) who consider themselves Buddhist. Not all of this extensive and varied literature is germane, of course, to a study of self and human development, and it will be simplest to discuss the relevant comparative points as they arise in conjunction with the Shan material. Nevertheless, a few orienting obser-vations about Buddhist studies and the anthropological approach to religion are appropriate at the outset.

First, what is the status of Buddhist doctrine in everyday religious life, and how should we regard any discrepancies between what is stated in the scriptures and what is said by contemporary Buddhists? While an earlier generation of writers on this subject may have identified the canon of Bud-dhist scriptures as the "true" Buddhism and tended to view any deviation from this in actual practice as aberrant and inferior, contemporary scholar-ship has pointed to several reasons why the doctrines as stated in scripture cannot be taken as equivalent to what the average person knows, believes, or understands. For one thing, communities often choose to highlight dif-ferent aspects of the canon (elaborating this but not that portion of the scripture into a ritual object, a ceremony, a basis for popular legend, etc.). In addition, religious ideas are used selectively by individuals, sometimes strategically, for their own ends. Further, ideas, once selected by individu-als for strategic use or by communities for cultural elaboration, must be (continuously) interpreted, and this process of interpretation and reinter-pretation, spanning a series of generations, offers manifold opportunities for creative revision and amendment.

This same process occurs in urban areas and in rural villages, in areas close to the institutional centers of religious power and in those far removed from it. Hence, the Buddhism of the cities or of Bangkok is no closer to some hypothesized true Buddhism than is the Buddhism of the countryside (nor, as is sometimes thought, is the rural version more authentic than what is seen as a corrupted urban version). Rather, they are simply the results of different sets of local actors applying received Buddhist traditions to somewhat different circumstances. Hence, throughout this book, I have been unwilling to privilege doctrinal or canonical Buddhism (that is, the Buddhism of the religious scriptures as interpreted by religious specialists) over customary practice and local interpretations (see Gombrich 1971, Lehman 1972, and Collins 1982 for insightful discussions of these issues). At the same time, I am convinced of the centrality of many Buddhist ideas—when defined in local terms—for people's everyday thinking.

A case in point is the Buddhist doctrine of *anattā,* or "not-self," which teaches that the belief in any sort of enduring soul or essence for individual human beings is an illusion. How can I possibly write a book about Shan conceptions of self if they do not believe they have one? The key here is to attend to how the teaching of *anattā* is actually understood and used by laypeople. In the community I worked in, as in many other Buddhist communities (see, for example, Spiro 1970, Gombrich 1971, and Tannenbaum 1995), the belief in some aspect of personhood that is enduring and that even survives the transformation of death is commonplace. To allow for this, *anattā* is defined variously as "having no control over oneself," "being unable to keep oneself from changing," and so on.[6]

This does not mean that more sophisticated understandings of *anattā* have no effect on local understandings. It simply acknowledges that, as with any complicated system of thought, there are specialist and lay understandings of important concepts. To ask, for example, what the average Shan villager knows about the doctrine of *anattā* is akin, in my view, to asking what the average person in Chicago knows about Einstein's theory of relativity. Each has at least heard of it and believes it to be true, but they do not pretend to understand it fully, if at all. If questioned about it, a few people will be able to give a satisfactory account, but most will repeat an abbreviated version that they've been told and then direct you to the appropriate local specialist (monk or physicist, as the case may be). Meanwhile, they go about their lives, secure in the knowledge that someone, somewhere understands these things, while relying for their own needs on a less complicated and more intuitive understanding of the way things work. Does this mean that our hypothetical Shan villager is not a Buddhist or that our friend in Chicago does not participate in the culture of science? Not at all. But it does mean that we cannot define Buddhism or any other complex tradition solely on the basis of what its virtuosi believe and do.

A related issue has to do with the use of Buddhist discourse and Buddhist ritual forms to legitimize social and political inequalities both within and between communities and social groups. As many researchers have documented, Buddhism has been a powerful tool of state building in Thailand, used both to reinforce the hegemony of Bangkok and to help justify local inequalities (see, for example, Tambiah 1976, Reynolds 1978, Keyes 1987, O'Connor 1990, and Tannenbaum 1995). As someone who has worked on the periphery of the Thai state, I have absorbed certain lessons from these writings that are reflected in this work, including a certain degree of suspicion toward cultural forms emanating from the center and a reluctance to assume that the dominant religious institutions can adequately encompass local meanings. At the same time, I recognize (and try to show) that this is a stance Shan villagers cannot always afford to take. To the extent that any particular version of Buddhism enjoys prestige and authority in the larger culture, adherence to which is reinforced by certain incentives and sanctions, it becomes, among other things, a hegemonic discourse that can perhaps be resisted (or creatively interpreted) but not ignored.

Finally, how should we regard the non-Buddhist elements that exist in the religious life of any given community? In Shan villages, as elsewhere in rural Southeast Asia, rituals involving local "spirits" are especially commonplace and sometimes quite elaborate. Are we dealing with two separate religions here, or a syncretic form that incorporates elements from different traditions, or something else entirely? If such practices are mentioned in the scriptures and occur wherever there are functioning Buddhist communities, are these elements really non-Buddhist? When our informants say that they are, what do they mean? Many writers have sought to uncover the underlying principles and logic that would account for the totality of observed ritual forms, and they have offered various strategies for reconciling the presence of so-called animistic elements with a more translocal Buddhism (see, for example, Tambiah 1970, Lehman 1972, Mulder 1979, Davis 1984, Wijeyewardene 1986, and Tannenbaum 1995). From this work, I have learned much about the common content and range of religious belief and practice in Thailand, and this knowledge has guided my inquiry into local understandings of selves and human development. Tannenbaum's work on Shan religion and overall Shan ethnography (1987, 1989, 1990) has been particularly helpful in this regard.

However, there is an additional problem entangled in this muddle that has to do with the very category of "religion." What makes spirit-related practices a "problem" is our assumption that they, like Buddhist practices, fall unambiguously into the category of religion (thus necessitating some sort of reconciliation between the two). But this assumption may derive more from the society of the researcher, where there is often a marked distinction between the religious and the secular (and between the supernatural and the natural), than from anything found in the society being investigated. Sorting this out will have impacts beyond the Buddhism/animism conundrum. In the

Shan case, for example, it may well be that spirit-related beliefs and practices more closely approximate the category of natural science than that of religion.

There is, in short, a solid ethnographic literature on ritual, religion, and worldview in Thai studies, but I think this material will have to be approached from a somewhat different angle if it is to be useful for a study of self, human development, and, more broadly, indigenous psychology. By what criteria does one separate spiritual, mental, and physical well-being? How does knowledge about the world (including cosmological knowledge) impinge on knowledge about people and human nature (i.e., on indigenous psychologies)? Is there a nonarbitrary way (i.e., a culturally motivated way) to separate the religious from the nonreligious? If we leave these issues unexamined—or, worse, assume they are irrelevant—we may simply further reify the dichotomies between the individual and society, and between culture and psychology. Instead, we need to attend to the way putatively religious concerns enter into people's everyday talk about human nature, emotions, mental health, and so on, and to consider how (and when) the very notion of a separate psychological realm of human experience has itself been constructed.

This is an inquiry that is fundamentally ethnographic, one that requires the production of detailed descriptions of alternative formulations of selves and their development, and how these formulations are related to, among other things, what some might call religious talk and/or ritual practice. Hence, although a fair amount of space is devoted to it, this book is concerned not with Shan ritual, religion, and worldview per se but, rather, with the way such beliefs and practices are used, sometimes strategically, in people's constructions of themselves and with what they might reveal about Shan theories of human development and human nature.

The Comparative and Historical Context

Although the historical research on this topic has not consistently been in dialogue with the anthropological research, it should be, for they have much to offer one another. By asking similar questions about the history of concepts of personhood and the life course in Europe and North America, cultural historians have begun the task of documenting when, where, and how the seemingly monolithic Western notion of self was constructed. Like those engaged in ethnopsychological research, historians have made a case for how our subjective sense of self—in particular, the sense of being an individual with an inner life—has varied through time, along with our perspective on different segments of the life course (especially childhood), but these differences have been theorized differently from those reported in the cross-cultural record. Where anthropologists have traditionally taken a culturalist approach to explaining difference, appealing to the logic of the cultural system and the tacit assumptions of the prevailing religion or worldview to explain any given view of self, historians have been more likely to focus on social and economic institutions that have been transformed by historical events as the key responsible agents. Among those who have investigated the history of European and American notions of self and personhood, the critical social institution has been the changing family structure, and the relevant historical event, frequently described as a watershed, has been the industrial revolution.[7]

The portion of this scholarship that has most influenced my thinking for this project is the work that has been done on changes in the family structure of the urban middle class that occurred in Europe and North America in the nineteenth century, and their consequences for modern ideas of selfhood and human nature (see especially Zaretsky 1976 and Demos [1978] 1997). This body of research is helpful because it illustrates how a particular ethnotheory of self and human development (the paradigmatic "Western" view of the person) grew out of a specific set of social and economic conditions. These conditions can be briefly summarized as follows.

Due to people's increased involvement with factory work under industrialization and the gradual removal of both children and women from that arena (a process that occurred to varying degrees and at different rates for different social classes), "work" eventually became separated to an unprecedented degree from the rest of everyday life, including domestic life, while the family retreated into a previously unknown level of privacy. "Home" became the haven or refuge from work in a world that was increasingly viewed as heartless and corrupt, and women were assigned the new task of "emotion management" in the household, providing emotional succor and repair for family members engaged in work outside the home. Those who worked under the alienating conditions of industrial labor did not identify with their jobs, and any notion of authenticity, including the concept of self, became identified with home. Home was the new site of "personal life," the place where the "true self" could be cultivated and displayed.

Gender stereotyping and culturally exaggerated differences in gender roles became the norm, with men and women each becoming closely associated with their newly created separate spheres. The removal of children from the workplace encouraged a new view of them as "tender" and in need of nurturing and cultivation. This, coupled with the new emphasis on "character education" that would prepare them for work under these vastly altered circumstances, created a child-centered family with an increased emphasis on "quality parenting," a concept that eventually translated into an ideology of full-time mothering, supplemented by a plethora of new advice manuals for parents written by (mostly male) child "experts" (Ariès 1962; Demos [1978] 1997; Schnog 1997; Hareven 2000).

The consequences of this separation of work and domestic life were profound. As the opposition between what was now understood as an authentic self and an artificial, "man-made" society became increasingly polarized around the turn of the century, a new ethnopsychology arose and eventually gained popularity under the writings of Sigmund Freud (see especially Freud [1930] 1961). Society, or "civilization," was necessary but repressive of the authentic self, which was now conceived as harboring antisocial tendencies. The resulting tensions between self and society, which were increasingly seen as natural, spawned a view of the self as having interiority, depth, or emotional complexity—themes that emerged in late nineteenth-century and early twentieth-century literature, art, and academic writing (see the collection of papers in Pfister and Schnog 1997 for examples and an overview of this period).

Views of the life course also changed, in response both to the above factors and to changing demographic factors (such as longer life span and decreased infant mortality rates). Childhood, now recognized as a special stage of life, became prolonged; adolescence was given new significance; "middle age" was identified for the first time; and the status and authority of grandparents was greatly reduced (Ariès 1962; Tufte and Myerhoff 1979; Lowry 1997; Shweder 1998; Hareven 2000).

Obviously, this sketchy history does not do justice to the subtle arguments presented in the sources mentioned above, nor does it begin to capture the complexity of the changes that occurred in people's conceptualizations of themselves and their expectations regarding the process of human development, but I hope it at least suggests the sorts of structural factors that might impinge on any society's leading concepts of self and the life course. For those of us who have conducted research in communities that are not yet fully industrialized, it raises important questions about the connections we might investigate between the organization of work, gender, and domestic life, on the one hand, and people's conceptualizations of themselves as persons with a certain kind of life trajectory, on the other. In my description of Shan village life below, and in the chapters that follow, I have tried to highlight those aspects of social and economic organization that are implicated by this account.

The People and the Place

The people called Shan by English speakers, and who call themselves Tai,[8] do not fit easily into the categories most often invoked to describe ethnic groups in Southeast Asia. Not quite "hill people" and not quite "valley people," they have chosen to live in the narrow upland valleys halfway up the mountainsides. Originating in the northeastern part of Burma (Myanmar) known as the Shan States, Shan have been migrating out of Burma and into the northern and northwestern provinces of neighboring Thailand for well over a hundred years—a process that continues today and has, in fact, been accelerating due to the ongoing political troubles in Burma. Although they are one of the most populous ethnic groups in Burma, in Thailand they are an ethnic minority, living on the periphery of the Thai state. They share the border area with other ethnic minorities—such as the Karen, the Hmong, and the Lahu—most of whom live farther up the mountains, where they have traditionally practiced swidden (slash-and-burn) agriculture and have followed their own local religious traditions. The Shan of this region have made their share of swiddens too but prefer whenever possible to cultivate the narrow upland valleys with irrigated rice.

Unlike most other highlanders in the area, Shan are practitioners of Theravāda Buddhism[9] and, as such, share a certain cultural affinity with their lowland neighbors elsewhere in the region, including the Burmese and the Thai. However, like all nominally Buddhist communities in Southeast Asia, they operate within their own local traditions of interpretation that are linked in intimate and complicated ways with other practices, including beliefs and rituals related to spirits. Living in the hills as they do, and yet practicing Theravāda Buddhism and wet-rice agriculture, Shan occupy an interesting social niche that participates in both the upland and lowland cultural traditions of Southeast Asia.

The specific community that is the focus of this book is a place I will call Baan Kaung Mu (a pseudonym), a well-established Shan village in Mae Hong Son Province, Thailand, where I have lived for a total of three years. Two of these were in 1979–1981, when I was conducting research on culture acquisition and moral development, and the third year was in 1990–1991, when I focused more explicitly on the concerns that led to this book. Although the community witnessed significant changes during the interim, as well as since then, many features of the place have persisted.

Situated in one of the many narrow valleys that line the hills of the province, Baan Kaung Mu is about twenty kilometers from Mae Hong Son town, the provincial capital, and about a two-day walk from the Burmese border. Teakwood and split-bamboo houses form a dense cluster pressed into the side of a west-facing mountain, leaving the maximum possible amount of precious irrigable land free for cultivation. In 1980, Baan Kaung Mu still had no electricity or running water, cooking was done over a wood fire, and all but a handful of the 69 houses were built on stilts in the traditional way, using the

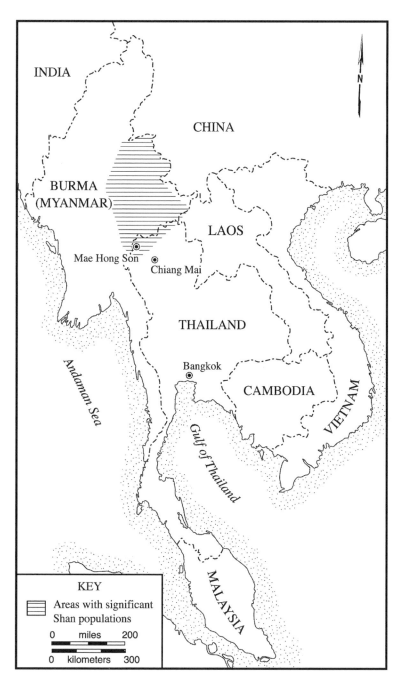

Mainland Southeast Asia. (Map prepared by Susan Brannock-Gaul.)

KEY

Areas with significant
Shan populations

0   miles   200

0   kilometers   300

space underneath to stable water buffalo, oxen, pigs, and chickens. By 1990 the population had grown from 300 to close to 400 people arranged in 99 households, many more of which had adopted the Northern Thai style of architecture that features a cemented ground floor used as a living area. Charcoal had replaced firewood as the fuel of choice in most kitchens, supplemented now by an electric rice cooker, but the houses were still arranged in fenced compounds along dusty paths lined with carefully tended flowers, bushes, and lime and coconut trees.

Most of the residents of Baan Kaung Mu continue to be born and raised in this or other nearby villages, although a few more come each year from the Shan States in Burma. A handful of Northern Thai and Red Karen have also married into the village and settled here. In addition to the houses, there is also an elementary school with six grades (where children are taught to read and write not in Shan but in the Central Thai language[10]), a small health clinic staffed by part-time health workers from town, a few small stores, and the occasional impromptu noodle stand, set up to sell lunch.

Near the center of the village within a clearly demarcated area lies the local Buddhist monastery. In 1980 it was home to a rustic but graceful old temple, or "preaching hall," where services were held and where the monks and novices lived. There were also three smaller and simpler dwellings for the three *mae khaao*, or Buddhist nuns (all local women); a modest but well-kept pagoda; a banyan tree; a shrine for a place-spirit; and the foundation for an ordination hall the villagers were building. By 1990 the ordination hall was complete, and the old preaching hall had been replaced by a larger but otherwise similar building—all built by hand using local labor—with beautifully polished teakwood floors that felt cool and smooth on one's bare feet, an open-air pavilion style of architecture that captured each passing breeze, and several imposing new Buddha statues, brightly covered with gold leaf and donated by well-wishers from Bangkok who had come to "make merit" in this upcountry temple.

During the years I lived in Baan Kaung Mu, the population of the temple grounds fluctuated, but there was always at least one monk and sometimes two in residence. Novice monks, and younger boys studying to become novices, were present less regularly and for shorter periods. Shan religious services follow a lunar calendar, observing the day of the new moon, the full moon, and the half-moons between each of these as *wan sin*, or precept days, something similar to a Sabbath.[11] A set of standard Buddhist holidays (most of which fall on either a full moon or a new moon *wan sin*) are celebrated locally, often including elaborate festivities at the temple the evening before and food preparations in the temple kitchen that go on well into the night.

Unscheduled, household-sponsored ceremonies (such as offerings for a

View of Baan Kaung Mu in 1980, with pagoda in foreground and monastery grounds toward the right.

The same area in 1990, with new buildings on the monastery grounds.

deceased relative, scripture readings upon the donation of a new manuscript, and so on) are also often held at the temple, especially if the entire village has been invited to attend. If a smaller ceremony is held in a person's home, villagers may nevertheless rely upon the temple's supply of dishes, teapots, and cookware. Beyond its use for religiously oriented activities, the temple also serves as a sort of community center for many other activities. Travelers passing through may spend the night there. The public address system is used to make village-wide announcements on a variety of subjects. Village meetings are also usually held at the temple.

Surrounding this cluster of houses, monastery, and other buildings that make up the village itself lies a patchwork of cultivated fields, gardens, and forested hills. Although the forest is still used as a supplementary food source (for gathered plants, mushrooms, small game, and so on), and gardens are an important source of fruits and vegetables for home consumption, the economy of Baan Kaung Mu continues to be based on the production of irrigated rice, an activity in which almost every household is vitally involved.[12] A generation ago, village production was geared almost completely toward subsistence agriculture, although even then sesame (grown on hillside swiddens) served as a major cash crop. Current production is still focused primarily on subsistence, but the developing infrastructure of the region has strengthened the village's market orientation. During the past twenty-five years, Baan Kaung Mu farmers have produced soybeans, garlic, and sesame for sale as well as for domestic consumption. Construction companies with government contracts for road building and repair in areas near Baan Kaung Mu provide some villagers with cash earnings from day labor (an opportunity that has also attracted some workers from the Shan States), and young people of both sexes increasingly seek temporary wage labor in Mae Hong Son town and other urban areas. For those who remain in the village, though, cash is not generally plentiful. After the sale of a cash crop, a substantial portion of the earnings is usually invested immediately in clothing and household staples, with another portion set aside for religious observances.

The exceptions to this state of affairs are the schoolteachers, whose government salary provides them with a steady source of capital. Although the number of schoolteachers residing in the village has fluctuated during the years since I began conducting research there (some commute from Mae Hong Son town or live in state-sponsored housing on the school ground itself), those who do opt to live in the village have invariably used their access to capital resources to operate small shops selling sundry food and household items. Two or three other households have, from time to time, operated diesel-powered rice mills, another source of cash income.

Shan women transplanting rice seedlings in the gently terraced rice paddies that surround much of the village.

Although located in one of the least developed areas of Thailand, Baan Kaung Mu is not without links to the rest of the world. In 1976 a new, all-weather road was built, linking the village to Mae Hong Son town and providing reliable, year-round access to it for the first time. When I first arrived a couple of years later, villagers were in the process of making a series of local adjustments occasioned by this new access to the town's hospital, post office, larger schools, daily produce market, and social/ceremonial life. More attention was being given to cash crops, for example; more people were trying to buy motorcycles; and the one local owner of a "minibus" (a converted pickup truck outfitted with two benches in the back) had begun to do a brisk business of daily runs to and from town. By 1990 several drivers were servicing the area, some making more than one trip to town a day, and those families who could afford it were often bypassing the village school altogether and sending their children to town to begin their education. Tourist activity in the province, especially in Mae Hong Son town, has also increased dramatically, bringing villagers into much more frequent contact with foreign guests. Meanwhile, caravan trade back and forth across the Burma border continues, bringing with it more news and occasional refugees from the troubled area in the eastern Shan States.

In addition to these sources of contact and information, there are the news media. During my first stay in Baan Kaung Mu, most households relied on shared newspapers and on battery-operated radios, which provided access to news and other programming in the national language, Central Thai. When I returned in 1990, nearly every house had electricity, and a few had purchased television sets that everyone was invited to watch, giving villagers access not only to national and international news but also to the broader commercial world of urban middle-class life as depicted in soap operas, sitcoms, and advertisements filmed in Bangkok.

In short, during the time I have been observing it, the village economy could be described as "in transition," moving toward greater engagement with regional and national markets and toward greater disparities in wealth between households. In 1991 most of the households owned at least some rice land, although the size of their landholdings varied considerably. All engaged in both the production of rice for subsistence and the growing of soybeans or garlic for cash crops, supplemented by wage labor when such jobs were available. Although some households were certainly on the margin, the village was not, on the whole, poor, and most people had at least some discretionary income. Much of this discretionary income was used for the increasingly available consumer items sent out from the urban areas, but a significant portion was set aside for traditional Buddhist rituals and merit-making ceremonies.

Finally, because Baan Kaung Mu is the "county seat" (*tambon* village) of a cluster of villages, its headman is also the *kamnan* (*tambon* head). He and his assistants attend monthly meetings in Mae Hong Son town with provincial officials of the Thai government and return with information on national and regional events. This information is communicated to the rest of the community in village meetings that are attended by both men and women— at least one adult representative from each household.

As this last statement suggests, the household is a significant administrative unit in village social organization. A household representative must be sent to all community workdays as well as to village meetings. Further, participation in certain village-wide rituals entails the contribution of an offering, or "tax," from each household, along with labor. Households are also the main unit of production and consumption in the local economy, pooling the income from their farm labor for the most part and making joint purchases for the household. However, individuals retain the right to control any wealth or property that they bring into a household through inheritance or their own efforts. Women, for example, may own land in their own name and decide independently of their husbands, fathers, or brothers what they want to do with it.

Although an old couple (or even a single widow or widower) sometimes chooses to live alone in a separate household, most households in Baan

Kaung Mu consist of at least two generations—a married couple and their children, often supplemented by additional relatives on a temporary or relatively permanent basis. Since kinship is reckoned bilaterally, these "extra" people may be relatives from either side of the family, including the husband's or wife's parents, the spouse and children of one or more of the couple's grown offspring, or one or more collateral relatives of either the husband or wife. The availability of reliable birth control since the 1970s has resulted in smaller families, but villagers still find it convenient to have three generations living close to one another—under the same roof, if possible. Grandparents who are willing to stay home while their adult children go to work in the fields all day can care for young children, perform useful tasks around the house, or simply housesit *(pan hoen)*—a valued service, for villagers do not like to leave their houses unattended, if they can help it.

Children, for their part, can run errands, help with meal preparation, care for younger siblings, do laundry, carry water from the well, and perform other relatively simple but valued tasks. As a result, children are sometimes invited to change households in order to help another relative or, on occasion, even a nonrelative. The children themselves are often allowed to determine their own choice of residence. Some children, for example, decide to leave their parents' household (perhaps temporarily) and join that of their grandparent(s). Others may leave to join an older married sibling who needs help with laundry and child care. When a couple divorces (which is easily done and common), their children usually end up living with the wife (and/or her mother), although the children continue to visit regularly at their father's house. Mothers generally encourage this contact as a way of inducing the father to help buy clothes and other necessities for the child.

Furthermore, there is a considerable amount of visiting back and forth between households during the day, especially in any given neighborhood. Shan houses are built with a large open porch that faces a courtyard in the front of the house. Since these porches function as work areas for everyday household tasks—such as food preparation, tool repair, craft production, and so on—it is easy for passersby to see what is going on and to initiate a conversation with whoever is at home. Houses are close enough that neighbors can often carry on conversations in a normal tone of voice without leaving their house. (In fact, if one wishes not to be overheard, one must drop one's voice to a whisper.) Yet it would be misleading to portray the family as the site of personal life. Socializing between nonrelatives is, on the whole, a same-sex affair in Baan Kaung Mu—men visit men, and women visit women. This carries over into other activities as well: people generally work, travel, and sit in same-sex groupings at rituals, at village meetings, when participating in group agricultural labor, and on other public occasions. Hence, one's marital status and household membership are largely irrelevant for everyday work and socializing, and women, in particular, are not isolated in any way.

In short, household membership is fluid and, to a significant degree, voluntary. During the course of a lifetime, most people have the experience of living in more than one household and learn to feel comfortable in many more. Daily life is structured by a combination of the annual cycle of agricultural work and the annual round of religious ceremonies, and what leisure time there is occurs at the interstices of these events. When activities permit, the preferred form of recreation is still visiting at each others' houses, and it is there—in the intimate context of peoples' homes and among friends—that much of the data for this book was collected.

The Fieldwork Context and This Project

During my 1990–1991 stay in Baan Kaung Mu, I rented a room in a house that belonged to a middle-aged widow, who I will call Aunt Ying, a strong and energetic woman who still worked her own land and was active in all temple affairs. Her son and daughter-in-law, whom I was close to from my previous stay in Baan Kaung Mu, used to live with her in this house, but they now lived independently in another part of the village, making it possible for Aunt Ying to rent some space to me. I hired a young woman from the neighborhood, Nang Kaew, to help with cooking and light housekeeping, and she decided to move in with us as well. This proved fortuitous on many counts, as Nang Kaew quickly became something more akin to a research assistant, accompanying me on my daily outings, "translating" for me (from more advanced Shan to simpler Shan phrases) when my language facility needed a boost, and offering counsel of all sorts. More than this, she soon became my closest friend, a relationship nurtured by constant companionship and late-night chats as we fell asleep on mattresses laid out next to each other on the floor, just outside Aunt Ying's bedroom.

In fact, my decision to use pseudonyms in this book has been a difficult one, largely because it prevents me from being able to thank and acknowledge people like "Nang Kaew" by name. Pseudonyms are not as necessary in a book that is focused more on concepts and events than on individual persons. But in order to provide a credible account of Shan thinking about selves and how they develop, I needed to talk about real individuals in some detail. Although some of these people may have liked to have seen their real name in print here, I wanted to allow those who might prefer to stay anonymous the possibility of doing so. Pseudonyms for everyone seemed the best way to accomplish this. At the same time, I am acutely aware that this decision is largely symbolic, since anyone persistent enough would be able to figure out the location of this village. I have therefore occasionally changed a few non-essential details about the persons described, in the hope of providing them (or their descendants) with a kind of plausible deniability, should they wish to invoke it.

As recent scholarship in anthropology has observed, the results of any given fieldwork project are affected in highly significant ways by the particular historical circumstances in which it was conducted, including many aspects that are not wholly within one's control. These include the gender or racial dynamics of the community, the local attitudes toward foreigners in general and anthropologists in particular, and myriad idiosyncratic and/or random events that can and do affect one's access to people, information, and particular settings. In order to provide some context for the account that follows, I will try to specify some of the factors that may have affected my results.

My situation in Baan Kaung Mu was a lucky one in several respects. First, in addition to being well known from my prior stay in the village, I was the indirect beneficiary of the rapport that had been established by three previous anthropologists who had worked elsewhere in Mae Hong Son Province: my former teachers F. K. Lehman and E. Paul Durrenberger and my good friend Nicola Tannenbaum. Their legacy meant that I was the recipient of the general goodwill, trust, and tolerant bemusement that villagers had come to extend toward the anthropological profession. Few anthropologists labor under such benevolent circumstances; I count myself among the fortunate.

Second, I think villagers' expectations of me were also colored, in part, by their situation as an ethnic minority in a multiethnic state. In this context (and despite my repeated attempts to explain my research agenda), I was widely understood to be there in order to record "traditional Shan customs," and people were constantly coming by my house to call me to witness some event that they deemed worthy of my camera and notebook. This was consistent with a rising self-consciousness among some of the more educated and traveled villagers about Shan culture, a process that was cross-fertilized by the increasing numbers of Shan refugees from Burma whose presence (including any perceived variations in style of speech, dress, customs, and so on) complicated local understandings of tradition and raised curiosity about authenticity and origins. My job, in this context, was to record the "real" Shan customs for posterity—an impossible task, of course, but one that they seemed to perceive as an honorable endeavor.

Third, although I made consistent efforts to get to know as wide a range of people as possible, my gender undoubtedly had some effect on this, making it easier for me to talk to women and for them to feel comfortable talking with me. Men who were locally recognized leaders or ritual experts were important exceptions to this, for it was understood that I would have a reason to visit and interview them, and some of my most important informants fell into this category. And inevitably, when I visited many of my female friends, their husbands, fathers, or brothers were often around and entered freely into the conversation. In addition, those teenage boys and young men who, as children, had been some of my major informants during my first field trip in Baan Kaung Mu and with whom I seemed to have developed a permanent "older sister" status, also remained comfortable chatting with me. Finally, time spent participating in group agricultural labor, riding back and forth to town in the local minivan, or traveling with groups of villagers to ceremonies and events in other villages provided further opportunities to talk with men in a relaxed setting. Nevertheless, it is probably true that my most intimate conversations were with other women, because it was possible for me to do things with them that were culturally impossible for me to do with men, such as to be alone in a house with them, to spend the night with them while traveling, to work with large groups of them during sex-segregated work parties, and so on.

My marital status was probably also significant. During my first stay in Baan Kaung Mu, I was a new bride accompanied by my husband, a status that made me privy to a kind of joking, sexual banter frequently carried on among young, married women (and not done with unmarried women who are presumed to be innocent of such knowledge). When I returned in 1990, I had been widowed and then remarried, events that villagers were eager to talk with me about.

Finally, and perhaps most significant for this particular project, my continued correspondence with people from the village in the intervening years, along with our mutual sharing of major life events—joyful and sorrowful—that occurred along the way, meant that by the time I returned ten years later, we had shared a significant chunk of our lives, a process that has continued right up to today. We have mutually advised, comforted, and congratulated each other on a wide variety of events, a process that, more than once, has prompted me to question my own first reactions. It has also made me more self-conscious about my own particular ethnotheory of self, emotions, and human development. Under Shan tutelage, I have learned much about the possibilities for how to interpret life's vicissitudes and have come to appreciate and value the alternatives they have to offer.

It was in this context, then, that I undertook my investigations. In the chapters that follow, I attempt to lay out a view of human development and the life course that is rooted in indigenous practices, discourses, and—to the extent they can be inferred—beliefs. It is based on listening to what people say, watching what they do, and talking with them about what it all means. What I consider my "best" data are the body of unsolicited comments about selves and human development that I overheard, or was party to, in the context of everyday life, but I have also made use of information I obtained in more formal interviews and household surveys, as well as my observations and analyses of various ritual practices and social events. The picture that emerges from these disparate sources is, of course, a partial one, limited both by my idiosyncrasies as an ethnographer and by those of the people who were generous enough to let me live with them and accompany them on their daily rounds. But I hope it will prove useful, nonetheless, in helping us imagine an alternative way of thinking about the course of a human life, and of highlighting the contingent and local origins of those seemingly inescapable issues that occupy our lives.

The Plan of the Book

In order to introduce and raise questions about some key features of Shan understandings of self, I will begin (in chapter 2) with a description of a healing session in the home of a local healer during which a troublesome spirit was chased out of an ailing body and the body's "souls" were called back. My purpose in beginning here is to draw attention to certain aspects of bodies and selves that figure heavily in Shan thinking, especially the concern with keeping spirits *(phi)* and souls *(khwan)* separate. Then, in the five chapters that follow, the book charts in rough chronological order the transformations that a Shan self experiences or endures over the course of a life and beyond, from "pre-" to "post-human" forms.

I have chosen to begin my description of this odyssey (in chapter 3) at the moment of death—both to underscore the cyclical nature of human development for Shan (a self does not begin at birth) and to draw attention to important aspects of the Shan self that are most easily seen in conjunction with death. The ethnographic focus is on two funerals. These funerals contrast in important ways that reveal the role of emotional attachment in creating "good" versus "bad" deaths. Building on the previous chapter, chapter 3 shows how, at the point of death, the concern with keeping *khwan* and *phi* separate intensifies. It also introduces important Buddhist concepts— such as karma, merit making, and rebirth—that figure prominently in Shan conceptions of self and human development.

Chapter 4 describes the segment of human development from birth (or rebirth, as Shan see it) to young adulthood, that is, the process of achieving social maturity. It begins with a discussion of the rebirth stories I collected and what these stories reveal about local ideas regarding emotional attachment. Young children, I suggest, are seen as both vulnerable and "wild." In an argument that draws upon the ethnographic material presented in the previous two chapters, I show how spirits, souls, and children together form an indigenous category of Other that is opposed to ideal notions of a mature self. I discuss the normative implications of this view, as well as the way it contrasts in significant ways with North American ideas about the nature of childhood and child development. The second half of the chapter, which continues the ethnographic description through childhood to young adulthood, is aimed at showing the significance of the local social structure and family organization. It ends with a discussion of some ideas about hierarchy that inform Shan social organization, showing how these articulate with an equally important value placed on personal autonomy.

Having survived the dangerous period of childhood and achieved some measure of maturity, a Shan enters a period of routine maintenance of that status. Adulthood is the time when people shore up control over the contested site that is their selves, by various means—some personal, some collective. In chapter 5, I present a sample of the techniques and ritual aids they employ, concentrating on examples from a single day in which three key rituals, held annually, were performed. In the final section of this chapter ("Self-Made Rituals and Ritually Made Selves"), I summarize the underlying logic of the practices I have described and their implications for a Shan concept of self.

Shan are well known in Thailand for their elaborate and theatrical version of the Buddhist ordination ritual that transforms a young boy into a novice monk. Chapter 6 examines an aspect of novice ordinations that has received scant attention in the literature, that of the role of the organizers, or sponsors, of these events. I argue that taking on this role is an anticipated and hoped-for event in a person's life, a goal that most people aim for, even if not all achieve it. As such, it constitutes a midlife project that illuminates both an official cultural consensus about idealized social relationships as well as the tensions that result when people attempt to enact these relationships. I give particular attention to the gender implications entailed in novice ordinations and to how women have responded to them.

Chapter 7 discusses old age, but it does so in the context of a larger set of values and practices to which all aspire but in which old people are considered particularly adept. These values and practices are embedded in a discourse of increased knowledge and self-control. The chapter begins with a discussion of local ideas about mental health as expressed in the advice people regularly give to each other (a kind of Shan self-help manual) and analyzes these ideas as providing the foundation for a Shan ethnopsychology.

This ethnopsychology is further explored by examining the arsenal of coping strategies that people have developed for restoring one's equilibrium when it is lost or threatened, strategies that prepare adults for a kind of re-tooling that occurs in old age. I then describe how old age is structured in this village, arguing that it is seen as an important developmental stage—a kind of second socialization during which people are expected to change in significant and highly valued ways, a process that is driven by old people's increasing involvement in Buddhist ascetic practices. The chapter ends with a summary of Shan thinking on human development and a discussion of the implications of this view for the sorts of explanations that Shan offer of people's behavior.

Finally, in chapter 8, I consider how the particular view of self and human development that emerged in the preceding chapters may be linked to broader issues, academic and personal, and I point to what I see as the most promising pathways for future research on the topic.

Chapter 2

Spirits, Souls, and Selves

The Body as a Contested Site

> The individuated boundaries thought proper to the self in Western
> culture are based upon a model of the body as a closed, self-contained
> unit. . . . But many societies have a model of the body as porous. . . .
> [T]he features of the body upon which people fasten (separateness or
> porosity) are tropes for their conception of self and, in circular fashion,
> validate them. Ontological premises are hegemonic; they are based on
> beliefs that wear the guise of biology.
>
> JEANNETTE MAGEO, *Theorizing Self in Samoa*

ONE OF THE MOST vexing issues in the study of indigenous psychological notions has been that of boundaries. What is to count as the psychological? In his study of how a psychologized self came to be depicted in
modern American portrait painting, David Lubin notes that, even in the
Western tradition, the term has not always held its contemporary connotations. In 1811, when the poet and literary critic Samuel Taylor Coleridge introduced the term "psychological" as an analogue to "physiological," the
meaning of its root word, "psyche," was still a significant part of its connotation. If physiology was the study of the physique, "psychology was the
study of the psyche: the mind, the emotions, the unique subjectivity of an
individual—in a word, the soul. A psyche was that which inhabited the body
and remained contingent upon it but nonetheless possessed an independent or transcendent status" (Lubin 1997, 134).

Over the course of the next century, a struggle would ensue between
those, like William James (in his widely read *The Varieties of Religious Experience*, 1902), who sought to retain a link between the spiritual and the psychological, and others who sought to redefine the psyche in mechanistic,
somatic terms (Lubin 1997, 144). Although the latter group eventually suc-
ceeded in separating the spiritual from the psychological in both the academic and popular discourses of Europe and North America, it would be a

mistake to assume that such a sharp distinction exists in all societies. In fact, in nonsecularized societies where "religion" has not been separated off from other sorts of knowledge about the world, it is hard to imagine how such a distinction could be sustained.

With this in mind, I want to begin this description of Shan ethnopsychology with a discussion of illness and some traditional healing techniques. As will become apparent, the Shan approach to healing does not respect facile boundaries between the "religious" and the "psychological." Healing sessions draw upon a diverse body of assumptions about the nature of the cosmos and the sorts of beings and forces at work within it, each of which has implications for the way an individual's subjective experience is communicated to others and ultimately understood. But first, allow me to introduce you to a traditional Shan healer, Uncle Pon.

A New Life for Uncle Pon

When I first met Uncle Pon in 1980, he was a rather forlorn figure. His tattoo-covered body was hard and thin, his hair always straggly, his clothes shabby. Impoverished from what seemed to be a long-standing drinking habit, he kept to himself and rarely appeared at village social gatherings. I felt sorry for his wife, Aunt Mim, whose hard work and ingenuity managed to keep the household together. They lived in the same house then that Aunt Mim still occupies today,[1] a large old-style structure with a couple of less substantial houses in the compound—buildings they shared with what seemed to be an endless extended family of adult children and their spouses, grandchildren, and various unspecified relatives who were always "visiting."

My primary connection with the household was through their two youngest boys, who, at that time, were both still attending the village grade school. The youngest, Lek, was a frequent visitor at my house in another section of the village. I was studying children during that field trip, and my house was always full of school-age kids. His older brother, Lom, was to be my *luk kham*–my "ordained son"—since I had agreed to be one of the ritual sponsors for his ordination as a novice in the Buddhist *sangha*. This relationship provided me with a permanent connection to the household and a good reason to look them up shortly after I returned in 1990.

I could not have been more surprised at the transformation the household had experienced since my last visit. Uncle Pon had stopped drinking entirely and—though still a quiet and socially reticent man—had somehow managed to become a well-known and highly respected healer with a vast clientele that drew on nearby villages as well as the people of Baan Kaung Mu.

The once struggling household now seemed stable and prosperous. During a visit to the house the following afternoon, Aunt Mim told me the story behind her husband's dramatic metamorphosis from humble derelict to esteemed practitioner. It all began several years earlier, she explained, when Uncle Pon decided to "drink the water of the *tsao moeng*."

The *tsao moeng,* or village guardian spirit, is a local deity with a shrine at the outskirts of the village, just inside the edge of the forest.[2] Based on the way people interact with him and listening to the way they talk about him, I have come to think of the *tsao moeng* as a kind of godfather figure—half Wild West sheriff and half rough-and-ready gangster. He acts as a strong and capable guardian for village residents, benevolent toward those who seek his protection and dangerous to all who neglect him. The *tsao moeng* is also a source of curing power for many traditional Shan healers, including Grandfather Tsing, the eminent old practitioner Uncle Pon was visiting in town at the time he decided to do something about his drinking habit.

"Drinking the water of the *tsao moeng*" is a procedure in which a spirit medium for the *tsao moeng* places a knife blade in an ordinary glass of water (thus infusing it with his power) while asking the patient to utter an oath, swearing that he will never drink alcohol again. If the patient agrees and then drinks the cup of water, he understands that breaking the oath means he will go crazy, become gravely ill, lose all his money, or experience some other sort of calamity or bad luck. As a result, this procedure is considered an extremely serious step and not one that is undertaken casually.[3]

According to Aunt Mim, on the day when Uncle Pon decided to go through with it, he was informed by the spirit medium that the *tsao moeng* also expected him to start attending temple services on *wan sin* (the Buddhist Sabbath) and to join those lay devotees who stay at the temple afterwards in order to meditate and practice other sorts of personal discipline. Grandfather Tsing even gave Uncle Pon a string of meditation beads to use when he went to the temple. However, Uncle Pon ignored this part of the instructions. He took the beads home and hung them on the wall. When the first *wan sin* came along, Uncle Pon went fishing.

At this point in her story, Aunt Mim became very animated. Acting things out, she described how Uncle Pon looked when he came back to the house a short time later—eyes wild, hands held taut in front of his face with his fingers curled like claws about to strike. He couldn't speak. Jaws clenched and teeth bared, the only sound that came out of him was a kind of low growl. A spirit had clearly possessed him.

Aunt Mim rushed him back to Grandfather Tsing's house in town, where the *tsao moeng* was again consulted through a spirit medium. "Why have you hung the beads on the wall?" the spirit demanded. This time,

Uncle Pon believed. When he recovered, he returned home and began staying at the temple on *wan sin*. He didn't drink again, and he had no more trouble with possessing spirits.

"So when did he decide to become a healer?" I asked. Aunt Mim laughed. "It doesn't work like that," she said. "You don't 'decide' to become a healer. The *tsao moeng* chooses you." Aunt Mim then explained that about a month after Uncle Pon returned home, with no prior study on his part, he had a dream in which the *tsao moeng* simply gave him the powerful verses, called *katha*, that are recited during a healing rite: "Nobody taught Uncle Pon. He just knew the *katha* automatically by himself, without studying. Grandfather Tsing didn't teach them to him. When he raises an offering to the *tsao moeng* [done at the beginning of each healing rite], they just come to him." Armed with these verses, Uncle Pon set himself up as a *saraa*, or traditional healer, and began to attract clients.

This story was later confirmed by another local man, Uncle Sanit. Referring to Uncle Pon's claim that the healing verses came to him in a dream, Uncle Sanit commented, "We could believe that Uncle Pon didn't study the *katha* anywhere, because we know he can't read or write—only his own name!" But people were still skeptical at first, he said, not quite ready to believe that this former ne'er-do-well now had the power to heal. Nevertheless, it seemed that everyone who went to Uncle Pon for treatment was cured, so more and more people began to go. "Those who went first were the desperate ones—people who had tried all sorts of treatments in many different places, all with no success," Uncle Sanit said. "When these people were cured by Uncle Pon, other people really began to believe in his power."

But why Uncle Pon? I persisted with my questions to Aunt Mim. After all, not everyone who drinks the water of the *tsao moeng* ends up as a healer. "Our life was miserable *(tukkha)*, and we were so poor," she said. "I think the *tsao moeng* felt sorry for him and that's why he chose him." Another woman visiting the house who was listening to our conversation added, "It's almost as if Uncle Pon died and was born again. Like he got a new life."

The Ritual Technology of Healing

The indigenous healing tradition that cured Uncle Pon of his drinking, encouraged him on a path toward greater self-discipline, and ultimately provided him with a new lease on life is a powerful package of beliefs and practices that is clearly capable of transforming lives. The repertoire of techniques this tradition uses for diagnosing and treating illnesses may be regarded as a kind of technology or tool kit from which we may learn something about Shan views of self-in-the-world. Every technology, medical or otherwise, can be viewed as the material embodiment of a tacit hypothesis about the nature of the world. Similarly, every technology that works, according to its users, can be seen as a vindication of that worldview. Hence, a society's ritual technologies become part of the everyday fabric of life for the people who use them, by giving concrete expression to a particular vision of the world and, as with all technologies (including scientific ones), by extending the effectiveness of the user in that locally envisioned world.

The healing rituals that follow are good examples of this mutual project of world creation and self-definition. They are part of a much larger repertoire of medical technologies—both traditional and Western[4]—that are available to the people of Baan Kaung Mu village. The knowledge that informs Shan thinking about health and illness (and, ultimately, about self and personhood) takes its inspiration from diverse sources that include the teachings of Theravāda Buddhism, the ancient lore concerning "spirits," and more recent borrowings culled from their exposure to the international practice of science and medicine.

Shan usually view these disparate sources of wisdom not as being in competition but, rather, as being complementary. When they choose to visit a traditional specialist such as Uncle Pon, it does not necessarily mean that they have ruled out a trip into town to visit the provincial hospital. They may, in fact, be planning to go the next morning. What it does mean, however, is that they have come to certain conclusions regarding the nature of their illness and have decided that their recovery will depend, at least in part, on the services that only a traditional specialist can provide. These visits to traditional healers, then, entail a prior self-diagnosis that implicates a certain view of the self and of the world in which that self acts. That Shan continue to use this traditional ritual technology in a context in which Western medicine is increasingly available indicates the ongoing importance to them of the worldview that underlies it.

Although a thorough discussion of Shan healing traditions deserves a book unto itself, examining some of the most common techniques used in a typical healing session will help illuminate key components of Shan thinking about the self in illness and in health.

A Curing Session at Uncle Pon's House

NOVEMBER 4, 1990: It is about 7 p.m. in the village, the air cool after sunset. Except for a few who worked late in their fields and are just now heading toward the stream with towel and washbowl in hand, most people have already bathed, have changed into a fresh sarong or pants, and are seated on the floor of their front room around a low table, finishing the evening meal with their families.

Visitors are beginning to drift into Uncle Pon's house. They climb the stairs, leaving their rubber sandals in a pile with others on the porch and pause as they reach the threshold to the house proper. Here they sit or squat for a moment and *waai*[5] in the direction of a complex of offering shelves set up along the east wall of the house under which Uncle Pon himself sits on a thin mattress. The other members of his large extended family busy themselves with various tasks—washing the supper dishes, caring for a small child, preparing tea to serve to visitors, chatting with guests. Over the course of the evening, anywhere from two to a dozen visitors will be present in the house, with others coming and going as the night wears on. Some of these will be patients, there for treatment; others will come simply to watch and to socialize. Although many of those who visit the house are ill or injured, this is not a somber place. The large nightly gathering ensures a convivial atmosphere, and people describe the house as "a fun place to visit."

The house itself is an old one, built in the traditional style. A lowered section of the floor running north to south, on the same level as the porch (and leading to the kitchen area in the back of the house), provides a kind of wall-less corridor that divides the main living space into two seating areas, on the east and west sides of the house, each about twelve feet square. Most of the casual visitors arrange themselves along the edge of the west side, near the middle corridor, leaving the east side of the house for Uncle Pon and his patients. Tonight, Nang Ing,[6] a young woman who has been suffering from stomach pains and general feelings of weakness, is scheduled to undergo the healing rites known as "sweeping away the spirits" *(pat phi)* and "calling the souls" *(haung khwan)*. She has spent the last three nights sleeping at Uncle Pon's house, receiving daily treatments aimed at preparing her body for tonight's twin procedures.

The operating assumption of this course of therapy is that the patient's body has been invaded by one of a class of invisible beings known as spirits *(phi),* causing some of the body's thirty-two souls (known individually and collectively as *khwan*[7]) to flee. The illness is caused both by the presence of the invading *phi*, which is said to feed on the body, and by the absence of the runaway *khwan*, which are needed to animate the body. (Shan say that when some of the *khwan* are missing, the result is poor morale or sickness; when all of the *khwan* are missing, the result is death.) For Nang Ing to get well, she must both rid her body of the unwelcome spirit and get her own souls back.

The key method for accomplishing this is a dual spirit exorcism and soul-calling ritual performed by the healer that is usually scheduled for several days after the original consultation. This delay is important. It gives the healer time to work on the spirit, "softening it up" through various treatments that will make expelling it easier at the time of the final exorcism. During this preliminary time, people often talk about the spirit in ways that provide interesting clues about what spirits are thought to be like and what they are expected to want.

At the initial diagnostic session, for example, the spirit that is determined to be responsible for the patient's illness is often referred to as *hai* (bad). Sometimes it turns out that the offending spirit is one that has recently gotten someone else sick or perhaps has caused this particular patient to be sick previously. On such occasions, onlookers are apt to remark, *"Phi nai hai na!"* which means, roughly, "This spirit is really active!" or "This spirit is always causing trouble!" If the patient's condition worsens during the time between the initial diagnosis and the scheduled spirit exorcism and soul-calling rite, one hears repeated complaints about how *hai* (troublesome) this spirit is. If the patient improves, people speculate about what the spirit might be thinking, making comments like "Ah! Now that we've consulted this healer, the spirit knows that it's going to get something to eat soon, so it's letting up a bit on the patient."

"Something to eat" refers to the basket of food offerings that are presented to the spirit at the time of the exorcism. Uncle Pon and his wife prepare these offerings, usually during the day on which the evening exorcism is scheduled to take place. Often there are visitors in their house during these preparations—patients and onlookers—who watch as the ingredients are assembled. While they watch, they chat about various people's illnesses and the spirits that caused them. The ambience on these occasions is one of purposeful activity but also is very relaxed. People watch Uncle Pon and Aunt Mim assemble the spirit offerings with the same relaxed confidence with which I would regard a pharmacist filling a prescription. There is no doubt here as to the efficacy of the procedure.

This confidence is based on the fact that, in contrast to the attitude toward invisible beings (such as gods, angels, and ghosts) often found in societies that separate religious and secular knowledge, Shan do not typically regard spirits as in any way mysterious. Although there may be some uncertainty over which particular spirit is causing the trouble, Shan seem to feel they have a good general understanding of how spirits operate and what it is they want from humans, namely, something to eat. Although Shan do recognize several kinds of spirits, the prototypical *phi* that is spoken of without some other modifying adjective is a hungry and restless being who, for one reason or another, is caught in a kind of no-man's-land, unable to be reborn. Like the wild tigers that plagued this village a generation ago (and are still vividly remembered), spirits are said to hang around the edges of human settlements, hoping to prey upon the weak and the imprudent.

The basket of offerings prepared by Uncle Pon, then, is intended as food for the spirit, as a kind of substitute for the patient's body. Two other offering sets must also be assembled before the healing rites can begin: a tray of food, clothing, and other paraphernalia for catching the wandering souls; and a basin of uncooked rice, money, and other gifts that will be presented first to the *tsao moeng* and then kept by Uncle Pon himself. His wife usually assists him with these preparations, which can be done earlier in the day or in the evening just before the treatment begins. In either case, these offering sets always contain the same items, described below.

For the *Phi*

For Nang Ing's healing session, Uncle Pon and Aunt Mim are working together to prepare the basket of spirit offerings. The frame of the basket is made from the stalk of a banana tree, cut and shaped into a tray about ten inches square, with side walls about two inches high. The first item to go in is a set of clay figures—some human, some animal—that Aunt Mim has made herself, using children's modeling clay. The number of these figures varies. Only the human figures are represented as having gender, and there is usually at least one male and one female figure. On what are otherwise identical-looking figures, Aunt Mim uses a contrasting color of clay—yellow on red, on this occasion—to add the gender-defining features. For the female, she adds bits of yellow clay to form breasts, a yellow topknot on the head, and a discernible slash at the crotch to denote the vagina. The male figure receives only one added feature, a bit of clay at the crotch to form a pointy, carrotlike penis. Figures of a chicken and a dog are also added to the basket.

In addition to the clay figures, other items are added, including bits of meat and fish, some chili peppers, garlic, salt, half a soybean cake, some rice (cooked and uncooked), and some crackerlike cookies or biscuits. Interestingly, when asked why these particular food items are the ones that are offered to spirits, people usually respond that the list contains "all the different kinds of things we [humans] like to eat," suggesting that spirits and humans are assumed to have similar appetites.

The remaining items in the basket consist of a few other human indulgences (cigars, tobacco, betel nut) as well as other items that Shan regard as basic human necessities (some coins, charcoal, candles). Reviewing this assortment, the overall impression one gets is that the items assembled here are intended to serve as a virtual compendium of the sorts of things that every person/spirit should always have on hand. In their talk and their actions leading up to the exorcism, then, Shan are clearly drawing upon their knowledge of humans and "human nature" as a guide for how to interact successfully with the spirit.

For the *Khwan*

The tray of items that will be used in the second half of the healing rite includes two bowls, one containing things needed to call back the *khwan*, the other containing food and flowers that, it is hoped, will entice it to stay. The tray also holds a cup of drinking water, as well as a shirt of Nang Ing's, folded and placed under one of the bowls.

The bowl that will be used during the actual calling of the *khwan* is filled with uncooked rice. On top of this, Uncle Pon places an uncooked egg and a 20-baht bill (worth approximately US$1 at the time) that was provided by Nang Ing's family. Four small candles and four ritual "flowers" (unspun cotton fitted into cone-shaped holders) are stuck into the rice to form a square around the egg. Uncle Pon adds to this a small "crossbow," about six inches in diameter, for use later in the rite. The bow is made of a thin, flexible wood that has been bent to form a horseshoe-shaped bow with a taut string running across its open end. A second string is tied midway along this first one, allowing Uncle Pon to pick up the wooden bow without touching it. The last item in this bowl is a bundle of white thread, laid on top until ready for use.

The second bowl on the tray is filled with things to attract and then keep the returning *khwan* inside the body: flowers, sweets, a hard-boiled egg, dried fish, a packet of peanuts, and cooked rice.

For the Healer

The final offering to prepare is a standard one called a *phoen* (table, as in "setting the table to invite someone to come"), which is used in many Shan rites, whenever the power for the ritual is thought to come from teachers (often deceased and/or mythic) who have passed on the knowledge and power necessary to perform the ritual and whose ongoing participation in the rite is being sought.

In the case of this healing rite, Uncle Pon prepares a *phoen* offering for the *tsao moeng*, whom he credits as the source of all his success in healing. The items are placed in a large white basin and include rice, a coconut, two bunches of bananas, and some packets of tobacco, betel nut, dried tea, and cotton.

Most, if not all, of these items, but in particular the rice, are provided by the patient. Nang Ing's mother hands Uncle Pon his fee, which will also go on this offering. In this case, it is 257 baht (numbers ending in 7 or 9 are considered auspicious), or about US$10—his standard fee for a *pat phi* (sweeping away the spirit).[8] Uncle Pon accepts the money, wraps it in special red and white cloths (colors associated with the *tsao moeng*), and places it between the coconut and a bunch of bananas. Now the preparations are complete, and the healing rites may begin.

Sweeping Away the Spirit

Uncle Pon begins by sprinkling the altar area of his house with fragrant water. He lights two candles and places them on one of the shelves along the east wall, then adds a few sticks of lighted incense. He lights a smaller candle and places it on the highest shelf, the one dedicated to the Buddha. Taking the white basin filled with offerings, he squats, facing the altars, and lifts it off the ground while softly uttering some verses of Buddhist scripture under his breath. These words invoke the help of his teacher, the *tsao moeng*, as well as a long line of other ancestral teachers that he inherits through the *tsao moeng*. He places the basin on the shelf reserved for offerings to the *tsao moeng*, then lights another small candle and affixes it to the coconut in this basin. Finally, Uncle Pon reaches for a sheathed sword (a weapon associated with the *tsao moeng*) that hangs on the wall near the altar. With the sword resting on his outstretched arms, he squats in front of the basin offering, touching it with his hand for a moment, and then performs the respectful *waai* gesture.

Having summoned the necessary powers, Uncle Pon asks his patient to move to the porch. Nang Ing takes a seat at the top of the stairs, facing away from the house. Uncle Pon brings the basket of offerings they have prepared for the *phi* and, holding it over her head, moves it in a clockwise circular motion three times above her before putting it down on the porch. Next, standing behind her, he rests his sword on her head for a moment, then begins to swirl it around her body in all directions, making his way slowly around her and chanting powerful verses all the while. He pauses now and then to poke the tip of the sword gently at various parts of her body—her back, her sides, her stomach—at one point tapping the back of her neck as if to cut off her head from behind.

In the course of these actions, Uncle Pon swirls the basket of food above Nang Ing's head to gain the attention of the *phi* that has been afflicting her. He then uses the power of the *tsao moeng*, symbolized by the sword, to intimidate it into leaving her. Employing this carrot-and-stick approach, he accomplishes the task of getting the invading *phi* out of Nang Ing's body. When he is finished, he allows Nang Ing to go back inside while he leaves the house with the basket of offerings, taking it outside the village proper and placing it along the road for the *phi*, which has presumably been following him. Nang

Ing is now free of the bothersome spirit and ready for the next crucial step to restoring her well-being, namely, reclaiming the errant souls that have wandered away from her body.

Calling the Souls

When Uncle Pon returns, he joins Nang Ing next to the prepared tray for the soul-calling part of the treatment *(haung khwan)*. As before, he squats and lifts the tray briefly in the direction of the altar, summoning the help of the *tsao moeng*, then puts it back down on the floor between them. His wife, Aunt Mim, comes over and sits down next to Nang Ing.

Uncle Pon unrolls the bundle of white thread, arranging it so that a piece of it touches everything on the tray. The ends of the thread rest in Nang Ing's open palms, making a circle that begins and ends with her and touches all the other items en route. Next, Uncle Pon takes the horseshoe-shaped crossbow and stands it up on top of the bowl of rice. The middle part of the wooden bow, where it is broadest and a bit flat, is resting in the bowl; the string side is up. He covers the flat part of the bow with a little rice, then balances the egg upright on top of it. Reciting powerful verses, he drops a bit more rice on top of the egg. Then, holding the string that is attached to the taut drawstring, he slowly tries to lift the entire bow out of its bed of rice with the egg balanced upright on it—a procedure that looks to me to be virtually impossible.

The egg falls over, but no one appears worried. Uncle Pon simply replaces it and tries again. Again, it falls over. He keeps trying. Aunt Mim is watching with a handful of popped rice. Each time the egg falls, she takes one of these "counters" and places it on the floor in front of her. After about eight attempts, Uncle Pon takes a bit of rice from the bowl and tosses it toward the entrance area of the house "to help the *khwan* find its way in." He tries again. The egg falls over. After another series of attempts, he instructs those watching to move away from the path that runs between the entrance to the house and the egg because they may be blocking the way, making it difficult for the *khwan* to find the egg. The people watching were already vaguely out of the way, but now they scoot back even farther.

Several more attempts, and still no success. Uncle Pon takes a stick of wood and lays it across the cup of water in line with the path between the entrance to the house and the egg. This forms a "bridge" intended to help the *khwan* get across the water. He repositions the egg and tries again. The egg falls. Nang Ing's mother reaches into the hidden pocket of her blouse and pulls out a coin, which she hands to Aunt Mim. Perhaps the *khwan* wants more money? Aunt Mim takes the coin but sets it aside for the time being.

A soul-calling ceremony conducted by Uncle Pon.

The trials continue. At one point, the egg surprises everyone by balancing for a moment or two on the raised horseshoe. This is the patient's cue to get ready to catch it, but Nang Ing does not get her hands underneath it in time before it falls off into the bowl. The onlookers groan. "You're moving too slowly!" someone says. "Sit closer!" says another. "Keep your hands close to the egg!"

Finally, after twenty-eight unsuccessful attempts, the egg balances perfectly for several seconds on the suspended horseshoe, then falls into Nang Ing's waiting hands. Her *khwan* has returned. Uncle Pon works quickly to secure its presence. He holds a length of the white thread between his two hands and gently brushes it along Nang Ing's inner arms, one at a time, beginning at the wrists and brushing in toward the torso, reciting verses as he works. He ties a length of the thread around each wrist, using the remaining thread for a long necklace around her neck. Only then does he remove the egg from her hands.

Meanwhile, Aunt Mim has been busy with the food in the other bowl on the tray—peeling the hard-boiled egg, unwrapping the sweets, and so

The egg finally balances and is about to drop into the patient's waiting hands.

on—getting it ready so that Nang Ing can eat it as soon as her hands are free. After Uncle Pon removes the egg, Aunt Mim asks Nang Ing to brush her hands into an open plastic bag in order to catch any grains of rice that might have clung to the egg. Into this same bag Aunt Mim also puts at least one piece of each kind of food and offering from the bowl, including all the flowers. This bag will rest by Nang Ing's pillow tonight to serve as food and an enticement to stay for the newly returned *khwan*.

Nang Ing proceeds to eat from each category of food remaining in the bowl. She drinks the glass of water that was on the tray and puts on her shirt that had been folded under one of the bowls. As she continues to munch on the food (some of which is also shared with the children who have been hanging around watching), Uncle Pon begins to disassemble everything. Working first on the large basin that held offerings for the *tsao moeng,* he removes all the wrapped offerings and candles and distributes a couple of the packets of tea to visiting adults in the room. The money wrapped in cloth he puts next to his pillow. Turning next to the bowl used in the soul calling, he removes the white thread and the crossbow and sets them aside. The egg that captured the wayward souls he places in an empty Five Rams–brand battery box that he stores under the altar area, along with other tools of his craft. The remaining rice in the bowl is added to that in the white basin.

The healing session is now over for the evening and the visitors resume their socializing. Nang Ing will sleep here at Uncle Pon's house tonight, as she has for the past three nights, and then return home in the morning. How long her souls will remain in her body, where they belong, no one can predict. But for the moment, at least, she is out of danger.

What Do *Khwan* Want?

Shan maintain that all people are susceptible to soul loss, especially as children (when the souls' attachment to the body is seen as most tenuous), and women are considered somewhat more susceptible than men. Within these general parameters, some individuals are perceived as more disposed to soul loss than others; these people are said to have weak, or soft, souls *(khwan un)* and are chronically ill. Nevertheless, it is a common enough occurrence that everyone will have had to have their souls called at some time or another, usually more than once. Most adults will also have accompanied their children or other relatives for treatment and will have witnessed the ritual on countless other occasions. Hence, they will have had many opportunities to absorb its lessons.

Based on my observations of other healing sessions at Uncle Pon's house and elsewhere, the session described above is fairly typical. The "sweeping away the spirit" segment has been virtually identical in every session I have witnessed. The "calling the souls" segment has also been very similar, with only trivial differences in placement of materials, style of "calling," and the like. There is one thing of importance, however, that is not predictable from session to session: how long will it take before the egg finally balances and drops into the patient's hands? Or, put another way, what will it take for the souls of the patient to return?

The unpredictable nature of this part of the ritual has become the occasion for a revealing discourse about the *khwan* in which onlookers try to guess what it is the *khwan* wants as a condition for returning to the body. For example, about two months after the session described above, Nang Ing was sick again and required another treatment. The following excerpt from my field notes on the event gives some flavor of the attitude people adopt toward an egg that refuses to fall.

DECEMBER 29, 1990: On the 9th trial, the egg stuck upright and Uncle Pon moved it so that it was poised directly over Nang Ing's waiting hands, but it didn't seem to want to fall. Aunt Mim bounded into action, coming around to the other side of the tray and grabbing a couple of sprigs of flowers which she then laid across Nang Ing's wrists "to entice the *khwan*." But still it wouldn't drop! (Uncle Pon was even jiggling the string a little.) Aunt Mim said it might be necessary to add some money, but Aunt Kham [Nang Ing's mother] said she didn't have any. Then Aunt Kham whipped out Nang Ing's gold necklace (which Nang Ing had taken off earlier and handed to her mother for safekeeping) and put it (as a "money-substitute") in Nang Ing's hands. At last, the egg dropped; the soul had been enticed home.

What I find most interesting here is the way people assume that souls have idiosyncratic desires that must be discerned and then placated in order for them to return. Another example will perhaps clarify this point. On this occasion, two people were scheduled for treatment on the same night. One was Aunt Kham (Nang Ing's mother); the other was Uncle Pon's teenage son, Lom. Uncle Pon did the rite in two shifts: the spirit-sweeping segments for each patient first, followed by the two soul-calling segments. In Aunt Kham's case, only four trials were necessary before the egg balanced, whereas it took twenty-one trials for Lom's *khwan* to return. During the latter, visitors who were getting tired and wanted to leave were not permitted to. Aunt Mim said they had to wait until it was over, apparently so as not to further confuse the *khwan* with a lot of commotion at the entryway to the house.

In both cases there were problems getting the egg to drop into the patient's hands once it had balanced on the crossbow, and in both cases those present speculated as to what the *khwan* might want. Aunt Mim always tries flowers first. When she did this for Aunt Kham, the effect was dramatic. The moment after the flowers were laid on her wrists, the egg dropped, producing audible gasps in the audience. The patient's daughter simply chuckled, "So! All it wanted was some flowers!"

With Lom, flowers were tried but with no effect, prompting more creative attempts to figure out the *khwan*'s desires. His mother tried adding a string of Buddhist meditation beads to his hands (which would have indicated that perhaps he—or, rather, his *khwan*—wanted to become a monk), but this didn't work. Neither did a coin, or a fancy men's wristwatch that someone in the audience lent to the effort. Throughout these attempts, people kept asking, "What does it want? What does it want?" After numerous failures, someone suggested, "It probably wants a wife." This was clearly a reference to Lom's youth and bachelor status. Interestingly, if this had been said about Lom directly, he would have been embarrassed, insisted it wasn't true, and so forth. Yet, on this occasion, he sat quietly and acted as if they were talking about someone else. His *khwan* was both "him" and "not him."

Responding to the suggestion that it probably wanted a wife, people asked if anyone present had a gold necklace (a standard item for a Shan groom to give his bride). No one did, so we all took off our wedding rings and other jewelry, adding them to his cupped hands until, finally, the egg fell. Lom kept these things overnight, wearing some and keeping the rest close to him, in an effort to persuade the *khwan* to stay.

In other contexts, Shan talk about certain features that seem to be common to all *khwan*. They are all rather skittish and easily startled, which causes them to flee. Their movements outside the body are portrayed more as aimless wanderings than as purposeful excursions. Although not headed anywhere in particular, *khwan* are easily distracted, confused, or led astray. Correspondingly, they are usually not too difficult to get back. You simply have to call them and coax them, like a shy child or reluctant pet.

Sometimes, getting their attention and informing them of your whereabouts are not enough, however. What motivates one person's *khwan* to cross the threshold and reenter the body may not work for another. In the cases described above, the *khwan* are talked about as if they had a personality of sorts, with their own tastes and preferences that are distinct from—but not unrelated to—those of the individual whose body they are supposed to inhabit. This indicates both that the *khwan* are an integral part of Shan constructions of self (without them the body would be lifeless) and, yet, that they are not the core, or true, self (as the concept of "soul" is sometimes understood). We are left, then, with a rather decentered view of the self in which an experiencing subject is intimately related to, but not perfectly identical with, a semiautonomous *khwan* that must be persuaded to remain in the subject's body.

Spirits, Souls, and Selves

If *khwan* want some place safe and appealing, *phi* want something else. They are usually portrayed in these rituals as perpetually hungry creatures that invade a human body primarily in search of something to eat. Although food offerings are prepared for both *khwan* and *phi* in the healing rituals described above, with some items in common, the *khwan* are given more sweets and snack foods that attract on the basis of their fancy quality and status as treats (as well as flowers, jewelry, and other pretty things to entice them to stay), whereas the much hungrier *phi* are successfully appeased with plainer fare, the staples of a Shan diet. As we have seen, people sometimes suggest that the mere act of visiting Uncle Pon's house in order to set up an appointment to begin treatment will cause the *phi* to let up a bit on the person's body "because now it knows that it will get something to eat." The *phi*, in a sense, kidnaps the body, holding it hostage for a ransom of food.

Although taken seriously as a danger to be reckoned with, *phi* are not portrayed in these rites as overwhelmingly powerful beings to whom we must submit. Nor do they have the delicate constitution of *khwan*, whose recovery requires skillful coaxing and endless patience. On the contrary: because they are hungry, they are relatively easy to manipulate—offer them food and they will follow you anywhere (right out of the village being the favored destination). They are susceptible to being threatened and intimidated, both in the final spirit-sweeping treatment *(pat phi)* and in the preparatory rites leading up to it. Throughout these maneuvers there is never any doubt as to the outcome of the encounter between *phi* and healer; the *phi* will leave, at least for a while. Equally certain, however, is that it (or another one like it) will return, looking once again to prey upon human bodies.

Hence, in Shan discourses of the self, the body is portrayed as a contested site, a place where opposing forces meet and do battle. The curing process itself is conceptualized as a "contest" between forces of differing degrees of power—namely, the agent of the illness, the *khwan* of the patient, the treatment that is being tried, and the power of the healer—with the assumption that the strongest force will prevail.[9] The body can be taken over by other predatory beings, but it can also be won back by still other protective or benevolent ones.

Essential to maintaining control over one's body (which, in the Shan formulation, includes having control over one's morale, or "spirits," as well as one's physical health) is to control one's *khwan*. Weak *khwan* are easily frightened off, vacating the body and making it easy for a hungry *phi* to enter. As long as one's *khwan* remain weak, any health one enjoys will be short-lived, and one will be repeatedly attacked by *phi*, necessitating repeated treatment. In contrast, strong *khwan* stay put in the body and, as long as they are there, no *phi* will enter.

A preferred or ideal ordering can be detected here that Shan strive to maintain. Although both *khwan* and *phi* represent a kind of invisible life force or essence, *khwan* are the version that life force takes when it is properly attached to a body; a *phi* is the disembodied version that life force assumes when it has been irrevocably separated from a body. Ultimately, this ordering breaks down, according to Shan constructions of death (where *khwan* are transformed into *phi*) and rebirth (where *phi* are transformed back into *khwan*). But a healthy life requires that we resist the blurring of these categories and strive to keep them separate. *Khwan* belong to the living; *phi* belong to the dead and not yet reborn. Illness can be an indication that this ordering has been violated—a *phi* has invaded the body, the *khwan* have left, or both. The logic of traditional curing rituals, as we have seen, is to reinstate the proper separation between the two.

Where is the self that is ill in this construction? The healing rites suggest an image of a fragmented self, parts of which are susceptible to both takeover and abandonment. And yet, paradoxically, the pragmatic force of Uncle Pon's treatments is a clear boosting of morale, an enhanced sense of wholeness. Ironically, it may be the very conceptualization of the self as permeable and capable of fragmentation that most lends itself to sensations of being strengthened or repaired. That is, the Shan construction of a decentered self, whose component parts can simultaneously be separated from one another and host to others, makes possible the subjective experience of reordering and literally re-collecting oneself, an experience Uncle Pon's patients find profoundly therapeutic.

In the following chapter, I will explore what happens when all such efforts at self-recollection fail, that is, what happens at the time of death. Doing so will give me the opportunity to elaborate on and clarify the nature of the distinction between *khwan* and *phi* in Shan constructions of the self, and to begin to show how these notions articulate with broader social forces at work within the society.

Chapter 3

Souls into Spirits

Death as Self-Transformation

ON THE MORNING of November 11, 1990, Grandfather Wang was doing what he loved to do—gathering wild mushrooms in the wooded hills near the village. His daughter, Nang Nu, had asked him many times not to do anything strenuous and specifically not to go mushroom hunting, because she was worried about his heart. Grandfather had a history of heart problems, and, now that he was seventy, she wanted him to slow down a bit. But, as was true for many older people in Baan Kaung Mu village, mushroom hunting was one of his favorite pastimes, and he was determined to go. So he waited until Nang Nu, who lived right next door to him, had left her house to do laundry at the stream. Then he stole off into the forest.

A few hours later he was dead, apparently from a heart attack. An old woman, herself out gathering mushrooms, chanced upon him lying on the path where he had collapsed, and she ran back to the village for help. By the time they got him into the pickup truck and arrived at the hospital in town, it was too late. Now, after an injection from the doctor that would help preserve the body during the coming days of funeral preparations, they had brought him home again. Nang Nu's loud wails could be heard all over the neighborhood. As people realized what had happened, they came to the house to comfort the family and to begin the work.

"Oh, my father is no longer!" Nang Nu cried when I entered the house. People were relating incidents from the past few days that seemed, with hindsight, to be connected to Grandfather's death. Nang Nu mentioned the family photograph I had taken at their house only the day before. As part of a village census I was working on, I had been trying to get a photo document of every household in the village, and theirs was one of the last ones left to do. Grandfather and his wife, who were not getting along well, had been resisting the idea until just the day before when, at their children's urgings, they finally agreed to sit together with the rest of the family for the portrait. Now Nang Nu understood their unexpected cooperation yesterday as an ungrasped omen of today's tragic events.

Pi Laeng, Nang Nu's younger brother, told another story. He had had a dream about five days previous in which some of his teeth fell out. This is a standard Shan dream, interpreted to indicate that a death or other misfortune is imminent. When he woke up, Pi Laeng told his wife to be careful when she went to work that day, never suspecting that the dream pertained to his father.

Other stories were told. Only a night or two ago, a niece of Grandfather's dreamt that Grandfather's house was on fire. "Someone's probably going to die," she said to her husband. Then, just moments ago, she had come to the house to buy vegetables from the little shop Nang Nu keeps in the front of their house, intending to tell them about the dream. When informed that Grandfather had died, she burst into tears and ran home.

"If he had died at home, I could accept[1] that," Nang Nu kept saying, "but to collapse in the forest!"

Grandfather's body was laid out on a mattress in the front room of his house with his head against the east wall, directly under the Buddha altar, and a white sheet covering him. Bowls of flower arrangements lined each side of the mattress. At the head, Nang Nu had placed a larger vase of flowers along with Grandfather's hat, a jar of drinking water, and a large beeswax candle. At the foot, she placed a board with a tray of candles and incense sticks.

A visitor to the house stopped here for a moment to say a prayer and pay her final respects to Grandfather. She lit a candle, held its bottom end over an already lit one in order to melt the wax a bit, then affixed it to the board. She lit a few sticks of incense and raised them over her head for a moment before sticking them into a waiting bowl of sand, then placed an envelope with a 10-baht bill into a silver bowl that had been set out to receive donations. Others did the same. Soon the board was full of burning candles.

Meanwhile, Grandfather's nephews were busy getting the rest of the room set up in preparation for the evening services during which monks would visit and a scripture reading would be held. Later in the afternoon, Uncle Samaun, a local elder and ritual specialist who was also a member of the temple committee, made an announcement on the creaky temple loudspeaker, informing the rest of the village that Grandfather had died and asking everybody, "old people and young people, men, women, and children," to come to the house and *het kau* (keep the family company). Hearing the announcement, one young woman commented, "It isn't scary to go to the house when it's an old person who has died. He kept the precepts."

If the illnesses discussed in chapter 2 pose a serious threat to the proper ordering of *phi* and *khwan*, death introduces an even greater challenge. At death, a person's *khwan* become a *phi*, which is then supposed to separate itself from the human community and "go to a good place." But that is easier said than done, according to Shan. Two things in particular can interfere with this important transformation: an insufficient supply of merit and an excess of emotion. Before returning to the death of Nang Nu's father and the elaborate ritual apparatus that is called into play when someone dies, we must pause to consider the Buddhist principles of merit, karma, and rebirth, as Shan understand them. Then, by comparing people's responses to a series of specific deaths, we can learn why some are considered dangerous and others relatively safe, and why both merit and emotional control are crucial for a successful transformation of self at the time of death.

Merit, Karma, and Rebirth

In their stories, sermons, and everyday talk, Shan depict a universe in which every purposeful action you perform registers on the cosmos and eventually returns to you. If you do good, you experience life's bounty; if you do evil, you suffer misfortune. The universe keeps track of all acts of kindness, generosity, and patience, as well as moments of selfishness, ill will, and indifference. Nothing is lost. The moral force of each act is held in abeyance by the cosmos and allowed to accumulate, creating an individualized inventory of positive and negative consequences-to-be-realized, until that unpredictable moment when it is returned to you in kind. You live, die, and are reborn a thousand times over, each life bearing the imprint of your accumulated moral history.

This is the subjective world Shan inhabit, the conceptual backdrop against which they interact with one another, seek their livelihood, and make the myriad choices that constitute everyday life. The invisible stockpile generated by their good deeds they call *kuso* (merit) and that generated by their evil deeds they call *akuso* (demerit). At any given point, one's overall standing with respect to accumulated merit and demerit is referred to as one's *kam* (karma). This trio of beliefs provides built-in incentives and life-shaping goals that have profound effects on people's behavior. For most lay practitioners, the overarching goal is to improve one's karmic status so as to enjoy a better rebirth next time round, and the primary way to do this is to accumulate merit.

There are many ways to "make merit," and Shan always acknowledge the potential merit to be had from performing virtually any good deed. Nevertheless, most people focus their energies on certain traditional and institutionalized ways of merit making that are perceived as unequivocally virtuous. In all of these standard merit-making activities, people make public gifts of their money, goods, and/or services. In most cases, these gifts are directed at the community of Buddhist monks and novices known as the *sangha* and at the group of village elders known as temple sleepers *(khon naun tsaung)*–two groups that are distinguished by their ongoing commitment to follow more than the usual number of religious disciplines or precepts. Since, like many other Buddhists in Southeast Asia, Shan expect that the amount of merit one receives for a given act of generosity will be linked to the moral quality of the recipient, the *sangha* and the devout lay elders constitute the best possible fields upon which to plant the seeds of productive merit making.

One of the most common ways of making merit, for example, is to offer food to the monks and novices residing in one's local temple. Early each morning, women of all ages can be seen streaming in and out of the village monastery compound with stacked containers of rice and curries taken from their household's breakfast preparations.[2] Throughout the year, village life is punctuated with a series of more elaborate collective merit-making rituals that focus on large-scale, organized giving to the monks, novices, and lay elders. By participating in these activities, people hope to improve their karmic status and to enjoy the benefits that derive from this.

Together, the concepts of merit, karma, and rebirth operate as a powerful theory of causality that can be used to explain the ups and downs of people's lives, as well as the broad differences among them. For the most part, villagers understand the doctrine of karma to mean that their efforts at virtuous behavior and merit accumulation will eventually yield some positive result for themselves personally, either in this life or in a future rebirth.[3] Although, theoretically, it is impossible to know what specific form this retribution (positive or negative) will take, the people of Baan Kaung Mu expect two areas in particular to be affected by one's karmic record, namely, the circumstances of one's birth and of one's death.

Consequently, whether one is born as a human or an animal, a male or a female, into a wealthy family or a poor one, in good health or crippled, quick-witted or slow, handsome or plain—all these are taken as leading indicators of one's previous accumulation of merit and demerit. Similarly, whether one dies of natural causes or of a violent accident, in old age or in the prime of life, surrounded by loved ones and at peace with oneself or alone and troubled—these circumstances are not considered accidental. Other events between birth and death are not typically explained by reference to karma unless they are of dramatic proportions (e.g., one's house and all one's possessions are lost in a sudden fire) or chronic (e.g., a recurrent illness from which one seems never to recover fully). In such cases, Shan are more likely to use the phrase *lai wot*, which means "to get one's due," or "to receive retribution." It alludes to karmic processes but does not employ the term *kam*. Even then, alternative explanations are usually available and considered.

As Shan villagers use the term, then, karma *(kam)* is not the sole causal force in the universe. It explains something about everyone, but never everything about someone. Gombrich found that Sri Lankan Buddhists (also Theravādin) interpret the doctrine of karma similarly:

> [K]arma is not necessarily responsible even for everything that happens to you: it operates, if I may so put it, in a gross way. One monk said that *karma* determines the station in which you are born, and your luck *(vāsanāva);* after that, it is up to you—the present you. (1971, 145)

It is this aspect of karma—the limitations of its causal power—that enables it to define a moral universe in which people may act. Without those limits, there could be no choice involved in human action, no control over one's behavior, and, hence, no possibility of morality. Obeyesekere has made a similar point in his discussion of the "psychological indeterminacy" of karma for Sri Lankan Buddhists:

> From a logical point of view *karma* is a highly deterministic theory of causation, but *karma* must be distinguished from Fate. A fatalistic theory of causation strictly implies that whatever one does has been pre-ordained by an impersonal agency. By contrast, the Buddhist theory places responsibility for each individual's present fate quite squarely on the individual himself—albeit in his past births. Since the quality of my current action will, with some leeway, determine my future birth, I am in control of my destiny. (1968, 21)

If karma is not fate, then what other sorts of causal forces participate in the shaping of human endeavors? What is that "leeway" to which Obeyesekere alludes? In a classic essay that applies equally as well to Shan as to the Thai about whom it was originally written, Lucien Hanks (1962) describes the interaction of merit and karma with something that people acknowledge to be a more mundane and amoral "power."[4] Individuals may obtain this power in various ways: from personal experience, from special knowledge (such as astrological knowledge), from protective amulets, and so on. While continued success in action suggests that an individual has great merit, as opposed to mere power, such a judgment requires time. On an everyday basis, as Hanks notes, assessing the reasons for a person's success is problematic:

> In principle one may easily distinguish power from effectiveness. Though both aid the success of an undertaking, power may belong to anyone, while effectiveness derives only from merit. Because effectiveness of action stems from enduring moral principles that govern the cosmos, gains made on this basis outlast gains

from amoral power. One may overcome a girl's reserve for a night or two with love magic, but an enduring marriage can only come from merit. In practice, effectiveness may be difficult to distinguish from power. Amulets, tattooed marks, verbal formulae, and a host of other devices enable the gambler to win, the boxer to beat his opponent, the soldier to win in battle, and the physician to cure a patient. In addition, a considerable proportion of the population seeks to insure the outcome of critical undertakings through offerings to various spirits. Hence, one cannot say directly from having seen a man win the national lottery for the month whether his success came from effectiveness or power. (1962, 1254)

Merit, then, is the preferred—but not the only—source of personal potency. As Hanks suggests, its usefulness is not restricted to achieving the goal of a better rebirth but can also be applied toward more mundane and immediate ends. In particular, a person of great merit is less susceptible to the hostile and aggressive powers discussed in chapter 2, such as those manifest in spirit possession; in the loss of one's vital life forces, or *khwan*; and in certain types of illnesses. Nevertheless, when Shan become convinced that their merit is weak, they do not hesitate to employ alternative sources of power. These include the use of protective amulets and tattoos, astrological calculations, and the propitiation of spirits—especially the *tsao moeng*, or village guardian spirit, who is perceived as both keenly interested in human affairs and immediately available for action.

All of these, and more, are used throughout a person's life to supplement the power of merit making. Once a person dies, however, these alternative sources of power are no longer available to him. There is only one kind of power that can reach a dead person, and that is the power of merit.

Making Merit for the Dead

> Once there was a very wealthy man who had a son. It was his only child and he loved him very much. When the child died unexpectedly, the father was heartbroken. He asked his servant to take a bowl of rice for his son's spirit to eat to a spot on the other side of a stream that ran next to their house. The servant did this every morning for many days. Then one day the stream flooded, and he was unable to cross to the usual offering spot. While he was wondering what to do, he saw a line of monks with alms bowls approaching along the road. The servant thought to himself, "I might as well give this offering of rice to these monks. It's a waste of food, anyway, to leave it out along the side of the stream." So that's what he did. He was afraid to mention it to the father of the boy, however, so he said nothing about it.

That night the father had a dream. His dead son appeared to him and said, "Father! Don't you love me? I haven't received any rice from you for a long time and have been very hungry. Today is the first day you gave me anything to eat!" After learning from his servant what he had done with that morning's offering, the father understood that he needed to give through the monks in order for anything to reach his son. When the monks eat the rice, his son eats the merit.

So, from this time on, people have made offerings to monks for their deceased loved ones.

REMARKS MADE BY A MONK *during a ceremony for the dead in the Shan village of Napatsaat, September 26, 1990*

At the conclusion of virtually any formal act of merit making, the person seeking merit pours water from a small container onto the ground (or into a bowl that will later be emptied onto the ground) while the monk or other recipient of the seeker's gift chants a blessing.[5] For Shan, this is the critical moment when one actually receives the merit, the moment when it is somehow cosmically credited to one's name. During this rite (called the *yaat nam*), it is customary to share the earned merit with one's deceased relatives, with hungry and wandering spirits, and, ultimately, "with all sentient beings." This is accomplished, Shan say, simply by stating who it is one wishes to share in the merit of this act. One's words have power—the cosmos listens.

When someone dies, this simple rite for sharing merit with others is expanded into a series of elaborate merit-making rituals, all of which are intended to aid the deceased (and, indirectly, the survivors). In fact, funeral rites can be seen as essentially a kind a communal merit making for the deceased; it is, one might argue, what Shan funerals are archetypically about. And merit making, in turn, is a concept whose core meaning is to help the dead. It can be seen as a practice that—no matter when it occurs—is essentially linked to the dead and the dead-to-be. Hence, even when a person is making merit for herself, she is doing it, at least in part, in anticipation of her dead self, that is, for the self that, when she dies, will experience the consequences of her current actions. The sequence of events that occur immediately after and within a year of a person's death illustrates these points and sheds light on the process by which a *khwan*-bearing body is transformed into a bodiless *phi*.

The Funeral of Nang Nu's Father

During the four days between Grandfather's death and the cremation ceremony, his family's house was filled with people, day and night. What would be frightening if alone—sharing a house with a corpse whose spirit has not yet fully departed—becomes bearable when one has lots of company. Each evening, just after sundown, a group of five invited monks arrived and proceeded up the stairs into the main room of the house where Grandfather's body was lying in state. They arranged themselves on chairs that had been brought in for this purpose—four to the right and parallel with the body, one set apart on the left. The rest of the room was packed with people, mostly temple sleepers, who had gathered to listen to the monks chant and to help make merit for Grandfather.

Different monks came each night—some invited from nearby villages, others from temples in town—but the service remained the same. After a brief sermon by the monk who sat apart, the other four began to chant, their faces hidden by four large red fans that they held up in front of themselves. Those of us in the audience could not see the monks' faces, but we could read the fans. Each fan had a verse in Thai inscribed on it in gold letters that, taken together, offered a piercing meditation on death: "a leaving with no return," "a sleep without a stir," "a recovery that doesn't happen," "an escape that is inescapable."[6] More chants and prayers followed, including a *sut mon* chant (*suat mon* in Thai) designed to generate protective and purifying powers, as well as a *yaat nam* prayer asking that the merit made that night be shared with the spirit of Grandfather. These prayers, together with the scripture reading by a lay reader that followed, were intended to facilitate Grandfather's passage to a good place in the land of the spirits while simultaneously providing protection for his family in case his *khwan* should linger awhile in the land of the living.

Meanwhile, underneath the house, a half-dozen different games of chance had been set up, each one attracting a small but intense group of mostly men and boys who had come to gamble. There is a long tradition of gambling at funerals and at *kotsaa*, the eleventh-month merit-making ceremonies for the dead, and village funerals often attract dealers and card sharks from miles around who join the local men in their all-night games. "If we didn't have gambling at funerals, not enough people would come," Uncle Samaun once explained to me. "Besides, how else could we keep people awake all night?" Entrepreneurial women, ever alert to an opportunity, set up food stalls nearby to sell sweets, roasted eggs, and spicy sausage balls on a stick to the hungry gamblers, giving the event the flavor and aroma of a village temple fair.

Next to this rowdy crowd below the house, a makeshift kitchen of open cooking fires and rough work tables served as headquarters for Nang Nu and the other women who showed up to help her. Food was being prepared around the clock. In the evenings, after they had finished their chants, the monks (who do not take solid food after noon) were served soft drinks while the rest of the guests were treated to cups of hot "oh-wan-teen" (Ovaltine), prepared in huge kettles by the volunteer work crew below and served by cadres of young girls who went up and down the stairs with tray after tray of glasses filled with the hot liquid. Many visitors left after this part of the evening services, but those who stayed for the long scripture reading that followed were served a midnight snack of rice porridge, also prepared by the women below.

During the day, the cooking chores continued, as regular meals had to be provided for all the visiting guests (some of whom had traveled from other villages) and for the workers themselves. Over the course of the four days, someone from virtually every household in the village showed up to help with the enormous amount of work this funeral required. Young men split firewood for the cooking fires and helped with the heavier tasks. Young women brought buckets of water from the well for cooking and washing dishes. Older women supervised the food preparations. Nang Kit, who lived directly across the street from Nang Nu and was her closest friend, was there every day, as were all the close relatives of Grandfather's family. Men who had been sponsored by Grandfather for their novice ordinations came to pay their respects, as did an older man who had been the sponsor of Nang Nu's husband when he was in the *sangha*.

In between greeting her guests, presiding over the merit-making rites upstairs in the house, and driving into town for more foodstuffs and offering supplies, Nang Nu directed the labor of the volunteers gathered under her father's house whenever she could, entrusting the job to her friend Nang Kit when her attention was needed elsewhere.

On the first day after her father's death, Nang Nu enlisted a local carpenter to build a simple wooden coffin, which was to be decorated with colored paper and placed inside a more ornate, gilded box until the time of cremation. When this was completed and the body placed inside on the second day, the carpenter organized a group of local men and boys in the building of a large, sleighlike palanquin upon which the coffin would rest during its journey from house to cemetery. These and other tasks filled the days prior to the final rites. Everyone was busy.

On the day before the cremation, Nang Nu sat on the floor in the back of her shop, surrounded by piles of offering supplies and by women who had come to help her assemble them. They were preparing *kho lu*, offerings to be given to each of the nineteen monks invited to participate in the cremation ceremony the next day. Each offering consisted of a group of useful, everyday items (detergent, candles, incense sticks, a bottle of fish sauce, a can of sweetened condensed milk, cigarettes and matches, and so on) carefully arranged on a plate and wrapped in yellow cellophane, then topped with 200 baht in crisp, new bills (about US$8 at the time).

As they worked, they discussed the monk's sermon of the night before, recalling his theme of the importance of keeping the old customs and his praise for Grandfather's efforts in this regard. Because of his generous involvement in so many religious ceremonies, the monk said, Grandfather had accumulated a lot of merit and, furthermore, had no negative karmic residue *(wot)* remaining, "so it was a good time for him to die." Nang Nu appeared to be comforted by these words. The sermons of the other monks on the two previous evenings had been similar, always stressing the inevitability of death and thus the importance of accumulating merit, while praising Grandfather as an example for us all.

Finally the day of the cremation arrived. The carpenter was up early, putting finishing touches on the palanquin that was to hold the coffin, after which the entire structure was lifted onto a wooden cart. Just after breakfast, three young boys (two of them grandsons of Grandfather) who had previously been in the *sangha* were reordained as novices in a simple ceremony at the home of Nang Nu's mother. Though they would remain in the yellow robes for only a few days, their actions would generate additional merit for Grandfather at this critical moment in his transformation from the living to the dead. Nang Nu's ten-year-old son watched them closely, wondering, perhaps, when his turn would come.[7]

With the ordinations complete, it was time for the coffin to be brought out of the house. Nang Nu's husband, Uncle Loen, led the way, carrying a silver offering bowl filled with flowers and popped rice. He was followed by a group of monks and the three newly ordained novices, each of whom was holding onto a long white string attached to the coffin. The coffin itself was carried by six men who were close relatives of Grandfather. After the coffin was positioned securely on the cart, Nang Nu placed three silver bowls filled with flowers on top of it and finished the decorations on the rest of the structure. Then she brought out an old enlarged and framed photo of Grandfather that I had taken ten years earlier and put it at the head end of the coffin, which had a place set up in front of it for people to light candles and incense sticks and say a short prayer. Paper cutouts of two feet, looking very much like footprints, were pasted onto the other end of the coffin so that people could keep track of which way the body was oriented. As in all Shan funerals, the coffin was positioned with the feet pointing in the direction that they were supposed to go, that is, away from the village and toward the cemetery, so that the spirit of the deceased would not wander back in the direction of the village.

As the time for the temple services neared, people slowly separated themselves from this scene outside the house and began to move up the road

Grandfather Wang's coffin is placed on the decorated funeral cart while newly ordained novice monks wait in the foreground.

toward the monastery grounds. In this, as in most large-scale Shan ceremonies, one's experience of the event was tied to one's age, gender, and relationship to the ceremony's sponsor. Older people went directly into the preaching hall. They were joined by most of the out-of-town guests and by local women whose infants and toddlers kept them from assisting with other preparations. This group constituted the audience for the merit-making rite of *thaum lik*, a ritual reading of a long, scripture-based text. (This was the same sort of reading that had occurred every evening since Grandfather's death at the home of Nang Nu's mother.)

Local women middle-aged and younger didn't even try to enter the crowded temple to listen to the reading. They went straight underneath it to help with the preparations for the huge meal that was to be served after the services as part of the merit making for Grandfather, a meal that was to feed several hundred people. Young men and boys from the village also helped with the project, as did out-of-town women who were close to Nang Nu and

Inside the temple's preaching hall, guests gather for Grandfather's funeral service.

her family. A fourth group who threw themselves into the work consisted of those who had recently sponsored a large ceremony themselves or anticipated sponsoring one soon. Although no records are kept of one's labors, reciprocity is the norm, and those who volunteer their help now know they can count on receiving help from others in the future.

Underneath the temple, people worked at filling dozens of trays with luncheon curries and hundreds of plates with rice, all of which would later be distributed among the guests upstairs. Nang Nu personally arranged bowls of food for the monks on low wooden tables, outfitting each one with generous portions of several different curries, a large pot of steaming rice, plates, spoons, and folded paper napkins. Because monks and novices do not eat after noon, organizers of ceremonies that are to include a meal for them must watch the clock. About 10:30, men were enlisted to carry the specially laid tables upstairs, and as the scripture reading continued, they quietly moved them up onto the platform near the monks.

The *thaum lik* ended at 10:45 and was followed by a few chants from the monks. At 11:00 sharp a bell rang, and the monks began to eat while the rest of the guests were being served. With so many people, the meal took a long time; some had already finished eating by the time that others were just being served. After the meal and a sermon by one of the monks from town, the nineteen wrapped offerings were distributed, one to each monk, and the novices

The funeral procession proceeds to the cemetery just outside the village.

were each given some cash in a white envelope. Chants from the monks in recognition of the merit that was being made for Grandfather punctuated each
of these activities and ended the service.

Now it was time to move to the cemetery. Everyone filed out of the
temple and returned to the crossroads where Grandfather's body lay waiting. They had gathered their resources to make as much merit as they possibly could for Grandfather, and all that remained was the final task of
sending him off on the next stage of his journey. The monks and novices led
the procession, again holding onto the white string attached to the coffin.
Others carried the silver bowls filled with flowers. Everyone crowded round
the cart—women in their white blouses and black sarongs, men in traditional dark shirts and pants—and tried to help pull the cart by the thick rope
that was attached to it, stopping every now and then for a mock tug-of-war
with the huge boatlike structure that seemed to float down the road.[8]

When we reached the cemetery, a site north of the village and just off the
road, Nang Nu and some helpers were there at the entrance to hand each of us
a little bundle of pine wood and incense tied with two strips of black and white
cloth, and a small breath inhaler wrapped in black netting. The inhaler was an
innovation for Baan Kaung Mu funerals, intended, no doubt, to address the
often voiced concern about bad smells at cremations. Small paper cups of cola
on ice were also available for those who were wilting in the midday heat.

We picked our way carefully down the tangled slope from the road and
through the underbrush that only partially concealed the broken pieces of

wood left from previous cremations. We added our bundles of kindling to the logs on the funeral pyre, then found a place to squat. Most women stayed close to the road, ready for their customary quick retreat as soon as the fire was lit. I opted to stay with the men and close female relatives of Grandfather who chose spots nearer to the pyre. Except for a few of Grandfather's older grand-children, no children were allowed in the cemetery. Because of their more frag-ile *khwan,* which are said to be less firmly attached to the body, most women and children avoid cremations when they can, or they at least try to stay on the fringes, for fear that the escaping life force of the deceased might seize them.

Meanwhile, a group of men were struggling with the coffin on its heavy and awkward palanquin. With effort, they got the elaborate structure down the slope and placed it next to the pyre. Monks gathered round it and, tak-ing turns, chanted and removed yellow robes that had been draped on the coffin for them to take, thus fulfilling the ancient admonition that monks shall wander and take as their clothing cast-off pieces that they find in the forest and in cemeteries. When the robes were all distributed, one of the se-nior monks took hold of the white string that was still attached to the coffin and, standing about five yards away under a beautiful, large yellow um-brella, recited the final merit-making chants for Grandfather.

Then, quickly, the palanquin was disassembled. The fancy outer frame was taken off the coffin and carried in pieces up to a waiting truck, revealing the simple wooden coffin that had been covered in gold paper. This was lifted up and placed high atop the pyre by a group of middle-aged men. One of them then climbed onto the logs that would soon be set ablaze. Balancing there, he pried open the coffin lid to expose the body. Then, using his machete, he split a fresh coconut over it so that the clear, fragrant liquid washed over Grand-father's face "to make him beautiful in his next life."

Finally, a monk lit a piece of pine wood and used it to ignite the funeral pyre. Within seconds, the entire structure was engulfed in flames. Most people left quickly now, if they hadn't already, leaving only a few men to watch the fire. Buckets of fragrant, cleansing water *(nam mak khaun)* were waiting by the side of the road for people to use on their face and hands as they left the cemetery, "to keep us from having bad dreams."

When I arrived back home, I noticed that my landlady, Aunt Ying, had taken in some laundry I had left out on the line, reminding me of the local custom: if, on the day of the cremation, the spirit of the deceased sees clothes hanging outside, he thinks they are the clothes of others who have died and calls whoever owns them to come with him to the land of the dead. Aunt Ying also reminded me that any clothes worn the day of the cremation must be taken off and laundered right away that day; and indeed, the bathing stream that afternoon was full of people washing their clothes.

That night at Nang Nu's mother's house, one more ritual reading was held, this one attended only by the local temple sleepers, all out-of-town visitors having returned home shortly after the cremation. The funeral was over now, but the merit making would continue. The next morning, Nang Nu would take a special set of offerings to the temple (called *haen saum tsaum*), with other offerings to follow at regular intervals. Later in the year, there would be additional public merit making with many more guests, a kind of second funeral known as the *kotsaa*. Only then would the sending off of Grandfather's life force be complete and the ambiguity over its whereabouts more or less resolved.

A "Different" Death

For Shan, death always signals the beginning of a process. It is not the end of a life force but the beginning of its transformation into something new. At death, a person's *khwan* must leave the body, become a freely mobile *phi*, and separate itself from the people and places it used to frequent. Failure to do this can both hinder the rebirth of the deceased and present certain dangers to those left behind. As we have seen in the case of Nang Nu's father, many aspects of Shan funeral rites are designed to facilitate this separating process while protecting the living during the interim. Nevertheless, some deaths are considered more problematic than others.[9]

The death of Grandfather was considered a normal, or ordinary, death, and, as such, it aroused only the most minimal concern for the behavior of his ghost. Even before hearing the monks' assurances, everyone assumed that Grandfather's life force would enjoy a relatively easy passage to the land of the dead and, from there, a good rebirth. There were two main reasons for this confident attitude. First, Grandfather's death, although sudden, was not the result of violence or of an avoidable accident. Second, Grandfather was an old man by the time he died and had been a devout temple sleeper for many years.

Understanding the significance of these two aspects of his death entails an appreciation of the defining role of emotional attachment in Shan constructions of "safe" and "dangerous" deaths. Simply put, Shan act on the assumption that the degree of danger that any given person's death poses to the rest of the community is directly related to the strength of that person's attachment to life in general and to certain people in particular. The stronger the attachment, the greater the danger. Those who die in the prime of life and/or with no time to mentally prepare themselves for their own death (as in the case of a fatal accident or a violent death) are presumed to be burdened by powerful, untamed emotional attachments to loved ones and home, a situation that is only compounded by a similar lack of emotional readiness on the part of their friends and family to let them go. Such deaths are considered extremely dangerous because they can result in other, living members of the community being "called" by, or drawn to, the deceased—an emotional tug that, if not checked, can have disastrous consequences. To see how these ideas inform Shan responses to specific deaths and, in the process, provide the basis for an indigenous theory of mental health, I want to relate the story of another death that was universally recognized as different from that of Grandfather's.

In this tragic case, Nang Yen, a young woman of twenty-eight, and her nine-year-old daughter, Tsip, were killed during a thunderstorm when a tree struck by lightening collapsed upon a roadside shelter in which the two had taken refuge. After the bodies were discovered by the woman's horrified husband, the *kamnan* (regional headman) and other village elders had to decide what to do. Bringing the bodies back to their house was out of the question, with a death as violent as this one. The leaders briefly considered bringing the bodies back to the temple so that they could hold services for them inside the village but ultimately decided that the village was "too small," with "not enough souls *(khwan),*" and that they "wouldn't be able to handle it" *(am pei lai).*

Instead, a group of monks was assembled to go with all the adult men of the village to hold a hasty cremation that very night.[10] The monks were asked to "chase the spirits out of the bodies" first, before the men tried to remove them from the rubble. Then the bodies were quickly cremated right there on the spot. No public service would be held until seven days had passed, at which time a merit-making ceremony would be performed in their honor. That night, and during the intervening days between the cremation and the merit-making ceremony, I listened to people talk about the tragedy.

Early in the evening, when there was still a possibility that something might happen at the temple, I expressed an interest in going. Nang Kaew, my young assistant who usually wanted to accompany me on such outings, said she didn't think she would be going because she was too scared. "When you're scared, you shouldn't go," she explained. "Your *khwan* might leave." Later in the evening, after the plans for an immediate cremation became known, Nang Kaew wanted to go visit her family (only a few houses away), but our landlady, Aunt Ying, cautioned us against leaving the house. As the evening wore on, I gradually realized that this was less out of concern for us than out of fear of being left alone in her house. Aunt Ying had been quite close to Nang Yen and her family for several years, so she had more reason than most to fear the "pull" of Nang Yen's ghost.

As we sat talking in the house, she told us of a dream she had had the night before in which she found herself in a dilapidated house (like the collapsed roadside shelter?) and heard a voice calling, "Mae Kham! Mae Kham!" (Mother-Sponsor!).[11] She clearly regarded the dream as an omen foreshadowing the evening's disaster, and she seemed to want to talk about it. Nang Kaew, on the other hand, although equally anxious, apparently felt the best strategy was to avoid talking about it. She buried her head in a magazine and responded testily to Aunt Ying's and my attempts to draw her into the conversation.

When we were all ready to go to sleep and it was time to make our final excursions down to the outhouse, Aunt Ying surprised me by asking to use my flashlight. (I had never known her to use one before, even on moonless nights.) I handed it to her. "Aren't you going too?" she asked. "I'll wait for you," I said. But she insisted, "If you're going to go, come on now!" Somewhat belatedly, I realized she wanted company. I glanced at Nang Kaew, who grinned and handed me her flashlight so we could go together. Safely back upstairs, as she was retiring to her own room, Aunt Ying surprised me again by instructing us to close all the windows in our room. (Normally, and often to Nang Kaew's distress, she asked us to leave them open in order to bring in the cool night air.)

Later, in the middle of the night, I was awakened by Aunt Ying's voice in the room next to ours. She had gotten up and was stamping her foot on the floor and yelling, "Go away! Go on! Get out of here!" This went on for some time. Downstairs the next morning, as we were all making breakfast, Nang Kaew (who later confessed to having slept all night with the blanket pulled up over her head) teased her about it, saying, "So, Aunt Ying was afraid of a rat last night, eh?" "It wasn't a rat," she replied soberly. "It was Nang Yen and Tsip. I heard them come into the house, downstairs. They were over there"— she pointed to her dressing area—"looking in the mirror."

As the days wore on, I learned that our household was not the only one that had been rattled by the sudden deaths. Everywhere in the village, people gathered in small groups at the local shops and at each other's homes to discuss the event, struggling both to make sense of what had happened and to control their own emotions. Two women mentioned, independently of one another, that they had not slept well the night of the deaths and, since then, had had trouble eating. One, whose house was fairly far away from that of Pi Non, the dead woman's husband, nevertheless insisted that she could hear him crying all night long, that the sound came to her "across the rice fields." A third woman, whose house was near the monastery compound, said that she had heard Pi Non crying at the temple and that she "couldn't bear to hear it," that it made her "want to run away." Significantly, perhaps, people didn't use the construction "I'm sad" *(tsau lek)* to describe their feelings. Instead, everyone chose "I feel sorry for them/I pity them" *(ilu man),* a formulation that expresses sympathy and compassion yet maintains some emotional distance and resists the temptation to fully identify with the victims and their distraught husband/father. Similarly, one might interpret people's expressed difficulties with hearing Pi Non cry as a desire to avoid situations in which it would be difficult not to feel sad and identify with him. Such emotional states are considered dangerous because they make one's *khwan* vulnerable to being scared off or, even worse, called to join the deceased.

Interwoven with this struggle to control one's emotions was a parallel effort to comprehend the meaning of what had happened. One man, after listening quietly to his wife tell a group of us how she had been unable to sleep at night because she could hear Pi Non crying, began to lecture us about the strange nature of the accident. "Why had the victims stayed out in an exposed area when the storm came up?" he asked rhetorically. The two of them must have "wanted to die," he went on; otherwise they would have waited out the storm in a ditch or some other safe place. Later, after more conversation, he remarked that "their time was up"[12] and, as proof, drew our attention to the fact that both mother and child had been born on a Thursday, the same day of the week on which the accident occurred. Later still, as people continued to talk about the incident, he warned them, "You just can't allow your heart to feel sorry for them constantly. One can't bear it. You must instead say to yourself, 'I, too, will die.'"

Meanwhile, Pi Non himself could be seen taking offerings to the temple early each morning to make merit for his wife and child. In the evenings, people gathered at his house to gamble and keep him company. Many observed him with some concern. "He's become somewhat crazy *(yaung),*" Nang Kaew commented after a visit from Pi Non in which he detailed his plans to make merit for his loved ones, including his intention to be ordained as a monk. "How can you tell?" I asked. "Because he talks nonstop and uses his hands a lot when he talks," Nang Kaew said. Others agreed with Nang Kaew's conjecture, though no one said anything to him about it at that time.[13]

By chance, the seven-day interval between the deaths and the public merit-making ceremony happened to include the day of the annual "feast of the *tsao moeng*" that was held in honor of the village guardian spirit.[14] One feature of this ceremony was of special interest to Pi Non—its gathering of spirit mediums that enabled anyone who wanted to do so to communicate directly with the village guardian spirit. Pi Non looked forward to this event all week, seeing in it an opportunity to find out about some matters that were troubling him.

When the day finally came, I sat waiting with other villagers for the spirit mediums (mostly elderly women) to assemble at the shrine of the *tsao moeng*. Pi Non arrived and sat down next to me. "I'm going to ask them about my wife and child," he said, adding that he hoped to learn where they were and whether they were getting the merit he had been sending to them with his daily offerings. He stressed that he wanted to ask these things not only for himself but also for the people of the village, so that they would know where the spirits of Nang Yen and Tsip were and would not be afraid of them. "I don't want people to be afraid of them," he explained.

As the mediums one by one fell into a trance, the attendants called to Pi Non to come and be the first to ask questions of the *tsao moeng*. Pi Non sat close to one of the possessed women and, in a quiet voice, asked, "What did my wife and daughter do wrong that they were killed by the falling tree? What mistake did they make? Who/what did they offend?" Speaking through the frail old woman who sat before him with her eyes closed, the *tsao moeng* answered, "They didn't do anything wrong. It happens that there is a spirit that haunts the spot where they were killed, the spirit of a young policeman who died on that very same spot about twenty years ago. This policeman had not yet married when he died, and now his spirit wants a wife, so he took Nang Yen." The *tsao moeng* went on to say that the spirit of this bachelor-policeman was in fact still there. It had taken other lives in the past and would no doubt take more. Pi Non asked for permission to chase it away, but the *tsao moeng* told him it couldn't be done; the spirit simply would not leave the spot.

Later, after others had had a chance to ask some questions, Pi Non resumed his inquiries. During one sequence, he asked whether the merit he had been making for his wife and daughter this past week had been reaching them. The medium/*tsao moeng*, who by now had moved into something of an entertainment-through-wisecracking mode, replied, "Yes, of course. Where else is it going to go?" which produced chuckles from the audience. Pi Non ignored the laughter and pursued his line of questioning with a grim determination. "And the ritual reading and offerings that I am sponsoring tonight and tomorrow morning—this is the right thing to be doing? The correct way to proceed?" "Yes, it is," the *tsao moeng* answered. "In fact, if you don't do these things, you might go crazy!" More laughter—the *tsao moeng* had noticed and called attention to the behavior in Pi Non that was of concern to his fellow villagers but, by making jokes about it, was relieving the tension it had produced.

Still ignoring the amusement of the onlookers, Pi Non continued, asking finally if he should become a monk. More gently now, the medium/*tsao moeng* reassured him that this was a good idea, saying once again that it would help keep him from going crazy. The *tsao moeng* suggested, however, that Pi Non try becoming a novice first and then, after seven days, if he still wanted to, he could become a monk. "And when should I be ordained?" Pi Non asked. "On *wan sin* (the Buddhist Sabbath)" was the reply.

That night and the following morning, the public merit-making ceremonies for Nang Yen and Tsip were held. The evening service consisted of a ritual reading *(thaum lik)* at the temple, including some gambling underneath and the preparation of a late-night snack for all those who came to listen to the reading. In this, the merit making was not unlike that done for Nang Nu's father. The service that was held the following morning, however, was quite different from the long temple service provided for Grandfather Wang.

After a brief series of scriptural chants and the serving of breakfast to the monks and other participants, the remainder of the service, which was the part most focused on merit making for the deceased, was moved out of the temple to a small clearing on the side of a nearby road. Mats were laid out for the monks to sit on, and all the offerings intended as part of the merit making for Nang Yen and Tsip were carried out of the temple and arranged on the ground in front of them. The reason for this change in venue was explained to me in this way: "The spirits of people who die the way Nang Yen and Tsip died cannot enter the temple to collect the merit being made for them. This is because, if they die that way, it means they have *wot* (negative karmic residue)."

To make up for this presumed karmic deficit, extra merit making is required, some of which is accomplished by symbolic-magical means. Thus, in addition to the regular offerings (which were similar to those offered at Grandfather's funeral), a series of 150 small mounds of earth decorated with flags, candles, and incense sticks were arranged in three rows. These were intended to be "sand pagodas," miniature replicas of the genuine pagodas whose construction is said to generate enormous amounts of merit. Ten larger mounds formed a fourth row, yielding a total of 160 "pagodas" to make merit for Nang Yen and Tsip.

Another prominent feature of the preparations was the presence of several distinctive *tam khaun*. A *tam khaun* is a funeral offering that is traditionally in the form of a decorated panel, perhaps ten feet in length.[15] The panel is attached by a piece of string to an even taller bamboo pole, which, at the end of the ceremony, is stuck into the ground, allowing the panel to sway, flaglike, in the wind. Grandfather's funeral offerings had included one such *tam khaun*, which, after his cremation ceremony, was set up on its pole in the monastery compound. Nang Yen and Tsip's funeral offerings, on the other hand, included six *tam khaun* of various sorts.

Tam khaun are used at funerals for two reasons. First, like the presentation of other objects to the monks at this time, the presentation of a *tam*

Monks leave the temple compound for the funeral of Nang Yen and her daughter.

The funeral service takes place along the side of the road.

khaun is an act that generates merit, and, because of this, a person may have more than one. Second, and more critical, is the role of the *tam khaun* in directing the flow of merit being made toward the spirit of the deceased. Attached to each *tam khaun* is a sheet of paper on which is written, in Shan script, the name of the person who died and a detailed list of all the various items that are being offered in the deceased's name, conveying the overall message: "This merit is for person X."

When the death is due to violence or an accident, the *tam khaun* often has the additional feature of a small wooden boat attached, complete with clay figures posed in the role of oarsmen. Others carry the figure of a bird perched on top of the pole. In either case, the boat and bird symbols are intended to "help carry the spirit [of the deceased] to a good place"; they "make it easier to get there." At the ceremony for Nang Yen and Tsip, two of the *tam khaun* had boats attached, two were of another, cylindrical design, and the final two were like the sand pagodas—miniature replicas drawn in the sandy earth. Once again, the point of such elaborate preparations was to provide a massive, merit-filled counterweight to the presumed karmic deficit that had produced this tragedy.

The roadside ceremony consisted primarily of a series of merit-generating chants by the monks, interrupted by a brief sermon. Afterwards, all the moveable offerings were taken back into the temple except for the *tam khaun*, which were supposed to be set up on the roadside clearing. Pi Non seemed reluctant to leave them there, however, and as people were beginning to disperse, he suddenly announced that he wanted to take two of them and put them up in the temple compound. "That would be all right, wouldn't it?" he asked nobody in particular. Everyone still within earshot replied kindly, "Sure, go ahead. That won't hurt anything. Put them up in the temple compound if you like." This he did, talking to himself as he worked, quietly explaining what he was doing to whoever walked by.

Like Nang Nu, Pi Non would continue to make offerings at the temple at regular intervals until the end of the year, when the final stage in the process of sending off his loved ones, the *kotsaa*, would occur.

Helping the Dead, Protecting the Living

Every year in the eleventh lunar month of the Shan calendar, which usually falls in late September to early October, a series of special merit-making ceremonies called *kotsaa* are performed for all those who have died in the previous year. It is said that, during this month, the spirits of the recently dead return to the village to pick up or receive *(hap)* the offerings prepared by

their surviving kin. The purpose of this rite, from the perspective of the survivors, is twofold. For still grieving kin, the *kotsaa* offers a kind of second
chance to do something tangible for their deceased relatives, something
that will benefit them in their new capacity as beings-in-transition. Many
people reported that only after sponsoring a *kotsaa* did they feel satisfied,
or content *(im)*.

Second, the *kotsaa* is regarded as the last step in the process of transforming a still lingering and potentially troublesome ghost into a benign, or
tame, spirit that is ready to be reborn among humans once again. This aspect of the rite is especially salient in the case of sudden or violent deaths,
but it is also present to some extent with any death.

Although many variations are possible, the basic format for a *kotsaa* is a
ritual reading *(thaum lik)* conducted in the temple by a lay reader, followed
by a meal for the monks and others present.[16] The monks are then presented
with the same sorts of offerings given at funeral ceremonies, including at
least one new *tam khaun* for each of the deceased, which the monks acknowledge with a series of chants and a sermon. When asked why *tam khaun*
are given again at the *kotsaa* ceremonies, Pi Non explained, "We do it to send
the merit to the person. Even if the person is already reborn by then, we ask
that the merit then go to that new person, to help him get a good start, to help
things go well for him."

Often, families in the same village who will be sponsoring *kotsaa* in a
given year combine efforts to hold a single grand and festive event with lavish
treats, nightly gambling, and many invited guests from other nearby villages.
This can be done, however, only for people who died an ordinary, natural
death. Just as in funerals, the spirits of those who died an untimely or violent
death cannot yet enter the temple to pick up their merit. Hence, the *kotsaa*
rites for such people, a much more somber affair, are held along the road and
separately from those of others who died more peacefully. At the 1990 *kotsaa*
in Baan Kaung Mu, relatives of people who died such deaths in the previous
year expressed their hope that, after the ceremony was over, their loved ones
would have received sufficient merit to cancel out whatever residual demerit
they might have had left and would, from then on, be able to enter the temple
and receive additional merit along with all the other sentient beings with
whom merit is customarily shared during ordinary merit-making rites
throughout the year.

Although the rhetoric and public discussions surrounding these and
other funeral rites emphasize helping the dead, a less talked about but equally
important function is to protect the living. Making merit for the dead to help
them "get to a good place" can thus also be seen as giving the spirits of the
dead whatever they need to make them go away. This darker side of Shan

funeral rites is barely noticeable during the festival-like activities accompanying a good death, like that of Grandfather, but its presence is unmistakable in cases of bad deaths, like those of Nang Yen and Tsip.

Thus, in addition to making merit to help the spirit of the deceased move on of its own accord, rites are sometimes performed to actually chase it away. This is considered especially appropriate in the case of a violent death that occurs at a spot normally used by others, such as a house or a cultivated field. When, for example, a young farmer from a neighboring village was found murdered in his field hut out in the rice paddies, special precautions were taken. As in the case of Nang Yen and Tsip, the body had to be cremated immediately. One of the man's older relatives told me, "I had to buy a lot of liquor for the men who were to deal with the body; otherwise they wouldn't be brave enough to touch it." Then, after seven days had passed and it was time for the public merit-making ceremonies (which were virtually identical to those held for Nang Yen and Tsip), monks were called in first "to send away the spirit" *(song phi)* from the site of the field hut.

As in the "sweeping away the spirit" section of the healing rite described in chapter 2, in which a basket of food is prepared for the troublesome spirit and used to lure it out of the patient's body and away from the village, five such baskets, containing the same sorts of food samples and clay figures but with the addition of miniature *tam khaun*, were brought to the field hut. A monk sat next to each basket—one in each of the four corners and the fifth in the center of the little room[17]—and chanted a series of powerful prayers and verses intended to drive away the possibly lingering ghost. Four of the baskets were then carried far away in the directions of the four corners in which they had rested, and the fifth one was placed along the road nearby. The field hut itself was then thoroughly sprinkled with sacralized water to purify it and protect it against a return of the ghost.

A similar *song phi* rite was held on the site of the mysterious death (and presumed murder) of a Chinese woman near some garden lands west of Baan Kaung Mu. Her funeral had already been held in Bangkok, where most of her relatives resided. Four months later, however, many people were still avoiding the site, making it difficult for those whose land was nearby to get anyone, especially women, to come and do exchange labor in their gardens. The solution was to hold a *song phi* rite, sponsored by the *kamnan* and his wife, after which people once again felt comfortable working in or near the area.

In some cases, even these sorts of measures are not enough to reassure people. When a young local woman, distraught after the recent death of her husband in a horrible accident, committed suicide by poisoning herself, people responded with a grief that was tinged with considerable worry. The incident occurred a few months before my arrival in 1990 but remained a topic of concern well beyond the time of her *kotsaa* several months later. The house she and her husband had shared with his parents and siblings (which was, in all other respects, an exceptionally attractive house by local standards) was abandoned by the family and remained empty more than a year later when I left the village. Not only would no one live in the house, but many also avoided even walking past it after dark. In cases such as these, when no ritual technology seems sufficiently powerful to counter the danger at hand, one must rely on one's own mental discipline and emotional control as the ultimate safeguard, a topic to which I return in more detail in chapter 7.

For now, the point to keep in mind is that, despite the many ways these diverse deaths might have been distinguished, a single criterion was used to evaluate the danger each posed to the rest of the community, namely, the degree of attachment the deceased was presumed to have toward life in general and toward specific people and places at the time of death. That the ghosts of undisputedly good or gentle people nevertheless aroused concern when they died prematurely indicates that the issue of attachment outweighs that of virtue in terms of the dangerousness of the loss. In other words, what makes a spirit wild or aggressive has less to do with the moral character of its most recent life than with that being's unresolved desires—desires that, one way or another, are destined to seek fulfillment among the living.

To recap the argument thus far, the funerals and related ceremonies Shan perform for the deceased, as well as their response to death more generally, tell us something about the way the self is conceptualized and understood. At least some aspects of the self persist after death in the form of a spirit, *phi.* Funerals are explicitly about providing the deceased with sufficient merit so that they can "move on to a good place," but the subtext or inference is "so that they will not haunt us." The dead are potentially dangerous to us, the living, since they will seek to continue ties with those to whom they are emotionally attached. To counter this tendency, we must do everything we can to make sure the dead are satisfied, content, and "not hungry." In addition, we must try to control our own emotional longings for the beloved so as not to encourage the *phi* to linger and try to take us with them.

The role played by emotional attachment at the time of death is intriguing here, not only for the way it contrasts with most Euro-American conventional wisdom and Western therapeutic practice—where active grieving is considered both cathartic and necessary to one's psychological recovery—but also for what it suggests about an alternative view of human relationships and capacities, that is, for the image it conjures up of hearts in motion, of the almost gravitational pull that exists between bodies that have an emotional tug on each other. According to Shan, we are always under the influence of our consociates—those who travel through life with us as long-term friends, partners, kin, and co-workers—and we are constantly susceptible to being moved by them, pulled by our emotional investment in each other's lives. This is a view of selves as co-constituted by others in a thorough and ongoing way. A self thus conceived will require an appropriate sort of maintenance to protect its physical and mental health. But before we consider that, we must first take a closer look at the way such a self develops, the subject of the next chapter.

Chapter 4

Domesticating the Self

Culture, character, and consociates weave a complicated fabric of biography. The process is not only lifelong; it is longer than life. Consociates begin to shape our personal course even before we are born, and may continue to renegotiate the meaning of our life long after we are dead. To this extent, a person is a collective product. We must all "author" our own biographies, using the idioms of our heritage, but our biographies must be "authorized" by those who live them with us.

DAVID PLATH, *Long Engagements*

HOW DO PEOPLE understand the vast personal transformations involved in going from infancy to adulthood? Is it a process mostly controlled by humans? By nature? By the gods? When does it stop? What counts as "maturity," and how do you recognize it when you see it? In this chapter, I consider Shan theories of human development from birth to young adulthood.[1] I look first at the early period of life, considering Shan ideas about newborns and young children. This is a period marked by a concern with children's vulnerability and by adult efforts both to protect them and to help them learn how to protect themselves. Interestingly, while exploring the way adults view children of this age, I found some unanticipated similarities between the way people talked about spirits, souls, and young children. I offer a way to think about the similarities and parallel constructions that occur in all three conversations and suggest that they constitute a persistent theme in Shan notions of self and personhood, a theme that I refer to as "domesticating the self." What I will ultimately argue is that the Shan categories of spirits, souls, and children together constitute a class of beings that functions as a kind of unacknowledged Other for the construction of an ideal Self.

I then turn to the periods of life that follow, those of older children, teens, and young adults. Shan view these as much less dangerous than the time of young childhood and, perhaps for that reason, have less in the way of indigenous theory about these times of life. The focus, instead, is on learning to work and be productive, the series of steps that eventually results in a certain measure of independence and adult status. My discussion of these periods of life aims at drawing attention to those aspects of the social organization of people and work—including aspects of gender organization and parenting—that are most significant for understanding Shan conceptions of self and personhood.

The process of "domesticating the self" and achieving adult status is not, of course, an individual odyssey but, rather, one that takes place in tandem with others, in a particular social context, embedded in a series of social relationships, and informed by certain images of what constitutes maturity and the ideal adult. In the last section of this chapter, I consider the importance of hierarchical social relations as the backdrop for a person's journey from infancy to young adulthood. I also consider some complications that result from the equally important but tacit assumption of personal autonomy, pointing to how the resulting tensions manifest themselves in Shan social life.

The Self Reborn

JUNE 1990: I have just arrived back in Baan Kaung Mu after a nine-year absence and am in the process of arranging for a place to stay. After an emotional reunion with members of a household Roland and I had been close to during our previous stay, I am introduced to the newest member of the family, a four-year-old boy whom many in the village believe to be my first husband reborn. We regard each other with interest. What is he thinking? I wonder. What does he make of all this talk, conducted in his presence, about his previous life? How does it affect his sense of who he is to hear talk of who he was? How will it affect his relationship with me?

Shan speak frequently about people's previous lives, especially when they are in the presence of babies and young children. Their talk assumes that reasons exist (however obscure) for why a given child was born into a particular household. Their rebirth stories also suggest that aspects of the self that is reborn persist across lives, and that these aspects can be recognized. Hence, by examining who is thought to be whom reborn (and why), one can begin to unravel some of the strands of Shan thinking on the nature of self.

The stories of particular individuals reborn are predicated on more general assumptions about the nature of rebirth. The most basic of these is the notion that every individual's life begins in an immaterial form as a spirit-being (*phi*) that is about to be reborn. This spirit-being has a history of past lives, all of which are seen as potentially, or theoretically, relevant to its next rebirth. Shan place most emphasis, however, on the most recent life. Two aspects of this life, in particular, are said to have a strong, almost determinative effect on where the spirit-being will be reborn: first, who it "made merit with" in its previous life, and second, the affective bonds it forged during that previous lifetime. Hence, one might say that the spirit-being, in effect, chooses its own place of birth.

In practice, this means that most people are believed to be reborn in their home village or one nearby, since the people living there are those with whom the reborn have most likely "made merit" and had the strongest emotional ties. Although the general circumstances of a newborn infant's birth—whether the baby is beautiful or not, whether it has been born into a relatively rich or poor household, whether it is healthy and whole or sickly and deformed in some way, and so forth—are attributed to the moral quality *(kam)* of the baby's previous life and the amount of merit *(kuso)* it accumulated, the more specific circumstances of the birth (such as why this rich household and not that one) are explained by reference to preexisting affective ties. In particular, people are born into households that allow them to be physically close to someone they loved in their most recent life, especially if, during that life, those affective bonds were thwarted or cut short. In other words, a person's unfulfilled attachments seek further fulfillment in his or her next life.

For example, one young woman who left the village and later died in childbirth is now said to be reborn as the daughter of her former boyfriend, a young man still living in the village. "She was in love with him and wanted to marry him," I was told, "but his mother wouldn't let him marry her."

Sometimes it is the persistence of such affective bonds that alerts people to who the child "is." One little girl, for example, is said to be the deceased wife of a man (her father's uncle) whom she "likes a lot." Her obvious enjoyment of his company, along with perceived similarities in disposition between her and the deceased woman, have persuaded many people (including the little girl's mother) that she is this man's former wife. Even so, I was somewhat surprised to learn that the adult daughter of the deceased woman, who lives in another village and visits only occasionally, seemed equally convinced that the child was her mother reborn. I ran into her at a temple ceremony in a nearby village that was attended by many people from Baan Kaung Mu. As we sat chatting in the temple, she pointed to the little girl, who was there with her mother, and told me with obvious delight that the child was her deceased mother. As evidence, she reported that when she arrived at the temple, the little girl had come right over to her and demanded, "What have you brought [for me]?" Later, during the service, I saw the child get up from her mother's lap and walk across the room to sit with my friend for a while, causing her to smile and say quietly, "Oh, so you've come to see me, eh?"

In many cases, the rebirth stories involve close relatives. My landlady, for example, who had been widowed for several years, spoke easily of her three-year-old grandson being her former husband reborn. Whenever she comes back from an overnight stay at her distant fields, she told me, her grandson asks, "How are the water buffalo doing?" and other pertinent questions regarding the condition of "his" property there. "He still remembers," she concluded. In three other cases, one boy was said to be his great-grandfather reborn, a girl was said to be her great-grandmother reborn, and another boy was said to be a paternal uncle reborn.[2]

Kinship relationships are not always involved, however, as the case of my first husband's rebirth in a local village household suggests. I interpret the preponderance of kin relations in rebirth stories as simply a special application of the more general rule that requires the presence of strong emotional attachments. A *phi* about to be reborn will "follow its heart" whether or not that involves a close relative. By the same token, rebirth stories told by members of the child's household can be read as acts that publicly lay claim to a particular kind of relationship with the deceased. Every such story in effect announces: "This person loved me (or some member of my household). We had a special relationship."

In this regard, the story of Roland's rebirth as Tsai—the youngest brother of my field assistant, Nang Kaew—was a typical one in every respect. Roland had indeed been very attached to Tsai's household during our previous field trip. He had gone fishing and hunting with Tsai's father, Uncle Sanit, and had shared with Tsai's mother, Nang Kham, the produce from his garden, which included everything from local varieties of eggplant to Iowa sweet corn. Uncle Sanit had taught him how to prepare fields with a water buffalo–driven plow (now no longer in use), and he had spent many happy days working alongside other members of their household in their rice fields and sesame garden.

When Nang Kham was pregnant with Tsai, her husband had a dream in which Roland said he was going to come and visit. Shortly after that, they received my letter with the news of his death. Other evidence that was cited had to do with Tsai's physical appearance at birth—he was "very large" and "covered with hair," characteristics associated with *farangs*, or Westerners. Though perhaps unusual in some respects, this case highlights the essential ingredients necessary for a credible rebirth story, namely, a widely perceived or publicly claimed emotional attachment felt by the deceased for his or her new home, along with some physical and/or behavioral characteristics of the child that are reminiscent of the deceased.

Rebirth stories such as these provide the child and its family with a link to the past and may help solidify or strengthen a preexisting relationship between two households. It is considered equally necessary, however, for the child to establish a separate and unique identity. This begins once the spirit-being has already chosen and attached itself to a particular household via a child-bearing woman of that household, who may or may not be the person with whom it has the strong emotional bond. Once attached, it begins to develop into a new individual. Shan recognize this new status of the life force by ceasing to refer to it as a *phi* and beginning to refer to it as *khwan* (soul-stuff).[3]

At this point, its previous self continues to influence the newly forming individual, and, indeed, it is the very persistence of some of these same character traits that allows others to recognize who the new person "is." But the attachment of the immaterial life force to a material substance—namely, a fetus in a pregnant woman—means that it is now undergoing new experiences, some of which will also shape the developing person. In particular, what a pregnant woman does during the pregnancy—who or what she associates with, the kinds of things she looks at or pays attention to, and, to a certain extent, what she eats—all affect the person developing inside her. Hence, pregnant women (like dying people[4]) are told to think only about "good things, beautiful things" and to avoid unpleasant scenes and associations. During this period, the pregnant woman and/or another member of her household may also receive clues about the fetus' identity in the form of dreams.

Even so, the fetus is not spoken of as a truly separate being until it is born. For example, Shan do not usually choose or even think about names for their children until after they are born, and then it may be several days or even weeks before a child is given one. One reason to wait until birth is that, traditionally, Shan names were associated with the day of the week on which a child was born (as well as, in some cases, the child's birth order). Although this custom is no longer widely practiced, people still wait and often choose a name that reflects something about the circumstances of the baby's birth, such as an unusual location or the co-occurrence of some significant event in the larger society. One man born during the time of the Japanese occupation of the area during World War II, for example, was called by the Shan word for "busy, troubled." Another, whose mother went into labor unexpectedly early while visiting the market in town and ended up giving birth in the town hospital, was called simply "town."[5] Later, when the child is more developed, it may also receive a nickname that refers to some physical or behavioral characteristic of its own, and, later still, male children who ordain as Buddhist novices may end up going by the name they receive at the time of ordination. At the moment of birth, however, people's attention is more often focused on the coincidence of the birth with time and space markers in the external world.

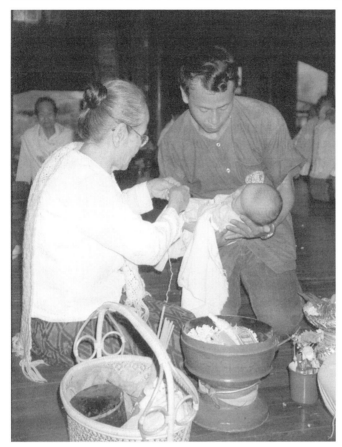

A respected elder ties a string around a baby's wrist while reciting a blessing during the traditional bathing ceremony held for newborns.

Children may also be named after someone else, such as a name that combines syllables from each of the parents' names, but I have never seen or heard of a child receiving exactly the same name as either parent. The idea seems to be to ensure that the child has an identity, symbolized by the name, that at once indicates its connections to others but differs enough to signal a separate self. In one case that occurred during my field stay, for example, the child happened to be born on the same day of the week as both its mother and father had been born. The parents decided that this was inauspicious, saying that the baby's health could be in jeopardy, and arranged for it to be ritually adopted (but not raised) by the father's older brother, who "bought" the child for the token sum of 20 baht. To complete the deceit, the baby was then named after its new adoptive father, by giving it a name that began with the same initial consonant as this man's name.

As this example suggests, a person's self is associated with both its name and the day of the week on which it is born—an association that continues

Because of their frequent need for soul-calling rites, babies and young children are often seen wearing string bracelets and necklaces.

throughout the life course[6]—and in each case it is important for the new being to be both linked with and distinguished from critical others in order for it to develop properly.

For the first few months after it is born, a baby is considered extremely vulnerable, or *un* (soft/weak), primarily because its *khwan* is not yet reliably attached to its body. Within a month or so of its birth, a bathing ceremony (the *ap loen* rite) is performed. Village elders are invited to the infant's home to help ritually bathe the baby with specially prepared fragrant water (*nam ngoen nam kham*, literally, silver and gold water) and to tie white strings around the baby's wrists as they chant blessings of protection and good wishes for its life to come. This ceremony helps strengthen the tenuous bond between body and *khwan* that is characteristic of the first few years of life.

Because of the weakness of their *khwan*, children are more generally vulnerable to the kind of spirit attack that results in illness than are adults. One type of spirit in particular, *phi mae ta laa,* afflicts only children under the age of twelve. Getting rid of the attacking spirit entails performing a curing rite, such as that described in chapter 2, in which the spirit is intimidated to leave the body and the child's *khwan* is called back and secured again with a white thread around the wrist. (This happens so frequently that most young children are perpetually walking around with white threads tied to their wrists.) Perhaps as a kind of compensation for their general vulnerability, children under twelve are also said to have two "spirit parents" *(pau phaan* and *mae phaan)* who watch out for it by, for example, keeping it from being badly hurt if it should fall down. These same spirit parents also sometimes entertain a baby while it is lying alone in its cradle, causing the baby to coo and laugh as if it were interacting with someone.

Children as "Wild": A Shan View of Child Development

It is an overarching concern of Shan parents of young children to do things that will protect them from predatory spirits and help stabilize the children's *khwan*. This means keeping them away from known spirit haunts (unless they are accompanied by an adult), keeping them home after dark, and trying to keep them from being emotionally upset or startled (conditions that can cause their *khwan* to flee). Very young children, however, remain blissfully ignorant of these dangers to their well-being and do not always want to cooperate with their parents' efforts at protection.

Perhaps because of this, as a baby grows and becomes more active, it is invariably described with the word *hai*–the same word that is used to describe active and troublesome spirits. In an early Shan-English dictionary written by the missionary Cushing ([1914] 1971: 659), *hai* is defined as "to be bad, not good," but I think a more accurate translation, at least in this context, would be "wild" or "uncontrolled." Behaviors that mothers and other caregivers are likely to label *hai* include leg kicking, wanting to stand up or jump up and down (rather than to sit quietly or lie down), random grabbing at objects within arm's reach, running around a lot (when they're a bit older), and, in general, any energetic body movements.

Caregivers do not necessarily try to inhibit such behaviors, especially in babies and very young children, for whom they are considered normal. During the first year or so, when the child is too young for its *hai*-ness to do much damage, one could even say that the surrounding adults enjoy it—cheerfully holding up an increasingly heavy baby that wants to stand and jump while complaining (through a smile) about how *hai* the child is. Eventually, though, this wild aspect of children's nature is seen as something that must be curbed. It will not subside on its own, as a natural part of the maturation process; rather, it is thought to require active intervention and instruction by the child's caregivers.

Shan adults also regard young children as essentially ignorant of the proper way to behave, a condition that the adults associate with the children's limited language ability. Hence, adults talk about child development as a process of going from a state of "not yet understanding words/speech" *(am pai hu kwaam)* to one of "understanding words/speech already" *(hu kwaam yao)*. The metaphor is elaborated in a number of related Shan expressions: A disobedient child is "difficult to say anything to" *(wa yap)* or "someone who doesn't listen" *(man am thaum)*. A stupid or stubborn child is "deaf" or "hard of hearing" *(nok)*. Accordingly, angry or exasperated parents who are scolding a child will ask it repeatedly, "Do you hear?" *(tsong mau yin)*. Correct or appropriate behavior is spoken of as following almost automatically from correct hearing and understanding. Conversely, Shan explain most misbehaviors of children as being the result of a combination of their natural wildness *(pen hai)* and their inability to understand speech *(am hu kwaam)*.

An additional aspect of Shan thinking about children that features in Shan theories of human development is the assumption of an independent or autonomous will in even very young infants and babies. This will is not something that develops; it is there from the start.[7] What develops is the child's ability to control or direct the will in culturally appropriate ways. A number of adult-child interaction patterns follow from this. The facial expressions, sounds, and random body movements of babies and toddlers are interpreted as meaningful and purposive, though sometimes obscure. Hence, one hears Shan parents saying things like "He wants to eat" (vs. "I think he's hungry") or "She wants to lie down" (vs. "She needs a nap") or "Why would he want to play with that?" (vs. "Who left that there within reach of the baby?").

Babies are thus treated as social agents almost immediately, and adults, especially women, interact with them as such. As the child grows and its desires and preferences for certain foods, activities, individuals, and so on become increasingly clear, these are sometimes taken as evidence of who the person was in a previous life. Here, idiosyncratic desires and preferences help define the self and make it possible for others to recognize it. Young children are also said sometimes to be able to remember (in a semiconscious way) who they were in a previous life, an ability that quickly fades as they grow older. As a result, otherwise incomprehensible statements from a three- or four-year-old are sometimes interpreted as references to its former existence as a different self.[8]

Note that this view of children is considerably distant from the tabula rasa view that has informed much of the child-rearing literature in North

America since the late nineteenth century.[9] Significantly, when children are viewed as highly malleable, the role of parenting is given more attention and cultural elaboration, a process that has important gender implications and consequences for overall family organization.[10] In the Shan view, however, children come into the world not as a blank slate but "preloaded" in significant ways. They arrive with a past—a history of former lives and accumulated karma to work out—and with a not unrelated bundle of desires and preferences that find expression in the exercise of an autonomous will. Parents have a role to play, but they are not the sole or even the most important influence on a child's life.

Accordingly, parents expressed a reluctance to overdirect a child's behavior, especially if this entailed going against the child's will or thwarting some expressed desire, for fear that they might be interfering dangerously with larger karmic forces. One woman, for example, expressed regret that she had not been able to persuade her youngest son to continue his schooling past sixth grade: "Now that he's farming all day long, he wishes he'd listened to me. Sometimes he says, 'Why didn't you force me to stay in school?' But I would have been afraid to do that, afraid I would suffer karmic retribution *[lai wot]*." Other parents cite examples where people did force their children, with disastrous or near-disastrous consequences—the child ran away, attempted suicide, subsequently had an accident, and so on. The general theme in all these cases seems to be that a very strong desire on the part of a child should probably not be opposed, at least not directly. It is dangerous to do so because no one knows in what form the thwarted desire will seek fulfillment.

Clearly, much is going on in these examples that could be analyzed in more psychodynamic ways than these Shan parents would choose to do. One might interpret such incidents, for example, as the result of hierarchical parent-child relations, where a child's only option for disobedience is some form of passive resistance. What is interesting for our purposes here, however, is the language that parents choose for talking about these events, a language that invokes both larger cosmic forces and an essentialized view of desires. For many Shan, a person's desires or preferences are not culturally/socially constructed but, rather, essential to the person—emblematic even—and, hence, somewhat arbitrary and mysterious. Who knows how deep-seated a child's expressed wish is, or what sorts of forces are behind it? It may be a whim, or it may be something much more than that. Therefore, one should be wary of forcing a child to do something that is against its will. Better to trick or deceive the child with little lies or distractions—a strategy that, in effect, changes what they want—or to induce fear in them, which has the same effect. By such artifices, a child who is believed to be vulnerable and too *hai* for its own good is kept safe and out of danger.

Related to this attribution of an autonomous will is an image of children as transparently self-seeking and easily frustrated when they do not get their way. That adults are often greatly amused by this dimension of childish behavior is related, I think, to its being the virtual opposite of the adult ideal of masking one's desires and maintaining a certain level of self-control. Although, for the most part, adults make an effort to indulge the desires of young children, this discrepancy with the adult ideal leads to a stylized pattern of teasing in which adults pretend to withhold or threaten to take from children some object of desire (especially food), laugh when the child inevitably shows distress, and then give in. It seems plausible that one of the things children might be learning from such experiences is that it is dangerous or unwise to reveal one's desires. The lies that adults tell children in order to manipulate their behavior ("Quick! Run home! Your mother is just back from town and has brought you a treat!") are similarly understood to work because of the transparency of children's desires—knowing what they want makes it easy to trick and deceive them.

Adults are also entertained by a kind of brazenness or lack of shyness that is sometimes found in young children and that adults associate with animal-like behavior—for example, eating greedily without regard for others who are present, exiting an interaction the moment one gets what one wants, or displaying personal immodesty in dress or demeanor. Indeed, young children are often jokingly referred to as monkeys. But eventually every child begins to show signs of being "appropriately shy/embarrassed" *(li aai)*, developments that are welcomed by adults as an indication that the child is now beginning to "understand speech" *(hu kwaam)*.

Given this attention to speech as the harbinger of maturity, it is not surprising that instruction in proper language use is an important vehicle for socialization. Polite expressions and proper forms for addressing elders are among a child's first words, and adults take great delight in hearing a child perform these social niceties. One often hears parents rehearsing a child in their proper performance and then coaxing the child to use them in the appropriate contexts.

When, for example, an adult gives a child a sweet or other treat, the child is encouraged to *waai* and say "thank you" in Thai *(khaupkhun kha/khrap)*.[11] A child who resists performing this little rite will hear the attending adults exclaim, "Oh, it must be a Karen child!"—referring to the upland Karen people who also live in Mae Hong Son Province. This is also said of a child who has been asked a common friendly question, such as "What are you eating?" *(kin phak sang)*, and fails to complete a reply with the standard Shan polite particle *(au)*.

As these examples suggest, the Shan socialization process makes use of the contrasting images—widespread in Thailand—of "civilized" valley people (who *waai* and use polite language) and "uncivilized" hill people in order to elicit certain behaviors from their children. Unwittingly perhaps, this strategy also forces the Shan participants to acknowledge the cultural dominance of the Thai, since it is the Thai language that is here being used as the symbol par excellence of polite, civilized behavior.

Nevertheless, the primary meaning of this process for the adults who initiate these and other such interactions with children is clear enough: the *hai* behavior that comes naturally to all children must eventually give way to a personal style that is marked by considerable discipline and self-control—a developmental transformation that Shan adults believe to be critical for the child's ultimate safety and well-being.

Spirits, Souls, and Children

How does this view of children and child development articulate with the images of spirits and souls prevalent in Shan discourse? Let me return first to that other class of *hai* beings—spirits. I want to suggest that Shan constructions of humanness are played out primarily in opposition to their ideas about spirits and, in particular, to what I have called the core notion of spirit as the hungry and wandering ghost. What is it that distinguishes humans from this core notion of spirit? In my view, it is the presence of some degree of self-discipline, especially of appetites under control, and, hence, of less vulnerability to manipulation by others—all of which are key notions in Shan and, more generally, Buddhist constructions of the idealized adult.

As we saw in the healing sessions described in chapter 2, spirits are portrayed—both in the rites themselves and in the talk that accompanies them—as troublesome but not very formidable foes; they have well-known desires and are susceptible to trickery, intimidation, and manipulation by humans. In many respects, they are anthropomorphized. But even more salient to Shan, I think, is the gulf that separates the prototypical spirit's existence from the way a human ought ideally to live. As is made clear in other contexts by the massive ritual apparatus of Buddhist-inspired ceremonies aimed specifically at helping people achieve a swift and agreeable rebirth after death, these common interlopers on the human domain represent Shan's own worst fears of what they might become—hungry and wandering ghosts. As such, spirits constitute an object lesson in failed transformations of self, beings who got stuck in the *phi* state and are unable to be reborn as *khwan*-bearing humans. Through Buddhist merit-making ceremonies and various other attempts at self-control, people work hard to ensure that they will avoid the miserable fate of these perpetually hungry beings. The otherness of spirits, then, is a contingent otherness, and that, I think, explains some of the fascination they hold for Shan.

When Shan talk about spirits and spirit-related events, the category of spirits seems to be used as a vehicle for reflection on what it means to be human. Not all distinctions between spirits and humans are given equal attention in these conversations, however. Some of what struck me as the most salient differences—for example, that humans are alive and spirits dead, that humans have bodies and spirits do not, and that humans consume the substance of food and spirits merely its essence—are simply taken for granted and not discussed much. Instead, it is the aspects of spirit behavior that impinge upon human life that most interest Shan and animate their conversations, aspects that can be discussed only after certain basic "facts" concerning their existence are accepted and, indeed, taken for granted. Only then can one ask questions such as, where does this particular spirit come from, and what does it want? as well as more general questions such as, what sorts of behavior can we expect from spirits, how can we protect ourselves from their predatory attacks, and, finally, how can we ensure that we will not become hungry spirits ourselves after we die?

Hence, the kind of knowledge and lore that Shan have accumulated about spirits is not the disinterested compilation of the naturalist or, for that matter, of the anthropologist. Rather, one might say that Shan "know" spirits the way ranchers "know" coyotes, which is not the same way that, say, a biologist "knows" them. In other words, the content of Shan talk about spirits gives much more attention to certain aspects of their nature than to others, namely, those aspects that bring spirits into contact with humans. The recurring themes of hunger, appetite, and uncontrolled desires are particularly emphasized, as is their connection to disruptive behavior, labeled *hai*. Significantly, these are the same themes that crop up, in somewhat altered form, in Shan talk about souls and children.

Souls are also spoken of as having appetites or desires and, like spirits, are often addressed as one might a child (though souls are "coaxed," whereas spirits are "scolded"). Like children, souls are susceptible to being led by others, especially by mature adults, who understand how to manipulate their behavior.

Spirits, souls, and children—though each are intimately associated with core notions of the self—are thus not fully human in the "best," or idealized, sense, precisely because of this shared vulnerability to manipulation by others. As a group, they represent what we adults might be like if we were not careful to cultivate our powers of self-control. What lies beneath the surface of the self we present to others? What would happen if we gave in and lost control? Shan do not worry about some kind of Jekyll-and-Hyde transformation, of turning into a beast or a violent, evil person. They worry instead about turning into a vulnerable child, a pathetic and hungry ghost, a lost soul who has been distracted by nefarious others.

What children, capricious spirits, and reluctant souls have in common, then, is that they are all desire-driven creatures, that is, beings whose behavior is almost completely governed by their immediate wants. This makes them potentially troublesome in some respects but also fairly easy to manipulate. In the case of children and spirits, being desire-driven takes on the connotation of being *hai*–wild and uncontrolled. In the case of souls, being desire-driven is more likely expressed as being easily distracted or led astray, a trait that children are also said to share, and one that makes them equally susceptible to getting themselves into trouble.

The problem with being desire-driven, then, from the standpoint of Shan adults, seems to be that it is associated with being vulnerable. It is for this reason, I think, that adulthood or social maturity is defined largely as having one's desires under control and that children come under increasing pressure (by persuasion, by teasing, and eventually by direct instruction) to learn to control or at least mask their desires. Thus, although children share certain qualities with souls and spirits, they are singled out as the group upon whom special expectations are placed. Spirits and souls may be incorrigible, but children are expected to develop.

Shan thus view the developmental process, at least in part, as a process of "domestication," that is, of taming the *hai*, desire-driven aspects of themselves and their children. Further, this domestication process is understood to be a lifelong affair–something that begins with a child's first efforts at self-restraint but then continues with the adults' ongoing struggles to manage their emotions, culminating in the almost full-time efforts of the devout lay elders who engage in merit making and Buddhist ascetic practices in order to achieve maximal self-control before they die. These are the areas that form the subject matter of the remaining chapters of this book–the way this theme of domesticating the self plays out in later portions of the life course that are well beyond childhood.

What is important to note here, however, is not only the specific content of Shan talk about spirits, souls, and children but also how any such talk helps constitute people's sense of who they are and what they are like. People growing up in other societies, having different sorts of conversations, in which they find themselves being compared to different sorts of beings or things, will develop a very different sense of self from that portrayed here.

For example, in a provocative study of how the widespread use of computers has affected the way Americans think about themselves, Sherry Turkle (1984) describes how computers have become a source of both fascination and fear, especially as they are seen as a model for the human mind. Children playing with computers talked among themselves and with her, debating whether computers were alive and whether they were human. Older children and adults, having more or less settled these questions in the negative, nevertheless struggled to articulate what makes humans unique. Traditionally (that is to say, prior to computers), what was special about people had been defined in contrast to animals, and that led to an emphasis on humans as intelligent and rational. Computers, however, upset this traditional scenario and, as Turkle explains, have provoked Americans into new conceptualizations of what it means to be human, most notably a shift away from the view of people as "rational animals" toward one in which they are increasingly seen as "emotional machines" (ibid., 61–62).

The argument is not that everyone who comes into contact with computers (or spirits) necessarily ends up with the same understanding of what it means to be human but, rather, that by engaging in frequent conversations about these culturally designated Others, speakers are constantly rehearsing, or practicing, a particular view of what it means to be a person. Further, it makes a difference what sort of object is chosen to play this role. That is, the characteristics of the particular object (or category of beings) that is given cultural prominence as an Other to some locally defined Self have an "agenda-setting" effect on the kinds of conversations that can take place. Turkle, discussing how computer play has encouraged children to think about psychological issues, puts it this way:

> Some children think computers are alive, some think they are not, others settle on "sort of." But to the extent that they debate the question in terms of the machine's psychological attributes they are getting practice in thinking about, talking about, and defending their ideas about the psychological. As the world of traditional objects serves as material for a child's construction of the physical, the computer serves as a stimulus to the construction of the psychological. (Ibid., 50)

Similar processes are at work, I believe, in Shan talk about spirits, souls, and children. People may disagree, for example, about what a particular spirit should be fed or how best to entice a lost soul or coax a recalcitrant child, but to the extent that Shan consistently choose to debate the question in terms of tastes and preferences, they are getting practice in a certain way of thinking about and talking about individual selves, namely, as "desiring subjects" or "beings-with-appetites," a habit of mind that surfaces again and again in many other contexts of Shan thought and social life.[12]

Achieving Adulthood

Counterbalancing the disparaging talk one hears about young children who are *hai* is a series of approving remarks about somewhat older children and youth described as *kai* (industrious). The two terms are closely related semantically. Both have "energetic" or "active" as an essential part of their meaning, but one has negative connotations and the other positive. *Hai* can be more formally defined as "energetic in a wild or chaotic way with no usable (and perhaps even destructive) results." Its opposite is *li*, which means "good," "well-behaved," "proper," or "well." *Kai*, in contrast, means "energetic in a purposeful and orderly way, productively energetic, keen." Its opposite is *(khi) khan*, which means "lazy," "apathetic," "uninterested," "bored," "unengaged."

One of the hoped-for outcomes of the developmental process, as Shan see it, is that *hai* toddlers and young children will turn into *kai* older children and youth. Hence, parallel to the concern with achieving self-control is an equally important emphasis on working hard and being productive, on acquiring mastery of adult skills and competencies, and on being able to participate in community projects.[13] Ideology and rhetoric aside, the "on the ground" definition of adulthood in this community is closely linked with economic independence, with being able to provide for oneself and one's dependents. Since adult work is easily visible and accessible in Baan Kaung Mu (unlike, for example, the situation in the United States, where most adult work takes place in settings that are "child-free"), Shan children have many opportunities to observe, participate, and begin to identify with the goals of adult work projects. Further, children are regarded by adults as quite capable of productive work. Thus, work skills become an important yardstick by which both children and adults measure a person's progress toward adulthood. There is no clear-cut moment (such as marriage or the birth of one's first child) that marks this important phase of the life course. Rather, adult status is something that is achieved gradually, via a series of steps.

Children officially begin to attend school at about age six, though younger children may tag along to the village school with their older siblings. Attending school is recognized as a significant milestone for children, and, to some extent, being a student *(nakrian)* is a recognized stage in life. The village school goes up to grade six, but the state has recently required that all children continue for an additional three years (the Thai equivalent of junior high school), something Baan Kaung Mu children must do either in Mae Hong Son town or in another nearby village that has a larger school. During these school years, parents recognize that children have homework to do and other extracurricular obligations, but they nevertheless expect their children to begin to help out at home too.

A little girl concentrates on her task as she helps her mother, aunt, and grand-mother make soybean cakes, a staple of the Shan diet.

Children, especially girls, are gradually given more and more domestic chores, such as fetching water from the well, doing some laundry, caring for younger siblings, sweeping the house, running errands, building a fire, and helping with various aspects of food preparation. Older children begin to help with the simpler subsistence activities such as weeding a garden, planting garlic, and carrying things back and forth to the fields. During school vacations, many older children spend a significant portion of the day engaged in some combination of subsistence or domestic tasks. Although parents rarely compliment their children directly for these signs of budding competence, they do praise their efforts to other adults while in earshot of the children. For their part, children often told me with excitement about some new skill they had just mastered, their growing abilities in the adult arena functioning as a clear source of pride and self-esteem.

Adolescence is not considered an especially turbulent or rebellious time. In contrast to the special protection that children under twelve are thought to require, primarily because of the fragility of their *khwan*, adolescents are

Above: A young boy tries to help his grandfather with a carpentry project.

Right: Two 5-year-old boys head off to hunt birds with their slingshots. (Note the strings tied around their necks and one boy's wrist.)

Two 12-year-old girls transplant rice while a teenage boy (in the background) brings bundles of rice seedlings from the nursery and distributes them to other workers.

assumed to be capable of looking after themselves. The most dangerous period of a person's life is past now, and in physical (but not yet social) terms the adolescent is considered essentially grown-up *(kau yau)*. Other than the Buddhist novice ordination (which, as we will see, is in many ways more a rite of passage for the sponsoring adult than it is for the boy), Shan do not mark the passage into puberty with any special rites.[14] The transition to full adult status *(khon long)* is a gradual one that parallels the gradual assumption of adult work responsibilities and the eventual establishment of an independent domicile. The instruction by adults that was considered crucial for the proper development of children is largely abandoned now, in part because adolescents are already presumed to know much of what they need to know in order to stay out of danger and in part because they are not considered as malleable as children; they are "harder to teach" *(saun yap)* and, in at least some sense, "already developed" *(kau yau yao)*.

Teenagers who have completed school (or have gone as far as they can afford to go) work full-time on agricultural tasks. Significantly, when exchange labor is performed, such as during the transplanting and harvest seasons, their labor counts as the equivalent of an adult's. Often, it is about this time that they are given control over some of the earnings their labor has generated. They may, for example, be allowed to keep the earnings from a garden they have made. Or they may be allowed to raise a pig, doing all the necessary work to feed it and care for it, and then keep the money earned from its sale. Some, especially boys, are also taking advantage of the occasional wage-labor jobs that are available in the area—for example, temporary work on a road construction crew. Girls may take temporary or part-time jobs doing domestic work or perhaps set up a roadside noodle stand. Usually, at least some of the money earned in this way is spent on personal items (clothes, a radio, a wristwatch, and the like), some of which their parents might have purchased for them anyway, and others that are probably not the sort of things their parents would have chosen to buy. Parents, however, are tolerant of these expenditures, since they see this kind of arrangement as educational for the child, something that will provide an incentive for hard work and that will help the child form the habit of working.

Teenagers are also given more freedom of movement and will often attend temple festivals or go visiting in nearby villages without their parents, traveling in same-sex groups with other teens. Although parents report some stress in dealing with their teenagers' new independence, it is largely offset by the parents' delight in the new source of labor they now have in the household. Since teens take on much of the heavy work formerly done by their parents, life actually becomes easier in many ways for parents of teenagers, and they are grateful for this. Their parental investment is finally beginning to pay off, and most parents speak about their teenage sons and daughters with great pride and pleasure.

The period of time right before marriage (late teens and early twenties) is recognized as a distinct life stage (marked by the terms *saao*, unmarried young woman, and *paao*, unmarried young man), but it is associated more with certain characteristic behaviors and activities than with any developmental problems or issues. Young people in this stage are thought of as being physically attractive and concerned with their appearance (both men and women), carefree in spirit, and prone to going visiting or wandering (especially young men). Aside from the small projects that give them some spending money, however, their labor is still usually under the supervision and direction of an older adult and will remain so even after they marry, at least until they establish a separate household. Although marriage is an important step toward achieving the status of a mature adult, it does not automatically confer any sudden change in status.[15]

Although the marriages I witnessed were rarely strictly arranged in the traditional sense, young people still welcome help from their parents in finding a suitable spouse and hope to marry with at least their parents' blessing. Where parents are adamantly opposed, however, the couple often elopes rather than capitulate, then works (often through intermediaries) to restore good relations before returning home. Most newly married couples live for a time with one or the other of their parents (more often the bride's, unless the groom was from a very well-to-do family), pooling their labor and earnings and dividing up the chores with the other adults in the household. Eventually, most couples move out into their own house, usually one they have been slowly building for themselves over a period of years.

It is at this point, when they establish a separate domicile, that they finally achieve some jural status as adults, even though they may continue to have close financial ties with one or both sets of parents. This change in status arises because village social organization places great emphasis on the household as an independent social-political-economic unit. When collective work projects are announced, for example (such as repairing the irrigation ditches each spring or helping with a temple project of some sort), requests are made for a laborer from each household. Similarly, whenever a village meeting is called, each household is expected to send one adult member. When offerings are being collected for a village-wide ceremony, contributions are requested from each household. By such means, the autonomy of the household unit and its members is continually recognized and reinforced. As the head couple making decisions for their own autonomous household, young people can finally be said to have achieved adulthood.

Production and Reproduction

The period of young adulthood is focused most energetically on productive work within the household and on parenting. Later (as we will see in chapter 6), adults turn their gaze more toward the organization of village-wide activities, especially merit-making ceremonies. But young adults participate in such events primarily as workers, not (like middle-aged people) as organizers and not (like old people) as part of the target audience for the religious services. This emphasis on productive labor applies to both men and women. For many tasks, there is a traditional sexual division of labor, although it is not always strictly enforced. Plowing, for example, is considered a man's job, and transplanting rice is considered a woman's job. Harvesting rice, on the other hand, can be (and is) done by both sexes. Women take primary responsibility for child care, cooking (including preparation of ritual food offerings), laundry, and other domestic tasks (many of which they delegate to their older children), while men do most carpentry and construction jobs. At social gatherings and work parties, which are often related events, men and women socialize and work in same-sex groupings for the most part. But, again, this is not strictly enforced, and to do otherwise is not considered unmanly or unfeminine. On the contrary, the main reason for staying with one's own sex is to avoid appearing sexually aggressive or flirtatious.

These sex-segregated aspects of daily life are counterbalanced, however, by the aforementioned emphasis on the household as the key unit in village social organization, a structural arrangement that tends to highlight the husband-wife pair and to treat them as virtually equivalent, if not equal. As an independent economic unit, the husband and wife who have formed their own household constitute a kind of mini-corporation and are motivated by common cause and joint interests in working for their mutual prosperity.

Most important to note is that people place a very high value on women's agricultural labor and other extra-domestic work. Aside from a brief postpartum period,[16] there is no cultural expectation that women should stay home, even after the birth of children. Many women nevertheless find that they must curtail their agricultural work for a time, especially when their children are nursing or very young, but they complain about this. Given that most agricultural tasks are done in groups with at least a few other women and sometimes with large groups, it is understandable that child care, by contrast, is felt to be a lonely affair. Women who stay at home to care for young children say they are bored and that they miss doing agricultural work. The task of mothering—far from being constructed as an all-consuming task that is the natural and most fulfilling work for women—is instead described as an interruption. Even more, it is seen as a sacrifice, an altruistic act that women do out of compassion for the helplessness of children (rather than a duty or obligation inherent in being a good mother). By construing it this way, children are cast as the beneficiaries of women's altruism and are thought to be literally in debt to their mothers in lasting and highly significant ways.

In sum, from the end of childhood on into the middle years of adulthood, people gradually acquire an increasing amount of both practical skills and more esoteric knowledge—the cultural competence needed to be fully active members of the community—but these steps toward maturity are not culturally recognized as a time when much development is happening. In fact, the next culturally recognized period of a person's life where development of a sort is said to occur is the period known as old age.

Discourses of Inequality and Autonomy

A child's progress toward competence and increasing autonomy takes place in a particular social context, one in which children receive early training in appropriate social relationships. Shan children are born into a world where asymmetrical social relationships based on age, gender, and social position are given much prominence, both in childhood and throughout the life course. Participation in these relationships has implications for the way people growing up in the community come to understand who they are and what sort of person they might become.

Within their own household, children encounter these asymmetries in their relations with their parents, in their parents' relations with each other, and even in their relations with their siblings. Beyond the household, hierarchical relationships in which one person is conceived to be in some sense higher than another (and, hence, entitled to certain privileges and held accountable for certain responsibilities) provide the basis for village social organization. It is not that more peerlike relationships do not exist. Shan of all ages talk about "being friends with" *(pen kau kan)* particular individuals, and it is clear that these friendships are valued. The difference is that such relationships are not given the same social salience or cultural elaboration that is granted to more asymmetrical ones. One type is seen as relatively informal and transitory; the other, as formal and enduring.

Hierarchical relationships in Shan society are also more institutionalized. They have an accompanying body of lore, including lists of the duties each party to the relationship owes the other, stories about people who failed to fulfill these duties and what happened to them, stories of those who were exemplars for the roles, and so on.[17] Hierarchical relationships also figure prominently in many rituals and are further reinforced daily by countless acts of deference in gesture, body posture, and speech. Nothing like this exists for relationships between peers. As a result, hierarchical relationships have an intrinsic "moral aura" about them; they are perceived as the appropriate site of moral behavior and moral obligation in a way that is not true of other sorts of relationships.

Growing children may be involved in numerous hierarchical relationships, but three in particular are virtually inescapable: that between children and their parents, that between students and their teachers, and that between older and younger siblings. In the brief descriptions that follow, it will be apparent that each of these is associated with similar responsibilities and privileges; in all three, deference and compliance are due from the junior member, while generosity and nurturance are expected from the senior member.

Parent-Child Relationships

Parents are expected to work hard and make sacrifices in order to provide for their children. And children, as soon as they are able, are expected to perform, expeditiously and without complaint, whatever tasks their parents assign to them. As the local gossip makes clear, parents do not automatically have the right to direct the labor and demand the cooperation of their children; rather, parents earn this right by the sacrifices they make for their children's benefit.

What gives parents the right to make demands on the labor and services of a child is not the biological relationship between them. It is their demonstrated willingness to accept responsibility for the child's care and welfare, their willingness to invest in the child. Hence, any adult with the necessary resources can establish this sort of relationship with a child. If a child's biological parents are very poor or are otherwise finding it difficult to provide for the child, there is almost always another adult ready and anxious to help out or, if necessary, even take over. This role may be filled by the child's grandparent, an aunt or uncle, or another close relative, but it may also be filled by a childless couple or other nonrelative who simply wants the opportunity to invest in a child.

Correspondingly, children are seen as being very much in debt to the adults who have taken the trouble to raise them.[18] The sentiment is perhaps more often directed toward one's mother, as it is thought that she "suffers" more for the sake of the child, through childbirth and nursing. The Shan children I worked with often expressed the desire to "pay back their mother's milk," a construction that does not take for granted a mother's care but, rather, casts it as a gift that has put them in her debt.[19]

How, then, are children to repay the debt they owe their parents? The most direct way is by contributing their labor to their parents' household. Male children can also agree to undergo a Buddhist novice ordination. This ceremony is thought to generate merit *(kuso)*, the reserve stockpile of good karma discussed in chapter 3. Since the merit accrues not to the boy but to the parents—especially the mother—and to any other sponsors of the novice, a willingness to undergo the discipline of monastic life for a period of time can be viewed as an expression of filial piety. (Indeed, young girls often express regret that they are unable to pay back their mothers in this fashion.) Finally, adult children are expected to return the debt by looking after their elderly parents.

The parent-child relationship is thus conceived as reciprocal as well as hierarchical. In its extended form, it symbolizes the mutually beneficial relationship that (ideally) holds between junior and senior generations. The kinship metaphor is extended further to encompass the entire community by the Shan system of honorific titles, according to which adults in the ascending generation are addressed as "aunt," "uncle," "grandparent," and so on, thereby recalling and reinforcing the cultural ideals for intergenerational interaction. Children become familiar with these honorifics quickly (by the age of four they can use most of them correctly) and understand the moral overtones they carry.

Teacher-Student Relationships

Like the parent-child relationship, the teacher-student relationship is also seen as a reciprocal one, but the nature of what is being exchanged is rather different. Whereas the obligations between parent and child are couched primarily in the realm of the tangible and material, the rhetoric surrounding the teacher-student relationship is more overtly moral. Shan consider it a teacher's explicit mission to effect a change in the attitude and behavior of his or her pupils. Parents expect that a teacher will impart to the child not only some specified body of knowledge but also a sense of respect for various social roles and institutions, along with actual training in the outward behavioral forms that will publicly display this respect.

Interestingly, parents say that although it is of course important for them to try to inculcate moral norms in their children, they believe it is generally much easier for teachers to do this effectively because teachers are less likely to succumb to sentimental indulgence. And, on occasion, I heard parents complain when they thought a teacher was being too lax in this regard.

Hence, teachers have the right as well as the responsibility to instruct and direct the behavior of their students in nearly all matters, not only those narrowly defined as school-related. At public gatherings and festivals, for example, I found children to be very much aware of their teachers' presence and concerned about their conduct in front of their teachers. When festivals were expected to continue late into the night, it was the teachers—not the parents—who imposed a curfew on the children.

Similarly, the obligations of students toward teachers are portrayed as diffuse and enduring and are understood to extend beyond the walls of the classroom. If students encounter their teacher on the street, for example, they are expected to behave even more respectfully than they would toward other adults the same age (by, for example, greeting them formally and with a *waai*). If their teacher becomes ill, they are expected to visit the house, make themselves useful, and so on.

Sibling Relationships

The relationship between older and younger siblings is an important one for illuminating the process of socialization because it is the first one in which Shan children learn how to perform both sides of a hierarchical relationship. Toward their older siblings (and cousins), children are supposed to be helpful, compliant, and at least somewhat deferential, duties that are already familiar to them from other roles. In their behavior toward younger siblings (and other close relatives of their generation), however, children must learn a new set of rules. Here—for the first time—they are supposed to be nurturing, indulgent, and constantly alert to matters that might impinge on the younger ones' welfare.

Training in the role of *pi* (older sibling) begins early. When speaking broadly, children are taught to refer to all of their younger siblings by the term *naung*. In a more restrictive sense, however, a child's *naung* is the sibling born directly after him or her. If, for example, "Laeng" has been the youngest child and a new baby is born into the household, Laeng's parents and older siblings will often immediately begin to refer to the baby as "Laeng's *naung*." Visitors to the house will tease Laeng, threatening to steal the new baby, and so on. Every effort is made to convince Laeng that this new creature, in some sense, belongs to him.

As a baby grows and becomes more demanding, one's duties as an older sibling begin in earnest. Shan children learn quickly that they are expected to share or surrender anything they have that a younger sibling wants. In fact, the phrase "give it to your *naung*" is probably the most frequently heard utterance in households with young children. You are accountable if your younger sibling is unhappy, and it is you who will be questioned closely, or even punished, if your younger sibling is found crying. Girls, especially, are often given almost full responsibility for the care of younger siblings during the day. They walk them back and forth to school, help them with their late-afternoon bath, and take them along on errands or visits to friends' houses.

In response, younger siblings generally do show a fair amount of respect and deference toward their older siblings, not least because they have learned to depend on them for help and advice in all sorts of matters. When they are teenagers or adults, younger siblings can also be counted on to be among those working longest and hardest at any collective projects (agricultural, ritual, or whatever) initiated by their older siblings.

As the first social relationship children have in which they are expected to perform as the senior, the sibling relationship is the initial training ground for performing that role in other hierarchical relationships throughout the course of the life cycle. It is also the first role in which children are cast as the bearers-of-culture with responsibilities for helping to transmit that culture to others less knowledgeable than they, a role that offers children their first taste of status and prestige.

These three hierarchical relationships, then—parent-child, teacher-student, and older and younger siblings—articulate deeply felt and reciprocal obligations. Later in life, they will also serve as models for other hierarchical relationships in which the affective and behavioral components associated with these three are extended, by analogy.[20]

This emphasis on the presumed inequality of all social relationships—a presumption so strong that even twins must be assigned *pi-naung* statuses[21]—is accompanied, somewhat paradoxically, by an equally strong presumption of personal autonomy. That is, even in a hierarchical relationship, it is never assumed that the social superior controls the social subordinate or that such control would even be desirable. Juniors owe their seniors public deference

but not absolute obedience. Each person, as we have seen, is assumed to be a
sovereign bundle of thoughts, feelings, and predispositions, working out its
accumulated karma even as it creates more "deposits," a situation that puts
all social rankings in a tentative mode and subject to flux.

In such a context, there is a limit to how thoroughly a high-status person
can direct the behavior of a lower-status one, and the latter can always invoke a variety of nonconfrontational avoidance tactics, including the ultimate one of simply withdrawing or running away. Since there is no way to
compel compliance, no culturally sanctioned coercive power with which to
enforce commands, those who would be recognized as "high" must press
their case by using persuasion, by cultivating a kind of moral authority, and
by maintaining overall good and friendly (i.e., nonconfrontational) relations
with others.

This a priori positing of both social inequality and personal autonomy is
mirrored in a more prosaic on-the-ground version. On the one hand, it is assumed and socially accepted that each household is striving to get ahead ma-
terially and that this striving will inevitably lead to certain inequalities in
people's standard of living. On the other hand, there is a limit to the amount
of wealth disparities and nakedly self-serving behavior that people in the
community are willing to tolerate. It flies in the face of their carefully constructed ideology that grants social status in exchange for generosity and
claims to moral superiority. Since those in more privileged positions are supposed to "take care of" *(liang)* their subordinates, there should, in theory, be
no one who is not taken care of—that is, no one who is going without while
others have plenty.

The tension between these two pillars of Shan social structure—a tension
that has no doubt been exacerbated by the increasing exposure to urban consumer items—provides the backdrop for a discourse on "asking for things"
that is related both to the teasing behavior mentioned earlier and to the hierarchical relationships just described. If you are the junior member in such a
relationship, it is quite acceptable (and very common) to *yaun*—that is, to beg
or ask for—something you want (a food treat, a new item of clothing, some
"pin money" for an excursion, and so on) from the senior, who presumably
has more resources. Somewhat more cheeky but still in the realm of the per-
missible is to make such requests of anyone who has more of some desirable
commodity than you do. What this does, in effect, is to create a hierarchical
relationship between you two—it is, indeed, a way of demanding that the
other act as if he or she is in a personal relationship with you, with all the responsibilities that such a relationship would entail.[22]

In this connection, a common way of mildly teasing young children (under four years old) is for an adult to go up to them when they are eating some-

thing and ask them to give it to or share it with the adult. The child, who is usually not yet experienced enough verbally to counter the adult's demands, will often withdraw its hand (the one holding the food), causing the adult to laugh or smile and perhaps press the issue further, but usually not to the point of making the child cry.

A version of this teasing goes on between adults too. If an adult goes anywhere outside the village (to town, to a festival in another village, or even into the forest to hunt or forage, although this last one does not always hold), he or she is expected to bring back gifts—typically food or, if it is a big trip, food and clothes—for the children of the household and, if possible, other adult members of the household. This expectation gives rise to a kind of teasing between adults where the teaser puts himself or herself in the position of a dependent and asks/demands of the other, "Where are my *khamun* [treats]? I've come to eat *khamun!*" or "Are you going to buy me some new clothes?" "Bring me back some *khamun!*" "Bring me back some clothes!" and so on. These are said with a smile, but a similar point is being made in each case: if you have something that others do not, or have gotten to go somewhere when they have not, expect to be asked for something. Depending on the context, the teasing sometimes has a bit of an edge to it, indicating some underlying jealousy or resentment.

When someone engages in this kind of asking for things, there are only two culturally appropriate responses. The first and most straightforward is simply to give what is asked. The second is to say, in a tone that indicates surprise, *"am mii ngoen"* (I don't have the money [to buy that for you]) or simply *"am mii"* ([Contrary to your assumption], I don't have [the requested item]). What is not acceptable is to acknowledge having it but refuse to give or share it. Giving/sharing is mandatory when someone asks for it.

If it is food that is being asked for—food that is already present—it will always be given. In fact, it is rare that anyone even has a chance to ask for food that someone is eating, so strong is the cultural imperative to invite anyone one happens to see and with whom one makes eye contact (even someone who simply happens to be walking by outside one's house) to "come eat with me." Other items it is sometimes possible to finesse. Any food or money that you have but are not using at the moment is always vulnerable to such requests. Hence, if you do not want to share it, better to have it out of sight (preferably out of the house) so that you can respond with a credible *am mii*— "I don't have any!"

This kind of banter is a normal part of everyday conversation: it happens daily, not only between young children and their caretakers (*yaun*-ing money for *khamun* or whatever) and between other members of the family (younger and older siblings, adult children and their parents, and so on) but also between neighbors and friends. The further away from a personal relationship two people are, the more inhibitions there will be on engaging in such asking behavior, but even this culturally induced reserve can be overcome if someone is making a public claim to a high-status position. The more one is perceived as putting on airs or otherwise trying to claim a high-status social position, the more one will be asked for things. Hence, this asking discourse provides a disincentive for a flamboyant personal style and serves as a check on the aspirations of all but the most serious social climbers. As we will see in chapter 6, people who choose to be the main organizers or sponsors of large merit-making ceremonies become prime candidates for this sort of asking behavior, giving them many opportunities to practice the self-control and mindfulness of proper social relations for which the local socialization process has prepared them.

This, then, is the social context in which Shan children come to maturity. As they undergo their transformation from vulnerable, wild young children who "do not understand words" and whose transparent desires make them easily manipulated by others, into secure, productive adults with enough self-control to keep themselves out of danger, they do so with an ever-increasing awareness that power, knowledge, and material resources are not evenly distributed in their social universe. They learn to appreciate not only the local justifications for social differences (with all their religious and cosmic reverberations) but also how to act within that system so as to advance their own claims to position in a culturally credible way. By the time they are middle-aged, some of them will be ready to take this to the next level of play by accepting responsibility for the staging of village-wide merit-making ceremonies. Before we turn to the challenges and satisfactions that come from these midlife projects, however, it will be necessary to know a bit more about the general scope of Shan ritual life. A tour of these ritual practices and their implications for self-maintenance are the subject of the next chapter.

Chapter 5

Maintaining Health and Well-Being

ONE EVENING, upon returning home late and very tired from a healing session at Uncle Pon's house, I found my landlady, Aunt Ying, engaged in a quiet, unannounced ritual near the Buddha altar in the upstairs room, about three feet away from my mosquito net. The *tsalei* (lay reader) from a nearby village was officiating. Aunt Ying had asked him to "make a candle" for her, a special process that involves making a large, beeswax candle about fifteen inches high and one inch in diameter while imbuing it with the sacred power of Buddhist texts. The *tsalei* had recently finished it and had brought it to her house that night to be ritually lighted. After it was set up and going, he performed a separate reading (a *thaum lik*) of an unrelated text that Aunt Ying wanted to tape-record using one of her prized possessions, a large black boom box. I listened to the rest of the reading with her, then chatted with them afterwards.

When the *tsalei* had gone, Aunt Ying told me that she arranges to have this done "every year in the seventh month" so that she will "be healthy and thrive" *(yu li kin waan)*. She seemed to regard it as a kind of preventive medicine, rather like having an annual checkup with one's doctor. The candle was supposed to be allowed to burn down completely, until it extinguished itself. When Aunt Ying was ready to retire to the next room and go to sleep, she placed a small bundle of her clothes in front of the burning candle; her clothes, a "self-substitute," would witness the flame's going out. I fell asleep under the protective glow of the *tsalei*'s creation, which burned continuously until the wee hours of the morning.

In the course of their adult lives, Shan have occasion to use many such rituals. Having survived the more vulnerable period of childhood, they must nevertheless cope with the ordinary misfortunes—illness, financial setback, loss of loved ones, and so on—that threaten their well-being. If part of growing up is learning to think of yourself as a potential locus for the not always benevolent designs of others, then adulthood is a time when people seek to shore up control over the contested site that is their selves by various means—some personal, some collective. To do this, they have assembled an impressive array of ritual aids. In this chapter, I describe a sampling of these and discuss their implications for Shan notions of self.

Person-Oriented Rituals

Many people subscribe to the notion that a person's luck can be changed by invoking the power of Buddhist texts and by accumulating more merit. People who have experienced an unusual streak of bad luck will often organize a special temple offering or merit-making ceremony to reverse it. One wealthy man from the village, for example, had encountered a series of setbacks that culminated in a crop-damaging storm, during which two of his cattle were struck by lightning. Frustrated by his continual bad luck, he decided to arrange a ritual reading in his home. He solicited the help of the local lay reader with a special offering and monetary remuneration for his services, sent special invitations to all the village elders to come and listen to the reading, and served expensive snacks and beverages to everyone when it was over. In exchange for these acts of giving, he received substantial merit, which he clearly hoped would work to stop his current string of misfortunes.

For lesser problems or for problems belonging to people of lesser means, more modest responses are available. One can, for example, simply increase the frequency of one's almsgiving to the local monks, prepare a special offering to be delivered on one's day of birth (that is, the day of the week—not the date—on which one was born), or hold a smaller reading session in one's home, with fewer people invited. The village guardian spirit *(tsao moeng)* can also be applied to with a special offering taken to his shrine or, more simply, with a prayer said at night before a lit candle on the family Buddha altar. In this case, the power comes not from the generation of merit *(kuso)* but from the village guardian spirit himself.

With such a variety of possible courses of action, a person suffering from bad luck is never left without recourse; there is always something concrete one can do to change one's luck. Exactly how these ritual practices are thought to "work," however, is not so clear. Persistent questions about the processes involved produced polite but vague responses, often contradictory. I suspect the reason for this type of response is that, like most people, Shan are less interested in articulating a flawless abstract theory of causality than they are in constructing a workable ritual technology that allows them to get on with their lives. Nevertheless, one can detect some recurrent themes in many of these rites that hint at their tacit underlying assumptions. One of these is a theme that might be called the principle of cosmic alignment.

According to this principle, the fluctuating arrangement and rearrangement of super- and subterrestrial bodies of a certain mass (including the moon, the stars, the planets, and an enormous subterranean spirit known as *phi long*) have consequences for people's everyday experience of the world. What do all these objects have in common? Besides their mass, each is characterized by regular movement that can be plotted. This means that their position relative to one another is constantly changing, continually creating new configurations of heavenly (and earthly) bodies in the universe through which we all move. Furthermore, because the movement of each of these bodies is regular, it can be predicted and its position to other such bodies can be charted. By paying attention to the resulting configurations, some of which are thought to be more auspicious than others, and by coordinating one's own movements with these in mind, one can avoid actions that "go against the grain" of the universe while enjoying the increased efficacy that comes from proper cosmic alignment.

These are some of the assumptions that inform the ancient Shan arts of astrology, calendrics, and numerology. The knowledge is specialized and requires literacy in the old Shan script,[1] since much of the relevant information is contained in old paper tablets filled with complicated lists and charts, laboriously hand-copied and passed down from one generation to the next. As a result, villagers tend to rely on a few local ritual specialists, such as Uncle Samaun, to help them sort out the good days from the bad, the auspicious from the inauspicious. These specialists are consulted before making a journey, building a house, making a large purchase, setting the date of rituals—in short, whenever any important event has to be scheduled.

An example that illustrates the logic of the cosmic alignment principle particularly well is a ritual I watched Uncle Samaun perform in June 1991 for Grandmother Yai, an old woman who had not been well. This standardized, fairly elaborate set of offerings is designed to help people improve their health or overall situation. This one was done early in the morning at Grandmother Yai's home and used the household Buddha altar as the "stage" on and around which various offerings were placed, as follows:

- Three bowls of fruit and sweets, with specific numbers of pieces in each bowl, were placed on the altar itself.
- A small table holding a sand pagoda[2] and a vase of flowers was placed in front of the altar.
- Two bundles of wood, containing specially chosen varieties, sat on the floor next to the table.

Interestingly, each part of this offering is understood to have an explicit symbolic meaning that is known to all the participants. And it is, in fact, that meaning that makes the ritual "work."

The meaning of the three bowls placed on the Buddha altar is the most complicated; it has to do with the number of pieces of fruit and sweets in each one. The left-most bowl had 49 pieces in it to commemorate the offering of 49 balls of rice made by the legendary Nang Suchindaa (Pali Sujātā) to the Buddha himself while he was sitting under the bo tree and meditating, having just achieved enlightenment. Invoking this first, or "primeval," act of merit making in any other ritual serves to highlight or call attention to that ritual's merit-making function. The center bowl rested on some of Grandmother Yai's folded clothes, which were to be used in a soul-calling ceremony later that evening. It contained 73 pieces, a number which was "more than Grandmother's age" (she was about 70 years old at the time) in order to "make her age lengthen" (that is, so that she will not die now). The third bowl, placed on the right, contained 108 pieces, a reference to the number of *tso* (planets; also translated in some contexts as "luck") believed to be in each of our bodies. It is a number that signals completeness or wholeness.[3]

Significantly, the number 108 is also associated with the days of the week and with the arrangement of the planets, that is, with the movements of time and space. Uncle Samaun explained it this way: There are eight days of the week (Wednesday is split at noon to form two days), each of which stands for one of the planets. For ritual purposes, these days/planets are characteristically arranged in a certain pattern (see the chart opposite). Each of these is further associated with a particular number. When the numbers are added up, their sum is 108.

This pattern can be put to a variety of uses.[4] It is relevant to indigenous understandings of the life course, as well, since it can help people determine whether they happen to be in a lucky or unlucky stage of life. For example, to find out what planet (or state of luck) you are currently "in," begin at the day of the week on which you were born and proceed clockwise around the squares, adding the numbers until they reach your current age. When Uncle Samaun did this for me, we began on Tuesday and proceeded until we reached Thursday, where I will "remain" until I am fifty-four years old. According to Uncle Samaun, being in Thursday is a good, or auspicious, place to be for someone born on a Tuesday, because these two days "get along well." When I move into the Wednesday afternoon slot, however, that will be "not so good." By knowing such things in advance, people can do various things to compensate for an anticipated inauspicious period in their life and thereby protect themselves from danger.

The other parts of the offering followed a similar logic. On the table in front of the Buddha altar was a small sand pagoda surrounded by various

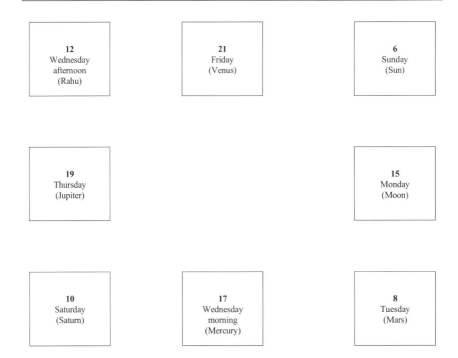

The customary arrangement of the eight "days" (each of which also stands for a different planetary body) and their associated numbers.

decorations and sprigs of greens that were meant to give added protection, as well as a flower vase filled with 73 stems (again, "to make her age lengthen") of a plant called *saup pei*. The *pei* part of the name here is auspicious because, by itself, *pei* means "to win" or "to triumph," suggesting that it will here triumph over Grandmother's condition.[5] Finally, one of the two bundles of wood on the floor next to the table also contained 73 pieces, while the other contained 4 much larger pieces of wood that, like the plant, had protective-sounding names.

Assembling such a large number of items and arranging them just so is, obviously, a carefully calculated act. But how could anyone believe that it would work to prolong life? What makes such a scheme compelling to many people in Baan Kaung Mu is the assumption that the internal organization of our own bodies mirrors the structure of the cosmos, a notion that is widespread in Southeast Asia. Further, the two are in a kind of dynamic tension with each other, such that changes in one compel changes in the other. Hence, by placing 73 ("more than her age") pieces of offerings in a ritual position that identifies the offering with Grandmother Yai herself (for example, on top of her shirt), the ritual is, in a sense, compelling the rest of the universe to adjust to this new, desirable reality, forcing it to "become true" in order to maintain its own cosmic alignment. Like a rubber band that, when stretched at one end and then released at the other, causes the entire band to spring into a new place, so does this ritual aim at changing one point in the cosmic circle (Grandmother Yai) by ritually "stretching" something at another, connected point—an effort aimed at "pulling" the ailing self into a new, improved position.

The view of the self that emerges from such a logic is one in which individuals are understood to be very much embedded in, and profoundly affected by, the larger structures that surround them. This includes social structures as well as physical ones. Just as one's well-being is enhanced by getting oneself into the proper cosmic alignment with the forces that be, the same must be done by regulating one's behavior in the social realm. This means taking care of and provisioning those for whom one is responsible, as well as prudently placing oneself in a position of dependence and respect toward those who are more powerful. The Buddha, the community of monks, and the Buddhist scriptures are included in this latter category, but so are the village guardian spirit, a host of nameless place-spirits, one's own parents and teachers, and, as we have seen, the structure of the universe itself. By putting oneself in the right relationship to these sources of power—by giving offerings, reciting prayers, paying attention to astrological conditions, and so on—one can empower oneself and ward off danger.

Certainly, Shan seek to do this in times of trouble, but not only then. This is also the stuff of everyday life—the sort of quotidian practice that helps create its own particular consciousness, a Shan view of self-in-the-world. In the following section on daily and weekly rites, I describe some of the most common ways in which the people of Baan Kaung Mu continually establish and reestablish their proper place in the scheme of things, all in the name of enhancing their health and well-being.

Daily and Weekly Rituals

Early each morning, as soon as the breakfast rice and curries have been prepared but before anyone has eaten, a woman of the household spoons a bit of each dish into small offering cups and takes them, along with a glass of water, to the household Buddha altar. There she sits on the floor, legs folded back and to one side in the polite posture that signals respect, raises each cup to the level of her head, and recites a short prayer before placing them on the altar (where they remain until midday). The entire rite takes about two minutes, yet it is sufficient to establish the household as one that accepts and respects the preeminence of the Buddha, while simultaneously laying claim to a certain access to power and protection implied by that status.

Following this, a portion of the morning meal is placed in a container (the favored utensil being a "lunch box" set of pale yellow tin dishes that are designed to stack one on top of the other) and taken to the temple as an offering to the monks and other residents of the monastery. Some households do this daily, others less regularly, but all participate. Each morning, a steady stream of people—often young and almost always female—goes in and out of the monastery compound with these alms, an act that generates merit for the entire household.

In the evening, candles and incense are lit at the household Buddha altar by one of the older adults (usually the oldest woman of the house), accompanied by a prayer. These prayers are fairly standard, having been passed down from one generation to the next, but can be varied by the individual reciting them. Here is a translation of one favored by my research assistant, Nang Kaew, who learned it from her great-aunt:

> *Sādhu!*
> *Sādhu!*
> *Sādhu!*
>
> I call upon the power of the Buddha,
> the power of the Dhamma,
> the power of Religion,
> the power of the lords of the village and the country,
> the power of my father and my mother,
> the power of the spirits who guard this house and room,
> the power of my teachers,
> and that of all other powerful beings
> of each and every place.
>
> Help us and watch over us.
> Let us be healthy and well,
> comfortable and cool.
> Let us avoid the things that are hot,
> the things that are not good.
> We ask that you protect us, please.

As this text indicates, the evening prayer is primarily aimed at seeking protection from illness and from any malevolent forces that may be out and about at night. Sometimes, when Nang Kaew has reason to be especially concerned (such as during a particularly violent monsoon storm), she adds a verse directed specifically to the village guardian spirit, who is generally regarded as the most immediately available source of power and protection.

On *wan sin* (Buddhist "Sabbath" days), these daily rites are supplemented by at least three others, all of which occur before the morning temple service. First, in addition to the regular offerings at the household Buddha altar, people fill small banana-leaf offering cups (prepared the day before) with cooked rice and sweets for the benign place-spirits of the house compound. Along with a few sticks of incense, these cups are placed (usually by women) at various "portals," such as a fence post at the entryway to the compound, at the top of the stairs to the rice barn, and at each entrance to the house proper.

A second set of these cups is placed, with candles and incense, at a simple wooden structure near the center of the village called the "heart of the village" *(tsau waan)*. This fenced-off area surrounds a heavy post, about four feet high. Connected to this post near its top are four small shelves oriented toward the cardinal directions. Other shelves are attached to the surrounding fence. The structure is a kind of power center[6] and serves primarily as a convening point for a vague category of benevolent spirits (or "angels") who are invited to share in the merit whenever the appropriate Buddhist ceremonies are performed.[7] Often people will leave offerings here whenever they take food to the temple, but on *wan sin* this area receives special attention. Additional offering cups of this kind are also placed on the pagoda in the monastery compound, on the railing of the temple veranda, and anywhere else these ethereal spirits are thought to congregate.

Finally, on each *wan sin*, a separate set of offerings is prepared for the *tsao moeng*, whose jurisdiction includes, but is not restricted to, Baan Kaung Mu village. These offerings consist of more banana-leaf cups filled with cooked rice and sweets, as well as fresh flowers, popped rice, candles, and incense sticks. Someone from each household takes these offerings to the house of the *phu moeng*, a title given to the man whose official job is to be the primary attendant of the village guardian spirit. When every household's offerings have arrived, the *phu moeng* takes them all to the shrine of the *tsao moeng* and presents them as a single group offering from the village as a whole. The effect, once again, is to enlist the ongoing aid and protection of the *tsao moeng* by showing the villagers' respect and appreciation for his presence and by simply reminding him that they are here and in need of his help.

Thus, on every *wan sin*, offerings are made to place-spirits at three levels: offerings to the spirits of the house site where one lives, offerings at the "heart of the village" post to benevolent spirits who frequent the village, and offerings to the guardian spirit who oversees the surrounding region (the *tsao moeng*). When questioned directly about the purpose of these offerings to various place-spirits, people invariably say that they are "for our well-being" (*yu li kin waan*, literally, be well and eat with good appetite). Clearly, performing these offerings on a regular basis makes people feel stronger, safer, and less prone to illness.

There are also community-wide rituals that draw upon a similar logic, the most frequent being the temple services that are held shortly after breakfast on each *wan sin*. Attendance at these services fluctuates considerably with the season. During *wa*–the rainy season retreat sometimes known in English as Buddhist Lent–attendance is swelled by the group of village elders who have taken on the status and responsibilities of being temple sleepers *(khon naun tsaung)*. During the rest of the year, attendance is sporadic, consisting primarily of a few older people who are regulars and a handful of young mothers with their babies and toddlers. (The full moon and new moon *wan sin* attract somewhat more people than do the two half moon *wan sin* that alternate with these.)

The service itself is simple and informal. There is no set time to begin, so people come whenever they have finished breakfast and chat with each other and with the abbot until everyone known to be coming has arrived, a process that can take an hour or more. They bring with them their offerings (flowers, popped rice, a bit of uncooked rice, and some money for the donation box) and wear clothes that are more or less dressy, depending on the season and whether or not it is an important holiday. Men and women sit separately– the men closer to the altar, the women farther back. When it is time to begin, the abbot or one of the resident novices moves to a special seat centered in front of the altar and begins the opening chant, answered by members of the congregation. He reads from the scriptures, delivers a sermon, and ends by reciting the *yaat nam* text through which people receive merit for this activity and share it with those already departed.

This is the basic framework for the service, but because most of the important holidays are linked to the Buddhist calendar and scheduled to fall on a *wan sin*, any actual *wan sin* service can be more or less elaborate, lasting anywhere from fifteen minutes to several hours, depending on the occasion. Like the other rituals described earlier, participation in these collective merit-making rites is perceived as beneficial in multiple ways: it will enhance one's overall well-being; it will prepare one for a good rebirth in the future; and it will establish one's social status in the present. Significantly, these rites also help establish the connectedness of people to each other, as people who "made merit together" and who, as a result, will probably be reborn together.

These rituals bring us back, then, to a notion that was encountered earlier in the context of people's attitudes toward death, namely, that the well-being of any given individual is linked in significant ways to the well-being of his or her consociates. This is especially true of individuals who have lived together in a single household, but it is also extended to the village as a whole. That is, the well-being of any one person is assumed to be affected by the overall welfare of the community.

Almost as if to dramatize this, the people of Baan Kaung Mu perform three rituals every year that have the explicit aim of helping the individual by enhancing the well-being of the village as a collective unit. These are the rituals of Sending Away the Spirits *(song phi)*, Feasting the Village Guardian Spirit *(liang tsao moeng)*, and Repairing the Village *(mei waan)*. In 1991 these three rituals were all performed on the same day, making the interconnections between them even easier to discern. In structure, if not in format, these collective rites are strikingly similar to the exorcism and soul-calling rituals performed for an individual in the healing session described in chapter 2, and they share similar goals. In the following account of that one, ritual-saturated day, I have highlighted those aspects of the day's activities that are most relevant for Shan theories of self and personhood, including what constitutes wellness and what constitutes a threat to personal well-being.

Three Annual Rituals

MAY 16, 1991: It is about 6:30 on the morning of what promises to be one of the stickiest days of the hot season. This is the day that was identified by Uncle Samaun (the local specialist in Shan calendrics) as a *phi kin kai* day, or "a day on which spirits can eat chickens"—hence, an appropriate day for the annual *liang tsao moeng*, or Feasting the Village Guardian Spirit ritual. It is also a Thursday, the birth day of Baan Kaung Mu village, and therefore a good day on which to hold the annual *mei waan*, or Repairing the Village ceremony. Before these two ceremonies can get under way, however, a preliminary one is necessary, one that will ritually evict all troublesome spirits from the village. This is the *song phi*, or Sending Away the Spirits ritual, and that is what is happening now.

I set out with a group of about a dozen men, laden with small packages, who are heading north along the road out of the village. The packages have been prepared by each household and are filled with the sorts of things spirits can use: a bit of rice in all its forms (unmilled, milled, and cooked), a chili pepper, some salt, a dried soybean cake, a little bag of cooking oil, a cigar, a coin (any denomination will do), some small onions and garlic—in short, all the accoutrements of everyday life. Some of the packages have been bundled together and attached to the center of a long pole that is then balanced across the shoulders of two men; others are simply carried in bunches by individuals.

Leading the spirits out of the village during the annual *song phi* ritual.

As we walk along the road, Uncle Samaun beats a large gong and calls to the troublesome spirits: "Come along, all of you, and leave this village! Come with us! We have food here for you to eat. Don't bother the people of the village. Eat this food instead!" At one point, the young men carrying the packages on the pole, who have been walking out in front, begin to turn off into the adjacent forest. "Wait! Not yet!" call the older men in the rear who are concerned that we have not yet gone far enough. "The farther the better, when it comes to sending off spirits," one of them remarks. They decide to take the provisions a bit farther to the fork in the road that heads off toward the next village. When we get there, everyone turns into the woods to hang their packages on tree limbs while Uncle Samaun beats the gong and repeats his call to the spirits.

On the way back, the men talk about the ritual for my benefit. "We do this once a year, on the same day as the *liang tsao moeng* ceremony," one man says. "In the past, it was more elaborate," another one observes. "People sent knives and other things as well as the food and money." Uncle Samaun's explanation gets to the heart of the matter: "In those days, there were no hospitals, no doctors, and no modern medicine—just our traditional healers and the medicines that we made ourselves. People got very sick. So this custom was even more important then. It was one of the few things we had to keep sickness away." When I ask whether it was ever done more than once a year,

Uncle Samaun answers, "No, just once a year." They talk about the sorts of illnesses that were common in the past, mentioning skin diseases in particular. As they talk, one man remembers that each household used to weave little rattan baskets to hold the spirit supplies instead of the plastic bags that were used this morning, adding "but now we're too lazy." This was not so long ago, I think to myself, remembering the woven spirit baskets used in the *song phi* ceremonies I witnessed in 1980 and 1981.

As we get closer to the village, most of the men head off to their respective houses to have breakfast before the *liang tsao moeng* ritual begins, but—afraid I might miss something—I proceed toward the path that leads to the shrine of the village guardian spirit. It is at the outskirts of the village, just inside the forest, about a hundred yards from the road.[8] The shrine consists of a small fenced compound containing a one-room building constructed on stilts in the traditional style. Although it is referred to as the guardian spirit's "palace" (and the small mattress and pillow inside as his "throne"), it looks more like a miniature Shan house. It is here that offerings are brought to this "lord of the realm," not only for this annual rite but also throughout the year.

The requirements of this lord are simple enough. He must be notified of all births and deaths and of anyone moving into or out of the village, as well as of any changes in status among the inhabitants (for example, when someone gets married or is ordained as a monk), all of whom are presumed to be under his care and protection. On *wan sin* he expects to receive a small offering of food and flowers from each household and enforces a ban on certain activities that are proscribed for the day, such as working in one's fields, slaughtering animals, collecting firewood, and making loud noises. In return, the guardian spirit takes a special interest in the concerns of Baan Kaung Mu villagers and can be applied to for a number of special services, such as protecting them when they travel away from the village, arranging nice weather and an absence of fights during festivals, helping a person avoid detection by the authorities for some minor infraction, or providing protection during a violent thunderstorm.

Once a year, the villagers renew and reaffirm their relationship with this spirit lord by mounting a major feast in his honor, after which people are given the opportunity to communicate with him directly through the intercession of spirit mediums. As I near the path that leads to the shrine, I notice a man constructing one of the roadblocks that is always placed across the roads leading into the village for the duration of the ceremony. This barrier is to prevent "bad things," as well as all motor vehicles, from entering the village during the time that the village guardian spirit is distracted from his usual patrols around the community by the festivities. Villagers are also not supposed to go in and out of the village during the time of the ceremony.

Preparing offerings for the village guardian spirit and his entourage at the annual *liang tsao moeng* ritual.

Following the overgrown path from the road to the shrine, I find several men already there, clearing the brush around the guardian spirit's compound and constructing small, makeshift offering platforms at the base of three large trees. Like any respectable lord, the village guardian spirit travels with an entourage of lesser spirits, and these will be feted at the smaller platforms. Women stop by with a plate of offerings from their household, but most do not stay for this portion of the ritual.[9] Offerings of rice, sweets, chicken, and liquor are assembled. Eventually, around 8:15 and well after all the households' offerings have arrived, the man who is his special attendant (the *phu moeng*) formally offers everything assembled to the guardian spirit and lights a good-sized candle near his throne. A portion of the food and liquor is placed at each of the smaller platforms for the spirit members of his entourage, and candles are lit at each of these too.

While the candles are burning, the spirits are "eating," so we all settle in to wait, the men resting comfortably on their haunches above the damp ground, chatting amiably in anticipation of the party that is to follow. When the candles finally burn down, the men form small, convivial groups to eat and drink the "remains" of the offerings,[10] after which a gong is sounded to alert the villagers who have remained at home that the *liang tsao moeng* ritual is complete and the roadblocks may be removed.[11]

At this point, some of the men leave. Others wait around for the spirit mediums to arrive so that the village guardian spirit can talk to us, and we to him. Although this is a fairly common accompaniment to *liang tsao moeng* rites in larger Shan villages and in Mae Hong Son town, it is a relatively recent innovation for Baan Kaung Mu. Visitors from other nearby villages that still do not employ spirit mediums for their *liang tsao moeng* rites are also arriving now, having come to take advantage of this opportunity to communicate with their respective village guardian spirits too.

Finally, about 9:30, Nang Nu's bright blue pickup truck, carrying two female spirit mediums brought from town, is visible at the edge of the road. Uncle Pon, the local healer, has also come to serve as a "chair," or medium, for the village guardian spirit. Escorted by the older women of the village, who are dressed in their "going-to-temple clothes," they make their way from the road into the shrine. Mats are set up in the guardian spirit's compound for the mediums to sit on, and a set of gong and drums is positioned under the "palace" itself, out of the way of where the mediums will be dancing. Several village women go into the compound too, slipping off their sandals first, then sitting on the mats. Some are there to attend to the mediums, sprinkling fragrant water on them and helping them get dressed as they become possessed. Others are there to be cured of something or simply to watch. Meanwhile, most of the men and some younger women prepare to watch from outside the compound fence.

Uncle Samaun and some of the other male ritual specialists join the group inside the compound. As the musicians beat out a strong, hypnotic rhythm, Uncle Samaun sprinkles the mediums with specially prepared fragrant water,[12] and, one by one, they begin to dance. While they dance, they may become possessed by various spirits, including any of the thirty-two village guardian spirits who watch over Shan communities.[13] When a female medium becomes possessed by one of the male guardian spirits, she signals this by taking on a masculine persona—moving, talking, and behaving in a way that is noticeably different from her earlier manner. She asks for swords to hold while she dances in a martial arts style. Uncle Samaun questions her respectfully until he ascertains her identity, then invites people from the village under that particular guardian spirit's jurisdiction to come and ask questions. As they move into position to do this, the medium sits back down, ready now to talk to "his" people as the guardian spirit.

Much of the initial questioning of the Baan Kaung Mu guardian spirit is taken up by Pi Non, regarding his recently deceased wife and daughter.[14] Then there are a series of questions about the other rituals that were performed today. "Did we do them right?" "Is there anything else you want?" The Baan Kaung Mu guardian spirit answers that the *liang tsao moeng* was done correctly "except for two things." The "hitching posts for elephants and horses" (the mythical mounts for the guardian spirit and his entourage) that are supposed to be placed on the stairs of the smaller offering platforms had been forgotten, and some uncooked, milled rice, as well as some unmilled rice, should have been placed in each corner of the guardian spirit's palace. Nevertheless, it was acceptable for this year. The *song phi*, however, would have to be done over. The villagers sent the spirits away in one direction only (north), whereas the correct way to do it is to divide the stuff into four piles and send one to each of the four "corners" (that is, northeast, southeast, northwest, and southwest). In addition, each of these corners should get a square basket—similar to the ones used in healing rituals—in which various figures (male, female, animal) have been placed.

People accept this unexpected news with surprising equanimity, considering the amount of labor that a repeat performance will entail. If the villagers follow these instructions, one man tells me a short while later, "people in the village will be healthy, there will be no fighting or quarrels, and there will be lots of water buffalo and cattle"—in other words, the village will prosper. Plans are made immediately to do the *song phi* over again in the late afternoon, in conjunction with the ceremony to repair the village.

Individuals ask other sorts of questions, mostly about various chronic pains and illnesses, which the mediums deal with one at a time. As a medium gets tired (or senses that there are no further questions), she announces, as the guardian spirit, that she wants "to return" and then—unless someone rushes up with another question right away—lies down flat on her back, "blacks out," and awaits another possession. Each new guardian spirit who "descends" is greeted by handing the medium a fresh sprig of fragrant flowers, which the medium sniffs almost nonstop during her possession. Throughout, the attendants continue to sprinkle the mediums every minute or so with more fragrant water.

The overall tone of this event is difficult to describe. Onlookers behave respectfully and attentively to the possessed mediums but seem to find the persona of the guardian spirits amusing. These spirits say whatever they want, whenever they want, and do not stop to bother with the social niceties. They are, in effect, still somewhat *hai*. This is part of their power and appeal, but it also makes them appear a bit childish. One of the possessed mediums entertains the crowd by purposefully provoking a woman known to have *khi*

Mediums being possessed by village guardian spirits.

kwaang, a condition that causes the sufferer, when startled, suddenly to begin to mimic the movements and speech of those near her.[15] People find this hilarious. Eventually, around noon, the group decides to break for lunch. Afterwards, some reconvene at Uncle Pon's house, where the mediums are staying, in order to continue the séance. Others go to Uncle Samaun's house to begin work on the new *song phi* ritual.

I decide to go first to Uncle Pon's house, where I find a rather more sedate session in process. There is no music and no dancing, just the continuous possession of one medium—the oldest and most frail, yet clearly the one with the most authority—who is "holding court" for an audience of mostly women and answering people's questions. Nang Ping, a young friend of mine, asks the medium to blow on some white string (the kind used for soul calling) and to tie a length of it around her wrists and neck. She wants this done, she says, because she has a twitch in her eyelid that has been bothering her for a while, and also because she had been anxious lately, "thinking a lot," and unable to sleep well at night. But Nang Ping gets more than she bargained for. After tying her wrists, the medium tells her that she should not go out visiting at night and that there are two people, a man and a woman, who are out to get her. If she goes out at night, there will be bloodshed.

This news greatly disturbs her, and she immediately discusses it with me and with her mother, who is also present. Trying to find something to which the guardian spirit's warning might refer, Nang Ping tells us that she has been riding back and forth to town a lot recently in Uncle Ut's truck and has been very friendly with him. "But he's not my boyfriend! We're just two people who get along well and enjoy each other's company," she says. Because they are friends, he has given her some discounts on the usual fares for heavy loads, she continues, "like the time I went into town to get the roof sheeting for the new house, and he only charged me one baht per sheet to transport them back to Baan Kaung Mu. He asked me to keep quiet about this, because his wife might be angry if she found out." Now Nang Ping is wondering whether the wife did find out. Perhaps the two of them are now planning to do something to her?

She goes back up to the medium and asks if the man and woman she was talking about are husband and wife. No, the medium answers, they are not. Nang Ping then arranges to have the medium "make a candle" for her to be lit on her next birth day, a Saturday. She will go into town tomorrow to pay for it. Later, she tells me that she will also ask for more details about the man and woman when she visits the medium in town. "If it is someone in the village, she wouldn't mention it there [at Uncle Pon's house]," Nang Ping says. "There were too many people present. But at her own house, when we're alone, she might tell me." If it turns out not to be someone in the village, she muses, then her second guess is that it might be some young man who is interested in her but not brave enough to ask for her outright and who therefore plans to "kidnap" her, perhaps with the help of some woman. In the meantime, she resolves, she is going to try to be very careful. She will not go visiting at night, and she will say a prayer to the village guardian spirit every night before going to sleep. "I used to do that all the time," she tells me, "but I've gotten out of the habit. I'm going to start doing it again."[16]

The mediums take a break for a late lunch, so I leave and head back toward the center of the village. I stop to visit at another house and chat with Uncle Tsat, the father of the household, mentioning that I hadn't seen the village headman at either the *song phi* or the *liang tsao moeng* rites this morning, although his wife had shown up for the session with the mediums afterwards. Was the headman out of town? "He's at another village's festival," says Uncle Tsat. His wife interjects, "Yes, but early this morning, he was here in the village. He could have gone to the *song phi* at least. He just doesn't believe in this stuff." Uncle Tsat, in an effort at diplomacy, turns to me and says, "It's the same with all religions, right? Some people believe, and some people don't. Some believe a lot, others only a little."

Trying to stay on the subject by moving to more neutral territory, I ask whether he thinks the people from a neighboring village, who had been told by a medium this morning that they should redo their *liang tsao moeng* and change the date of their *mei waan* ceremony, were really going to do it. Uncle Tsat hedges, "I don't know. If they believe it, they will, but I don't know if they really believe it. Some people believe when the village guardian spirit speaks; some don't." He pauses for a moment, then adds that it is also a matter of who from that village had been present at the guardian spirit's pronouncements. As I consider the significance of this, I begin to recall that it was mostly young people and some older women—including one who was well respected in that village—but no older important men. Although I would regard this as a highly mixed group of people, Uncle Tsat proceeds to refer to them as "just kids" *(luk aun lai lai)* and seems skeptical as to whether the rest of their village will be persuaded to redo and reschedule their ceremonies on the testimony of a group of "children."

Stopping back at my house briefly, I find my landlady weaving green grasses into little bundles to add to the bucket of items that will go under the chanting tower during the ceremony to repair the village. Once they are "charged" by the monks' chanting of Buddhist scriptures, she explains, she will put them at the entrance to the house compound and at the doors at the bottom and top of the stairs. "Spirit screens" of woven bamboo strips— designed to foil the attempts of malevolent spirits to enter—will also go into the buckets and then be placed at each of these thresholds, along with the woven grass. Other items that each household will include in the bucket of things they wish to have empowered are a ball of white string, some sand, kindling wood for starting a new fire (each household's hearth will be fully extinguished before the ritual begins), some matches, a bowl of *mak haan* water (water mixed with a special kind of seed, to be used for shampooing after the ritual), and a host of other idiosyncratic items that their owners hope will somehow be improved, or made more effective, by the ceremony. These can range from the garden seed one household hopes to plant this spring, or the brightly colored nylon rope a cattle trader uses for his livestock, to the pencils and notebooks that a schoolchild relies on for doing homework.

I continue on to Uncle Samaun's house where the preparations for the second *song phi* are under way. Uncle Samaun is supervising the preparation of the special baskets the guardian spirit has ordered, and the headman's wife is busy shaping a veritable army of little clay figures that will be divided up among them—so many miniature men, women, cattle, water buffalo, elephants, and horses to each basket. As they work, men arrive with a fresh supply of offerings collected from each house in the village (plastic bags filled with the same items used in this morning's version of the ritual) and work at attaching them to four carrying sticks in preparation for sending them to the "four corners of the earth."

Uncle Samaun has made one basket for each "corner," or direction, and one for the center. When the five baskets are ready, he takes them up into the chanting tower, which is directly across the road from his house and right next to the "heart of the village" post. The tower consists of a small, roofed pavilion, about ten feet square, with a much smaller porch at a slightly lower level—rather like a tiny traditional Shan house. The whole structure is raised to a height of about thirty feet and is accessible by a long, steep ladder-staircase leading to the porch. When Uncle Samaun returns, I ask him if putting the baskets of spirit offerings in the tower is a new custom. "Actually, it is an old one that we have neglected," he replies. "The guardian spirit reminded us that we should do it."

As I watch and listen to everyone scurrying to complete the preparations before the scheduled Repairing the Village ceremony, it seems to me that people are pulled in two directions by their ritual involvement. On the one hand, there is a sense in which keeping the customs is experienced as somewhat burdensome—hence, the tendency to streamline rituals over time, to use plastic bags instead of homemade rattan baskets, and so on. On the other hand, there is considerable worry that failure to do them properly will result in various kinds of disasters, diseases, environmental problems, crime, and the like. So there is a tug in each direction, a cycle of ritual lapses followed by a period of rectifications.

Meanwhile, the tower platform is being readied with other paraphernalia—mats for the monks to sit on, a curtain to block the sunlight streaming in from the west, the large beeswax candle that will burn during the chanting, and many other items. As soon as all the invited monks from other villages have arrived at the monastery, the village roads are closed off again. Villagers—mostly women and young children (the older ones are still at school)—begin to arrive with their buckets of items to be blessed. Many households bring two buckets: one with the specially prepared *mak haan* water, the second with all the other items. They place these directly underneath the tower, then take a seat on mats placed on the grass next to the tower or somewhere else close by. Mothers fan themselves with their large conical hats and yell at the children to stay out of the sun.

Finally, about 4 p.m., Uncle Samaun walks over to the temple to formally invite the monks to begin the ceremony. Shortly thereafter, a line of monks walking in single file moves from the monastery to the tower and climbs the

Monks ascending the tower to begin the annual Repairing the Village ritual. Underneath the tower, villagers place items to be blessed and empowered by the monks' chanting.

steps to the platform. Sitting in a circle, each of them holding onto a length of white string that passes through all their hands and ends in a bowl of specially prepared water, the monks begin to chant. The villagers sit politely—legs folded back, hands placed together in a *waai* and holding a sprig of flowers and a bit of popped rice, the customary attitude of devotion. Halfway through the chanting, the schoolchildren arrive and take their seats next to their mothers.

The chanting is said to generate merit for the participants while also channeling "positive energy" of sorts into the things placed underneath the monks and the people sitting nearby. It is not necessary to listen to the words being spoken, and, indeed, most people do not know the meaning of the verses that are being recited in Pali, the language of the Theravāda Buddhist scriptures. It is enough just to be present and to hear the sound of the words being spoken. The words have an efficacy of their own that is activated simply by their being uttered.

After about forty-five minutes of continuous chanting, the ceremony comes to an end. People gather round the base of the tower as the head monk, a much-beloved abbot from a neighboring village, stands on the platform's porch and, grinning, sprinkles everyone below with sacralized water from the bowl they have used in their chanting. People squeal with delight at each sprinkling, jumping to catch the sprigs of flowers and handfuls of popped rice that are being thrown overboard from the tower. Finally, when the water and flowers are gone, the crowd collects the buckets and begins to disperse while the monks prepare to go home. Uncle Samaun stays to supervise the putting away of temple paraphernalia and also to organize the dispatching of the baskets of spirit offerings to the "four corners."

When people get home, they take the things out of their buckets and use them to ritually "power up" their households: The sand is thrown onto the roofs of their houses, rice barns, and outhouses. (My landlady also throws a little in each corner of the room "to chase away spirits.") The white string is used to encircle the house. Spirit screens and woven grass bundles are strung up at all portals. The kindling wood and matches are used to start a fire for cooking supper. And everyone at the bathing area that evening is using the *mak haan* water to shampoo their hair. It is a fresh start for the village, its annual ritual obligations having at last been met successfully.

Self-Made Rituals and Ritually Made Selves

In the healing session described in chapter 2, we saw, in essence, a collapsed version of this day's activities that followed an identical logic: first, evict the offending spirit(s); then, invoke a power source (such as the village guardian spirit or Buddhist monks); and, finally, secure the newly restored order by tying white threads around the body or other thing-to-be-made-whole. Similar correspondences can be found between many other aspects of the three annual rites and the much more modest everyday rituals directed at the Buddha, the monks, or place-spirits, and in such practices as making a candle. All of the rituals mentioned have similar goals of achieving well-being, with only minor variations on how this is to be accomplished. They have a normal or routine quality to them (as opposed to being mysterious or awe-inspiring)—a kind of tool-kit approach—and are considered as necessary to health and well-being as eating and sleeping.

That the same sort of logic or reasoning continues to reappear in many different forms, and on many different levels (that of the body, the household, the village, and so on), suggests that the ritual complex as a whole is pointing toward some very basic assumptions about the way the world works. Three sorts of assumptions are particularly relevant for my purposes. First, many of the rituals make implicit claims about the nature of the self (for example, that the self can be possessed, fortified, intimidated, protected; that personhood is not unique to humans; and that persons—human and spirit—behave in predictable ways). They also make claims about the nature of the social order (for example, that more powerful beings should help the less powerful, that the less powerful should be grateful and dutiful, and that respect should be accorded those who, like monks, exhibit great personal discipline and self-control). And finally, these rituals make implicit claims about people's relationship with the universe itself (for example, that people's luck waxes and wanes and can be changed by ritual, that anticipated misfortunes can be staved off with preventive rituals, and that current misfortunes can be alleviated with rituals).

Despite these commonalities, the rituals are not wholly redundant. They accomplish things in different ways, create different sorts of opportunities, and solve somewhat different sorts of problems. During the possession of the spirit mediums, for example, and during the subsequent attempts to interpret what was said, people can play creatively with their own ideas about self and society, propriety, and authority. When someone asks the village guardian spirit through a medium whether something has been done properly, they are addressing themselves and their fellow villagers in addition to the guardian spirit, seeking the sort of satisfying reassurance about the appropriateness of a given course of action that uniquely comes from mutual witnessing and public consent. Further, since interpreting the medium's instructions frequently entails judgment and discernment and requires that those affected reach a consensus about its meaning, it matters who is there listening. Hence, the ritual practice of consulting a spirit medium both sets limits to, and gives permission for, specific ways of conducting village business. As such, it is a kind of "politics by other means."

The *mei waan* (Repairing the Village) is different. It cleanses, purifies, and renews. It gets rid of the old—enables a clean break with it—and allows one to get a fresh start. It also energizes, invigorates, revitalizes, and makes potent all things that come in contact with its power. Unlike the *liang tsao moeng* (Feasting the Village Guardian Spirit), it has as its basis for power not a strong person but, rather, the power of Buddhist texts and monks and, more abstractly, the power that courses through the universe itself. Just as a person has a birth day that anchors him or her in the universe, so does Baan Kaung Mu village; by operating from a position that acknowledges its idiosyncratic place in the universe, both a person and a village can tap into sources of power greater than themselves.

It would be impossible to participate in such a large number of rituals (and I have recounted only a fraction of them here) on a daily, weekly, and annual basis—many of which rearticulate the same cultural logic—and not have that practice affect one's consciousness. Each performance constitutes yet another rehearsal of a particular view of self-in-the-world even as it offers opportunities for reinterpretation and (occasionally) rewriting the script. Armed with this arsenal of techniques for coping with the world, the adults of Baan Kaung Mu generally feel well prepared for most of what life throws at them. But sometimes it is not enough. In chapter 7, I will return to this subject in order to consider the personal coping strategies that people have developed for restoring their equilibrium when it is lost or threatened, a topic that will also entail a closer look at old age.

Before doing so, however, I want to explore one additional ritual complex, that of Buddhist novice ordinations. Like the large-scale community rituals recounted in this chapter, these are elaborate ceremonies that involve virtually everyone in the village. But unlike those just described, these are organized and funded primarily by individuals, not by the community. As such, they put the spotlight squarely on those individuals who choose to sponsor them, a process that can illuminate important aspects of Shan thinking about the ideal course of an individual's life.

Chapter 6

Marking Maturity

The Negotiation of Social Inequalities at Midlife

VISITORS TO THAILAND who express any interest in seeing Mae Hong Son Province will undoubtedly encounter images of Shan ordination rituals in the travel brochures available at any Bangkok tourist agency. Beautiful color photos of elaborately costumed boys sitting astride the shoulders of smiling young men advertise the charms of this remote province, alongside photos of poppy fields, mountains shrouded in mist, "the long-necked Karen," and other exotica. "Mae Hong Son—The Land above the Clouds—reveals its timeless cultures and traditions and a lifestyle unaltered in its innocence," promises one brochure.[1] If you're lucky enough to arrive in the provincial capital during the ordination "season," you may even see a colorful procession winding its way through town—young men with costumed boys on their shoulders moving rhythmically through the streets and alleyways, dancing to the accompaniment of a gong-and-drum band and followed by a crowd of joyful people.

Although all Theravāda Buddhist communities have ordination rituals for transforming men and boys into monks and novice monks, Shan are known for staging some of the most spectacular versions of this ceremony, and the recent promotion of these events by the Bangkok-based tourist industry has not diminished their significance to local participants. Indeed, most Shan would surely rank this ritual as one of their most important and enjoyable customs, a ceremony that is anticipated with great excitement and remembered long afterward with pride and pleasure. What are these huge, expensive, labor-intensive, and emotionally compelling events about? As with most complex social institutions, ordination rituals are revealing of many aspects of Shan social life, and any attempt to reduce their meaning to a single "explanation" should be regarded with skepticism. In this case, I am particularly interested in exploring what they might tell us about Shan conceptions of the life course.

One possibility would be to focus on the boys who are being ordained and to view the ceremony primarily as a rite of passage for them, a transition from childhood to adulthood. This is the approach that has been taken most frequently in the ethnographic literature, and I will return to it later in the chapter, mainly to raise questions about it. There is another possibility, however, for assessing the local impact of this ceremony on the life course, and that is to focus on the adult sponsors of the ritual, the patrons whose financial and logistical support enable the large-scale, elaborate versions of the ritual that Shan so love. In this chapter, I highlight the role of these sponsors and suggest that ordination rituals are as much a rite of passage for the sponsors as they are for the boys being ordained.

Becoming a Sponsor

Much of young adulthood, as we have seen, is spent in work aimed at getting a newly married couple established in an independent domicile and helping them achieve a certain measure of economic autonomy. But with regard to those who have attained this goal, we might still ask: What motivates a person in this community to work beyond the level of mere subsistence, and what makes their work meaningful? How is one's productivity tied to one's own developing sense of competence and self-worth, and how are the fruits of one's labors harnessed to a social system in which the differences between people—men and women, young and old, rich and poor—are granted cosmic significance? Having accomplished their economic independence, middle-aged and older adults who can afford to do so (and not all can) try to participate in the sorts of projects that bring status and prestige. The most traditional and still the most popular way to do this is to become a sponsor of a large-scale Buddhist merit-making ceremony, a role that confers both secular status and religious "merit."

What is entailed in the role of sponsor? On the most mundane level, sponsoring a ceremony means agreeing to do the lion's share of the work in getting it organized and, most important, paying for most of the expenses, including any incidental ones that occur unexpectedly in the course of putting on the ceremony. Other people will contribute modest sums so as to make merit along with the sponsor, but the sponsor agrees to take responsibility for making sure that everything needed is provided.

On a more symbolic level, sponsoring a ceremony—especially a large, village-wide one—means that one is temporarily setting oneself up as a "lord" (*tsao;* the Shan term for this role is *tsao paui,* "lord/owner of the ritual" or "master of ceremonies"), with those who attend being placed either in the role of "recipient of offerings" (usually monks and/or temple sleepers) or in the role of helpers and dependents (everyone else). As such, the sponsor takes on all of the usual obligations and privileges inherent in the senior role of any hierarchical relationship for the duration of the ceremony—most notably, to look after and provide for one's dependents while retaining the right to direct their labor. Minimally, this means providing meals and snacks for all who attend, as well as the special merit-generating gifts given to monks, novices, and temple sleepers. Often, especially if it is a large ceremony, it entails providing some sort of entertainment (usually musicians) as well.

In fact, the idea of community socializing for its own sake is still mostly a foreign concept here. There are no dinner parties, no outdoor barbecues or potlucks, no equivalent to the traditional American rural square dances, and so on.[2] As a result, village social gatherings take place mainly in one of three contexts: (1) in work-related projects (e.g., while doing exchange labor in the fields or while helping a neighbor build a house); (2) on excursions *(thiao)* to various sites of interest (e.g., a trip to a park or a religious shrine); and (3) during the preparations for a religious ceremony (and, to a lesser extent, at the actual event), both in one's own village and in others. In this sense, sponsoring a merit-making ritual has much in common with throwing a party, with all of the pleasures and headaches that such projects entail.

These ceremonies can range in scale from small affairs involving a few households to village-wide projects involving hundreds of people. Although the basic elements remain the same no matter what the size, the role-playing dimensions I have alluded to are most apparent in the larger ones. Ultimately, what makes the role of sponsor a status-enhancing one is that it involves giving to others. This generosity reflects more generally on one's productive capacity, which, in turn, is assumed to be related to one's overall karmic status. By the same token, if individuals can afford to sponsor such a ceremony and do not, it reflects poorly on them and, in fact, calls into question the source of their productivity, encouraging rumors that they are perhaps in league with less reputable sources of power and potency.

For all these reasons, most Shan adults are eager to sponsor ceremonies whenever they can afford to do so, an interest that begins in middle adulthood and continues into old age. And of all the possible ceremonies, big and small, that one might choose to sponsor, the one that always generates the most excitement is the *paui sang long,* or novice ordination festival. Shan women, in particular, are deeply attached to it. Why should this be? In this chapter, I provide a description of the ceremony that stresses its importance as a rite of passage for the adult sponsors, one that marks their maturity and status in the community. I also show how the event functions as a kind of social drama in which age, gender, and class hierarchies are displayed and sometimes challenged.

Sponsors as "Lords": Ordination Festivals as a Celebration of the Royal Style

The ordination ceremony that initiates a man into the Buddhist *sangha* as a monk—or, if he is under twenty years old, as a novice monk—is an important ritual in all Theravāda Buddhist societies, although in different communities the overall structure of the ritual varies somewhat in emphasis and degree of elaboration.[3] For the Shan of northwestern Thailand, the ceremony is typically a three-day affair held every two or three years, or whenever there is a good number of boys of the appropriate age (about ten years or older) to be ordained.[4]

A boy can be ordained as a novice at any time, without much fanfare, but the first occasion on which he is ordained is usually treated as special and deserving of whatever ceremonial elaboration the boy's sponsors can afford. It is these initial ordinations, called *paui sang long* in Shan, that I am describing here. The season for these sorts of novice ordinations runs roughly from March until May, just before the rainy season, when the weather is warm and dry.

The highly elaborate and visually stunning ordination festivals that Shan perform are based on a reenactment of a scene from the Buddha's life. It is the moment when the young Prince Siddhartha—who is destined to become the Buddha—has decided to renounce all his worldly possessions in order to devote himself to the pursuit of enlightenment. He steals away from the palace in the middle of the night, cuts his hair, sheds his princely garb, and takes on the robes of a wandering mendicant, carrying only a bowl in which to receive food and other offerings from the faithful.

In the ritual version of this drama, the boys who are to be ordained are taken to the temple in the middle of the night; their eyebrows are shaved off (their heads having already been shaved the previous day); and they are dressed in princely costumes. Then, they remain in this royal mode for several days (usually three), during which time they visit every house in the village and the festival part of the ceremony takes place. At the end of this, they complete the reenactment by "renouncing" their princely status, changing into the yellow robes of a novice monk, and taking their ordination vows.

Throughout this drama, the sponsor (or sponsoring husband-and-wife couple, as is often the case) plays a prominent role, beginning with the initial organization of the event. Some boys are anxious to be ordained and pester their parents about it; many more are actively "recruited" by an adult who wants to sponsor the ceremony in order to make merit. Although a boy's parents are almost always involved in sponsoring his ordination, it sometimes happens that a *paui sang long* is being planned in the village during a year when they are not quite financially ready to handle all the expenses. They can try to hold their son out of the festival until the next time it comes around (when they might be more prepared), but the more common solution is for a wealthier household to persuade the parents to let them shoulder the expenses as the boy's major sponsor, with the parents helping in whatever way they can. Thus, many ordination festivals end up with one or two major sponsors and a host of minor ones.

In the early days of the planning, the sponsors are the only ones involved. They must decide many things: which boys will be ordained and who will sponsor each of them, what date will be an auspicious one for the ceremony, which monks will be invited to perform the actual ordination, which other temples (and their respective villages) will be invited to attend, who will be responsible for food preparation, how they will handle latecomers who decide between now and the ordination date that they would like to have a boy ordained, and so forth.

Once the chosen boys have agreed to undergo the ceremony, the sponsors must arrange for them to receive regular, daily instruction (usually from the village monks) in learning the chants and other things they need to know to prepare for life in the monastery. After the date has been set, invitations have to be mailed out. Then begins nightly preparations—for weeks in advance—of the nonperishable items such as offerings and decorations that will be used in the festival. These nightly gatherings are usually held in the home of one of the main sponsors, who provides light snacks and refreshments. Volunteers from all the village households show up to work, entertaining each other with lively conversation, jokes, and sometimes some spontaneous singing and dancing in the special style associated with *paui sang long* festivals. During the weeks of preparation, gong sets are assembled (either by purchase or on loan) for use during the ceremony, and these may be brought out and played for everyone's entertainment during the evening work sessions. Meanwhile, the sponsors make frequent trips to town to purchase costume material and an endless list of supplies.

When the time for the three-day festival arrives, the sponsors' responsibilities intensify. It is the sponsors who decide when to begin the festivities with the late-night "stealing away" to the temple of the boys (in memory of Prince Siddhartha's midnight escape from the palace) and who, once there, supervise each boy's transformation into a *sang long*, the beautiful costumed young "prince." Each boy has an entourage, recruited by the sponsor, which includes a couple of young men to carry him from house to house (sometimes referred to as his bodyguard) and, perhaps, a dresser (a person in charge of his initial makeup and costuming, as well as touch-ups and adjustments along the way), although the sponsors themselves may also take on this job.

Dressing a boy as a "prince" during the *paui sang long,* or novice ordination festival.

Anyone who is interested may come to observe, and the temple is usually full of villagers of all ages, crowding round to watch.

From this point on, the agency of the boys is muted, while the sponsors and other "handlers" are clearly in charge. During the initial dressing at the temple, the sleepy boys are often treated like dolls, fussed over, photographed, and made into objects of beauty. (Later, when they begin the house-to-house visits around the village, people say they should be carefully watched, guarded, and brought in after dark because, like all beautiful and attractive objects, they might attract witchcraft, or *phoe.*) When all are ready, they form a line as *sang long* and pay respect to the assembled monks, reciting the chants they have been working on the previous few weeks. Their transformation complete, they are finally allowed to lounge about and nap a bit on mats their sponsors have brought to the temple, as they wait until morning. Then, after a few last-minute instructions from their sponsors ("hold on to the man's headband when he dances, and you won't fall," "if

The costumed boys are carried on men's shoulders and paraded around the village. The sponsors lead the procession, dancing to celebrate their achievement.

you have to pee, ask whoever's carrying you to let you down," and so on), they embark on their first shoulder ride as *sang long*–a predawn trek to the shrine of the village guardian spirit, who must be informed of their imminent change in status. (The sponsors usually take advantage of this opportunity to ask the village guardian spirit for his help and protection during the festivities, with requests for good weather and no outbreaks of fighting among the young men topping the list.)

As the first rays of sun are peeking through the mountain ridges, the jubilant procession emerges from the guardian spirit's shrine and noisily begins its tour of the village, accompanied by the gong-and-drum band. Over the next three days, the procession will stop at each house, dancing briefly in the courtyard before going inside, where the *sang long* will recite their memorized blessings and receive small gifts of money from each household. On the second day of the festival (called *wan kho lu*), the sponsors lead a grand procession to the temple, pausing to dance as they go, during which the offerings they have collected are displayed and presented with much fanfare. Throughout the three days, the mood is festive. The young men who are carrying the boys bring a bottle of whiskey along (provided by the sponsor) and indulge in a shot every now and then while their young charges are inside chanting. They return as a group to the sponsor's home for meals and a longer break during the afternoon heat.

Meanwhile, guests arrive in "delegations" each day from other villages and are announced on the temple public address system—for example, "Please welcome the people of Village X, who have just arrived and have made an offering at the temple in support of our *paui sang long.*" These guests usually then fan out to visit friends and relatives in the village. Young people roam around together, talking and flirting. Older visitors (some of whom may be planning to sponsor a similar ceremony themselves) check out the style and quantity of offerings the local sponsors have assembled in the temple for the ordination. Children beg their grandparents for change to buy a treat at one of the many food stalls set up by local women. Meals for these guests are provided by the sponsors and served at the temple each day, made with village labor under the sponsors' supervision. In the evenings, people gather in the sponsors' homes for conversation, snacks, and perhaps some entertainment by musicians who know how to sing and play in the traditional style.

On the night before the ordination, a soul-calling rite *(haung khwan)* is performed for the boys. During this rite the parents and other sponsors ritually feed the boys, an act that underscores their capacity to nurture and provide for *(liang)* the boys and, simultaneously, draws attention to the hierarchical quality of the relationship. After the ceremony, the boys will permanently acknowledge their debt to any nonparent sponsors they may have had by addressing them as "Mother-Sponsor" *(mae kham)* and "Father-Sponsor" *(pau kham)* and by taking on certain ritual obligations toward them. If there are significant economic disparities between the boy's household and that of his sponsor, he may also end up joining that household and working for them for a while after he completes his stay in the monastery.

The actual ordination on the third day is somewhat anticlimactic, with most of the guests having already departed, but the boys line up in front of the invited monks to receive their vows and change into the yellow robes that their sponsors have provided for them. They will now live at the monastery for as long as they remain novices, keeping ten precepts rather than the usual five required of lay Buddhists. (The boys I spoke with were unanimous in saying that the most difficult of these was the precept forbidding solid food after noon.) Any remaining guests depart at this point, and village life returns to normal.

Although this is only a sketchy description of the ritual, it is sufficient, I hope, to give some indication of the scope of the event. This is a huge festival that requires a lot of planning and labor to come off well. It is a genuine community project, on which everyone in the village works, with the leadership provided by the sponsors. Shan consider a successful *paui sang long* one in which lots of people attend, everyone has a good time, and there are no fights (always a latent concern when young men are drinking). To the extent that these conditions are met, it reflects well or poorly on the organizational abilities and overall charisma of the sponsors. People speak fondly, for example, of an old headman of a previous generation who used to sponsor "really good novice ordinations" with many boys being ordained at once, lots of guests, hired singers and dancers, and the ability to "keep the young men under control." This sort of rhetoric points to the way in which ordination festivals signal a suspension of everyday social reality and cast something of a feudal overtone on the event, a romanticized longing for a village ordered by idealized hierarchical relationships that is expressed in people's descriptions and memories of past ordination festivals. In this Camelot-like nostalgic reverie, the wealthy and powerful protect the poor and weak, no one is stingy, everyone is generous, and there are no fights and no bad feelings. In this sense, ordinations can be seen as an exercise in utopia building, and sponsors are implicitly challenged to meet the requirements of being "king" (or "queen") for a day.

At any point during the time leading up to and during the festival, for example, sponsors may be approached by various people who want them to spend more of their money on ordination-related expenses: traveling salesmen with religious paraphernalia; local parents who need help in having their son ordained; volunteer workers who need more refreshments; the boys' entourage and "bodyguards," who ask for more liquor; out-of-town singers and musicians who show up at the event but who then require special gifts in compensation for their "spontaneous" performances; and so on. Although these are the sorts of requests that well-to-do households are quite used to dealing with, they take on a special quality when they occur during a novice ordination. Sponsors spoke of the obligation they felt to be generous, to be willing to spend money, and "not to calculate the cost," in order to keep their minds focused on the religious aspects of the ceremony. "Otherwise," they said repeatedly, "you won't get any merit." During the planning stages, when people are trying to decide who will be the major sponsor(s) and who will be the helpers, the language used to describe the sort of generosity that will be expected of them is one of courage and bravery. "Do you dare to do this?" one major sponsor asked the others who were trying to decide what to do. "If we each have to spend twenty thousand baht [about US$1,000 at that time], will you be afraid?" Since sizeable sums may be at stake, it is not a game for the faint of heart.

In this way, a kind of dual disciplining goes on in the course of these ordinations. The boys who are to be ordained prepare themselves to be subjected to the discipline of the monastery, with its various restrictions on sleeping conditions, food intake, permitted activities, and so on. It is a further intensification of the "domestication" process all children are socialized into, in which one's emotions and bodily needs are supposed to be brought under conscious control. Likewise, the sponsors prepare themselves to be subjected to more than the usual number of requests, and they aim to control their emotions so as to feel no regret over any costs that may arise in the course of sponsoring the ceremony. This goal of detachment toward material loss is extended even to losses unrelated to the ordination itself. One sponsor, for example, during the preparations leading up to an expensive ordination festival, lost an entire field of sesame (a major cash crop) because of a neighbor's negligence regarding a fence. Others in the village were horrified and said they felt sorry for her, but she denied being upset. Although she had no doubt intended to use the sale of this field's crop to help defray the spiraling costs of the ordination, she laughed it off whenever the subject was brought up, insisting, "I'm not even thinking about it," and went ahead with her plans.

Hence, being a sponsor entails some risk. People want to do it—for the merit and for the prestige—but they don't want it to bankrupt them. There are two basic ways to control the "asking" that accompanies this role. One is to decide to be a "minor" sponsor after someone else has already agreed to be a major one. The minor sponsors pay a fixed amount of money to the major sponsor, who then agrees to take on whatever additional expenses occur as the event unfolds. The other method is a bit trickier. It is to have a *lak* (stolen) *sang long* in which the boys are "kidnapped" (by sympathetic co-conspirators) early on in the preparation period, before too much money has been spent, and the event is allowed to take place ahead of schedule, with a reduced audience and on a much smaller scale.

This second method draws attention to the important role of reputation, or "face," in these proceedings. It is essential that the sponsors at least appear to be generous and ready to spend whatever money they have. If they appear to balk, they lose both merit and face. People assume that the more money that is spent, the more merit the sponsors make and, of course, the more status/prestige they get. The three concepts—merit, prestige, and money—are inextricably linked.

In some ways, it might appear that this system simply validates a sponsor's preexisting status, since only people of means could attempt to be a major sponsor. But the ceremony does indeed add to their preexisting status because it shows that they are generous. A person may be rich and respected for that, to some extent, but if he or she rarely sponsors anything, that status is tenuous.

Traditionally, when the ordination festival proper was over, there was an additional and even more dramatic test of the sponsors' generosity of spirit, a kind of final reckoning between the sponsors and those who had performed most of the labor. This encounter was known in Shan as the *tok su* (literally, to collect the prize or reward). In 1991, I saw no hint of this, but in 1981, when there was a "stolen" version of the novice ordination, I witnessed an abbreviated *tok su* that brought forth memories from those assembled about the more elaborate versions they used to do in the past. A group of young men who had been among those in the *sang long*'s bodyguard made the rounds to the house of each sponsor, including our house, asking for "a little liquor." People said this can be done after any merit-making festival, but that it is especially appropriate at the end of a novice ordination festival. Ideally, the group should be accompanied by an elder who is there to give the owner of the house (the sponsor, or *tsao*) a blessing, thus underscoring the link between a person's generosity (providing liquor, in this case) and accumulation of merit. However, in the 1981 version, the group of young men did not have an elder with them the first night. They drank, sang, danced a while, then moved on to the next sponsor's house, collecting their "due." The next night, they made another round, this time with both an elder and a professional singer. After presenting the sponsor with an offering tray with popped rice and flowers, onto which the sponsor was supposed to place some envelopes with "pocket money" for the young men, the elder recited a blessing for him and the singer sang a song. The sponsor also served liquor and provided snacks and cigarettes for the guests.

Since this had been a *lak sang long*, the young men's requests might be interpreted as a kind of compensation for not having been properly "hired."[5] However, there was reason to believe that the *tok su* could appropriately have been done in any event. Later that year, after sponsoring a different merit-making ceremony, I was treated to a more elaborate *tok su*. Two young men came to the house dressed as water buffalo (the draft animals still used to plow the fields in 1981)—wearing only *phakama* (men's traditional short saronglike cloth wrapped around the lower half of the body) and completely covered with mud (and, they claimed, manure). A rope around each of them was held by two other young men who were dressed as "farmers"—wearing traditional Shan pants, a conical-shaped woven hat *(kup)*, and a basket tied on their backs. The two "buffalo" (who were quite drunk) pretended to fight in our house compound, surrounded by a crowd of cheering men. Women came up into the house to watch and told me that this was the "really traditional *tok su*, the kind you're supposed to do after a novice ordination festival, but it's not done very often anymore." Traditionally, they explained, the "buffalo" demand one new set of clothes apiece from the festival sponsor, threatening to roll around in the sponsor's house and get everything dirty if the sponsor doesn't meet their demands. According to the women, a similar version of this custom was enacted for very large festivals by all those who helped with the food preparation (presumably mostly women). They would take all the dishes and pots and pans from the sponsor's house, cover them with mud and filth, and then threaten to strew them around the house unless they, too, each received a new set of clothes.

These traditional customs, though no longer always performed in their fullest versions, point to an ongoing tension in the symbolic structure of merit-making rituals, namely, the hierarchical relationship between the sponsor, who funds the ceremony, and the rest of the people, who provide the necessary labor. The sponsor gets the prestige, but the ceremony could not happen without the labor of the villagers. Whether the latter view their participation as a matter of "taking their turn" (with the hope that they, too, will someday be doing this in the role of sponsor) or regard their helping role as something more akin to a permanent subordinate status, there is an undeniable element of inequality and a recognition of the differential resources of the two parties that is dramatized and, to a certain extent, challenged by the custom of the *tok su*.

Mothers and Sons: Novice Ordinations as a Ritual of Maternity

It is not only inequalities of wealth and resources that are dramatized by these rituals. Gender inequalities are a further puzzle.[6] Although only boys and men can be ordained, countless observers of Thai, Northern Thai, and Shan ordination rituals have pointed out that women are highly involved in all aspects of the ceremony and seem to be deeply attached to it—as much as, if not more than, the men. Why should this be?

I was prompted to ponder such things one day in 1991 as I sat listening to my twenty-year-old field assistant recount her day of exchange labor during the rice-transplanting season. She had spent the day with a crew of other young women, working on one of their fields. Despite the backbreaking labor involved, she had returned in good spirits. "We were pretending we were doing a novice ordination," she announced with a grin. "We said, 'Today is the day to display the offerings *[wan kho lu]*,' and 'Tomorrow will be the day to wash dishes!'" She was clearly entertained by this little role-playing game they had concocted, and I found it equally arresting. Although I knew that ordinations were important to older women, I had not guessed that the ceremonies were also a source of fantasy material for younger women and girls. What was it about this seasonal exchange of rice-transplanting labor—a decidedly secular, economically oriented, and predominantly female genre of group activity—that made it reminiscent of a novice ordination?

In the remaining sections of this chapter, I describe how novice ordinations look from the perspective of the female participants and suggest that
this perspective provides something of a challenge both to the usual interpretation of what novice ordinations are "about" and to our understanding of
how gender differences are usually constructed in Theravāda Buddhist societies. In the process, this discussion will provide a further illustration of how
people's efforts are shaped by the context of hierarchical social relationships
and gender asymmetries within which they work, as well as an example of
how they use these structures to achieve their own ends of gaining status and
demonstrating maturity.

Women's Involvement in Novice Ordinations

Traditionally, before the advent of state-sponsored education, the monastery provided instruction in basic reading, writing, and calculating skills, so
that the time young boys spent in the *sangha*–often several years–constituted
their formal education. After the introduction of public coeducational
schools into this part of Thailand, these tasks were taken over by the new village elementary school. Nevertheless, Shan boys continued to be ordained, albeit for briefer periods of time. Today the vast majority of adult men in Baan
Kaung Mu have spent at least a short time in the *sangha,* and the effort to ordain a new generation of boys shows no sign of stopping.

Given the high degree of participation from the male population of the
community, it is reasonable to talk about ordination into the *sangha* as a rite
of passage of some sort, and native exegesis provides support for this interpretation. The ceremony was traditionally said to transform an "unripe" boy
into a "ripe" young man, ready for marriage and other adult responsibilities
(Tannenbaum 1995, 130). From young boys themselves, however, the most
frequently heard motive is the desire to "pay back their mother's milk," that
is, to repay their mothers for the gift of nurturance. Since the merit that is
generated by this ceremony accrues primarily to the sponsor, which is archetypically the boy's mother,[7] agreeing to undergo ordination is indeed a way
for a son to "pay his mother back."

The ordination festival is obviously an event rich with interpretive possibilities on many levels. Scholars interested in issues of gender, however, have
focused on the fact that only boys (and men) are eligible to be ordained.[8] There
is no comparable ceremony for girls, and Shan have made no effort to devise a
complementary role for girls in the current male ordination ceremony.[9] Indeed, several authors have pointed to the nonordination of women as a key
element in their subordination to men (e.g., Kirsch 1982; Van Esterik 1982).

Hence, one might well ask: How have women dealt with this exclusion
from the *sangha*? To what extent has it functioned as an effective "gate-

keeper," keeping women from positions of influence and power? On the one hand, it is fair to assume that no single ritual or religious tradition can dictate what the lived experience of its female followers will be like. The material is too complicated, contradictory, and open to multiple interpretations for that ever to happen. Nevertheless, to the extent that people want to be identified as followers of a given religion—and the Shan women I lived among certainly wanted to be seen as Buddhist—they must at least confront and deal with those aspects of the religious and ritual tradition that have been highlighted by their own community. And it is here, in the confrontation with a particular lived tradition, that new interpretations, creative forms of resistance, and sometimes enduring innovations can occur.

In the Shan case, there are certain primary Buddhist concepts that the women cannot afford to ignore; these are the concepts of karma, merit, and differential rebirth, which together form the basis for a larger universe of social inequalities within which the specific inequality of male and female is subsumed. As we have seen, those with access to greater resources and greater productive capacities are assumed to be cosmically justified in this, having earned these advantages in a previous life. Hence, there is felt to be some cosmic justification for a "natural" social hierarchy of men over women, rich over poor, fertile over infertile, productive over unproductive. Although one can never be certain of another's karmic status, the inherent demerit implied by the female condition distinguishes adult women from adult men.

Women and men both explain the impossibility of ordaining women in terms of this presumed karmic deficiency. Interestingly, they do not link it with other things like intelligence or physical prowess. That is, they do not say that girls are not smart enough or strong enough to be novices. Instead, they say things like "Girls can't be ordained because they can't ride on people's shoulders," an indirect reference to the cosmic impropriety of having "lower-level" beings riding on top of "higher-level" ones. Similarly, women sometimes say that they hope to be reborn as a male in their next life so that they can be ordained and "pay their mother back"—as clear an indication as one could hope for of the perceived connection between karmic status, gender, and eligibility for ordination.

In spite of all this, women have been deeply involved in these ceremonies, both as sponsors—usually, but not exclusively, of their own sons—and as an enthusiastic audience for others. Why should this be? Why should women be so eager to participate in a ceremony that is a rite of passage for men and that specifically excludes them? In particular, why should they be anxious to ordain their own sons if, in doing so, they are enabling their sons to become independent of them, to "cancel the debt" they owe?

One answer has been that women have a greater "need" for the merit (Kirsch 1985) and so are always looking for ways to increase it, including sponsoring males who are willing to be ordained. Although women can (and do) gain merit from sponsoring any male, their own sons are the most likely target, especially given their sons' sense of felt obligation. By "giving" a son to the *sangha*, women are (according to this logic) simply extending their culturally assigned nurturing role to the *sangha* itself, while simultaneously obtaining the merit they so desperately need (Keyes 1984). Thus, according to this explanation, women's participation in ordination rituals does not really pose a challenge to traditional gender hierarchies in any significant way. On the contrary, it underscores women's karmic inferiority and portrays them as social actors whose social identity is bound up with being "mothers." Further, it portrays the aim and scope of their actions as largely personal (a better rebirth) and familial (a new status for their son).

While I think this interpretation captures some important aspects of the ritual, I would also like to consider an alternative possibility, namely, that novice ordinations are only nominally a rite of passage for boys, and that—even though everyone's participation in these events must be couched within the rhetorical framework of merit making—women's motivation to participate sometimes goes beyond the desire for merit and into the realm of the pursuit of a more secular kind of status and recognition.

I was led to consider this view by my participation in a fairly large ordination ceremony in 1991. I had observed many ordinations before and had helped sponsor the ordinations of several novices and even a few monks. But this time, I happened to be in the company of whom would turn out to be the two major female sponsors when the idea of performing the ritual was first discussed, and the level of my involvement both with these women and with the event was more complete and more intense than it had been in the past. Inevitably, I came to look at the event through their eyes, which, though offering only a partial truth about the meaning and significance of the ritual, was nevertheless a truth I had overlooked in my previous efforts to document the ceremony and tell the "official" version. From this particular vantage point, I was struck by a couple of things that had previously escaped my notice and that I have not seen adequately discussed in the literature on ordination ceremonies.

First, the nature of women's engagement with the planning process for novice ordinations was noticeably more intense than men's. In the case of couples who acted as sponsors, the men helped, but it was without a doubt the women who planned, organized, and, in general, took responsibility for the event. Even the local women who were not involved as sponsors were visibly animated by the task and, as a topic of conversation, found the subject compelling in a way I did not observe to be true of the men. In the early days of the planning, for example, when I sat at the corner shop with the major female sponsors (whose husbands were also, theoretically, cosponsors), women passing by on their way to the fields would stop when they heard what we were talking about and join the conversation for a while, discussing thoughtfully and judiciously all the various details that had yet to be decided, including which temples from the surrounding villages should be invited, what sorts of food and offerings should be prepared, whether there were any additional local boys or young men who might be recruited for ordination, and so on. It was hard to avoid the sense that virtually all of the women, young and old, took an intense interest in the logistics of the ritual and that they all identified strongly with the role of sponsor, either because they had been one before or because they anticipated doing so some day. That is, the women clearly regarded it as an anticipated rite of passage for themselves, a "ritual of maternity" or, even more broadly, a ritual of middle age to which any woman (whether she was literally a mother or not) could aspire.

Men's interest in the ceremony was noticeably different—the interest of those who had been through it already as boys or young men, when they themselves were ordained. The husbands of the main female sponsors and the male ritual specialists whose services were needed in the planning stage (or after) were the men who were most involved, but even then, it was at the level of a "support staff" for the women who were the primary initiators and decision makers.

Second, the female sponsors ended up directing the labor of others—lots of others—for weeks, even months prior to the actual three-day festival, first in nightly gatherings at the sponsor's home to assemble the nonperishable offerings and decorations that could be made well in advance and, later, as the date approached, in all-day work sessions to complete the final preparations. As is true for all large-scale village-wide ceremonies, but especially for ordinations, many ritual and decorative items are needed, along with lots of cooked foods, and most are still hand-made or prepared from scratch in a labor-intensive way. Everyone in the village feels obligated to help with these preparations to some extent, but the level and intensity of participation reflect directly on the sponsor. It is an indication of her leadership ability and, more generally, her charisma to be able to attract large groups of people to the task.[10]

As the local economy continues to change and people's labor time becomes more valuable, I expect this pattern of labor organization to change, and to some extent it already has for other rituals (e.g., funerals), with an increasing number of ritual items being purchased, instead of made by hand. When the commoditized versions of these foods and other items come to dominate the proceedings, as they inevitably will at some point, the social organization underlying the ritual as well as its meaning will change considerably, if imperceptibly. However, in the labor-intensive version that was still being practiced in 1991, the successful sponsor-organizer was someone with sufficient respect, status, charisma, friends, and relatives to be able to assemble a large workforce of volunteers. Each staging of the ritual displayed and reinforced the relationships among these people.

Finally, while I do not want to trivialize the religious significance of novice ordinations (which is obviously enormous, especially for the participants and major sponsors), the women who were in charge of the event clearly approached it as a cultural production as much as an act of piety. Although this is no doubt the case, to some extent, for other Theravāda Buddhist communities as well, I suspect it is especially important for the Shan of this region, both because of their own long-standing inclination to regard novice ordinations as somehow emblematic of Shan culture and because of the increasing tourist traffic in Mae Hong Son Province, which has reinforced this link and made the ritual into an icon for "Shan-ness." Hence, women regard the task of putting on an ordination festival as one that is fraught with significance for the entire group, not just for them personally (as sponsors) or for the boys who are being ordained.[11]

A fair amount is at stake here, especially for the sponsors. The sheer enormity of the task of planning, organizing, and presiding over a large novice ordination provides women with a very public arena in which to display their skills and demonstrate their knowledge of cultural appropriateness and correctness, as well as the more general industriousness, graciousness, and almost studied generosity that are expected of a Shan host. In a very real sense, from the moment they publicly declare their intention of putting one on, the women who sponsor a novice ordination are on display as much as their sons. There are correct ways for doing everything, and women are eager to show that they know how to do it "right" and to have their efforts validated by an appreciative audience of festivalgoers. The women in charge talk a lot about "making it fun" for the people who come. They worry about their guests' comfort and want to impress guests with their ability to pull it off well. They worry equally about the possibility of hearing criticisms or complaints from those who attend, and they do everything they can to anticipate problems and avoid them.

There is a competitive element to their preparations as well, with female sponsors often traveling to attend ordinations in other villages during the ordination season, where, among other things, they take note of how the sponsors there are doing things; they talk quite explicitly among themselves about what they want to copy and what they want to do differently. In other words, throughout the preparations and the actual event, the female sponsors act as if their own reputations were on the line and appear to be acutely aware of being under the gaze of their invited guests. In short, they act as if the ritual were somehow about *them*.[12]

As mentioned earlier, Shan couples who sponsor a novice ordination are thereafter entitled to be addressed by the honorifics *mae kham* and *pau kham* (Mother-Sponsor and Father-Sponsor). During the novice ordination itself, all sponsors—male and female—are continuously addressed by these terms. After it is over, the boy who was ordained usually continues to use these honorifics to address his nonparental sponsors and invariably uses these titles when he is making a request of them. In addition, the honorifics retain some use on ceremonial occasions (such as lay scripture readings and other merit-making rituals), where, for example, a server may use them to address a guest. It is these latter cases, where the use of the title "sponsor" is divorced from the actual event, that most closely approximate the acknowledgment of a separate and enduring status for people who have, in the past, been sponsors. In my experience, achieving this status and being addressed by this title were far more important to the women of the community than to the men. On many such occasions, for example, I have heard a woman seated alone be addressed as *mae kham*, but the only time I have heard men being addressed as *pau kham* was when they were seated next to their wives. Perhaps this is because men have access to other titles—including *sang* (former novice) and *nan* (former monk)—that are unavailable to women. For Shan women, however, achieving the title of *mae kham* is about as good as it gets.[13]

What Are Novice Ordinations "About"?

On the one hand, then, the ordination ritual appears to be used by Shan women as a vehicle for the pursuit of status and prestige. It does so by taking on some of the characteristics of a rite of passage for women who—at midlife—are ready and eager to demonstrate their productive capacities and leadership abilities. At the same time, there is some reason to question the wisdom of labeling what happens to the boys in these ceremonies as a "rite of passage." As the average age at which boys ordain has become younger (it is now typically about age ten, or just after the completion of fourth or fifth grade[14]), and as the amount of time they usually remain in the *sangha* has shifted from a matter of years to a matter of weeks or even days, most Shan boys are too young to emerge from the experience as the "mature sexual beings" hypothesized in the literature of other Theravāda Buddhist communities (e.g., Tambiah 1970) and, in some cases, in native rhetoric itself.

Furthermore, while in the *sangha*, the boys do not make much of a break or separation from the world of their families. Their mothers, in particular, visit at least once a day, bringing food and elaborately serving it to them—acts that, once again, deflect attention from the boys and focus it instead upon the sponsor-mother's role in making all of this happen. In doing so, it is a further illustration of Penny Van Esterik's (1996) point that the core meaning of the word *liang* (which has usually been translated as "to nurture" or "to bring up") should also be understood to entail a bid for power and control. If, in theory, the boys have now "repaid the milk debt" they owed their mothers, the mothers, for their part, do not seem inclined to "wipe the slate clean" but, on the contrary, seem intent on renewing and deepening the bonds of reciprocity.

Finally, those boys who (for whatever reason) never go through the ordination ceremony are still considered, upon reaching adulthood, to be fully "men," with no apparent diminution in their status as men. This suggests that, at least at this historical juncture, the importance of the ceremony for Shan men is less as a rite of passage per se and more as a celebration of certain key notions about masculinity—for example, the notion that males, by virtue of simply being male, are capable of taking on difficult restraints and disciplines, that doing so gives them strength and power that is evident beyond the strict confines of the monastery, and so on.

If it is the case that ordinations are now more a symbolic than an effective rite of passage for boys, it is possible that this is a relatively recent state of affairs and that, in the past, ordination ceremonies functioned as a more genuine rite of passage for them. Now, however, as ordinations are performed on relatively younger boys who stay in the *sangha* for considerably less time, its meaning may be changing. Two things in particular might have contributed to this situation. One is the advent of public schools and the consequent end of using the time in the monastery for one's education (so that now boys have to be ordained during school vacations and stay in for shorter periods). A second is the changing economic base in rural areas. In 1980, boys would be ordained after grade school—at about thirteen to fourteen years old—and then begin doing agricultural work full-time when they got out. Now boys who have just completed a stint as novices are no longer ready to commence their working careers.

One might speculate that although the original meaning of the ordinations has been retained symbolically, the real transforming power of the ritual has shifted away from the boys and toward the sponsors as the main protagonists in this drama. Alternatively, one might conceivably argue that the current significance of the ceremony for sponsors, especially female sponsors, was indeed always there and that it has simply been overlooked or downplayed by our attention to other aspects of the ritual.

In either case, once we acknowledge the significance of these rituals for women's expectations about their own social and political "careers"—a significance that goes beyond the quest for merit and beyond their traditional role as nurturers—we have added another layer of complexity that must be factored into our formulations of the role of Buddhist religion and ritual on Shan constructions of gender and the life course. Unlike most other public occasions—especially those associated with Buddhism—in which women typically work behind the scenes or on the sidelines (Eberhardt 1988), ordination rituals are ones in which women are allowed to be seen on center stage where they have a prominent, even commanding public presence. Women's avid participation in these events has a strategic and ambitious quality to it that, far from being simply a remedial effort to redress a cosmic imbalance, includes a bid for this-worldly power and influence. Further, it is often the women—rather than the boys or the adult men—who take the initiative in deciding to hold an ordination ceremony and in recruiting potential candidates for ordination.

Indeed, Shan women clearly behave as if they have rights in the ordinations of their sons and grandsons, sometimes even in those of other junior male relatives. These boys owe it to them to undergo ordination, in part because of their "milk debt" but, even more generally, because as junior kin they are indebted to all senior relatives who have nurtured them in some way. Hence, one of the sources of prestige for the women involved is that sponsoring an ordination constitutes an effective display of all their hard work, productivity, and prior investments—of the social debts that they are now "calling in." The more debts they can call in, the more powerful and productive they appear, and the more they can approximate the "royal" style that is fundamental to all merit-making rituals, but especially ordination ceremonies.

As a "ritual of maternity," then, ordination ceremonies reflect a very unsentimental view of motherhood. For Shan, motherhood begins, but does not end, with self-sacrifice; it is also about making an investment in children that can be cashed in at a later time. While this rhetoric is also used to describe father-child relations, I have heard it much more frequently with respect to mothers.[15] Reciprocity, then, is an important theme of novice ordinations—and one that is central to Shan constructions of motherhood. A mother is someone who gives a lot but who also is eventually entitled to some return. And it is precisely this that comes with the title *mae kham* (Mother-Sponsor)—an opportunity, one might say, for women to transform their status as mother (with a small *m*) to Mother (with a capital *M*).

Ordination and Subordination

As it stands, Shan women have the possibility of real material independence from men. They can (and do) own their own land, run their own shops, keep their own bank accounts, and accumulate wealth on their own. In spite of this, however, their ineligibility for ordination and, hence, inability ever fully to repay their obligations to their parents mean that they are, as Tannenbaum (1995) has pointed out, socially constructed as dependents. Thus, it is primarily in the arena of ideology that Shan women must battle for prestige and for some social recognition of their autonomy.

Women's participation in the ordination ceremony can be read as one attempt to do just that, even though the results are decidedly mixed. On the one hand, the ceremony successfully pushes the limits of traditional stereotypes by highlighting the leadership, ambition, and community-organizing skills of women and by portraying them as social actors on a village-wide or even regional scale (as opposed to more parochial "mothers" with an exclusive concern for the family). Even when women do not have the role of sponsor, the ceremony provides them with an activity that they find rewarding and engaging to work on and, as such, is a genuine source of pleasure and empowerment.

On the other hand, because the very nature of the ritual calls attention to and celebrates men's unique capacity to be ordained, it ultimately reaffirms women's second-class position. In this sense, it is a hegemonic institution of the classic sort wherein women themselves, by their devotion to the ceremony, help reproduce a gender ideology that gives them a long "leash" but insists that they can only go "so far."[16] From the time they are young girls, Shan women look forward to the day when they will have the opportunity to be in the role of sponsor. They play "novice ordination" with their baby brothers, carrying them on their shoulders and teaching them how to move to the distinctive rhythms of the music that is played when real novices are carried from house to house on the shoulders of young men, even as their baby sisters are left watching and wondering on the sidelines. Adult women will continue to try to use the ceremony for their own ends, in ways that are meaningful to them, but in so doing they risk reinscribing the very categories of gender difference they seek to transcend.

Further, as we have seen, gender differences are not the only inequalities that are highlighted by ordination festivals. A similar dynamic occurs for wealth differences among the households in Baan Kaung Mu, differences that are at once celebrated by the role of the generous and "royal" sponsor and challenged by the demands (both ritual and more prosaic) of those upon whose labor the ceremony depends. Although the challenges are significant and provide a potential avenue for resisting the ideological underpinnings of income inequalities in the community, I believe the ceremony is ultimately more supportive than threatening to this ideology, providing people with an appealing narrative that offers both cosmic justification for the status quo and the promise of personal transcendence.

Nevertheless, despite these complications, ordination festivals are useful to the men and women of Baan Kaung Mu primarily because they provide an arena in which to demonstrate their competence and social maturity. By sponsoring an ordination, even in a modest fashion as helpers, individuals are able to signal to the rest of the community that they are willing and able to shoulder the responsibilities that come with local definitions of mature adulthood. This much is within reach of virtually every adult in Baan Kaung Mu who wishes to attain it. And for those with the resources to serve as a major sponsor for a large-scale ordination festival, the opportunity is available to go beyond this and substantially increase their status and prestige.

Ordination in the Context of the Shan Life Course

Anthropologists interested in understanding adult aspects of human development (e.g., Plath 1980; Kerns and Brown 1992; Shweder 1998; Lamb 2000) have been quick to point out that the Euro-American model of "middle age" does not apply everywhere; midlife is a cultural construction. In many societies, midlife is not associated with a loss of vitality, nor is it defined primarily in biological or medical terms. Instead, it is often associated with increased responsibility and social seniority manifest in such spheres as family management, political power, civic duty, and moral leadership. The Shan case clearly lends support to this view, with sponsorship of ordinations providing one salient example of how mature adulthood can be demonstrated.

Weisner and Bernheimer (1998) have also suggested that, rather than being a function of one's chronological age, midlife is yoked to significant changes in the lives of one's children, usually during their adolescence. This view also finds support from the Shan material in the sense that sponsorship is often linked to the ordination of one's son, though the person being ordained may be considerably younger than adolescent and is not necessarily one's own child. Still, the general point holds and has been stated succinctly by Shweder:

> Within such cultural worlds one reckons and manages one's life not by reference to age per se (e.g., there may be no annual public recognition of the day of birth of mature adults) and not by reference to biological aging (back pains, menopause) per se, but rather by reference to family position and associated social responsibilities. Within such cultural worlds, changes in behavior are marked and regulated by transitions in family status, including transitions in the status of one's children. (1998, xi)

For Shan, then, as for many other societies, the course of human development entails a sequence of anticipated phases or stages, but these are not linked to specific ages or biological cues. What is important is the order of the sequence, not when the phases occur, and people may move through them at considerably different rates, determined in part by what is happening to other family members (especially their parents and their children) and in part by their own ambition. As we shall see in the following chapter, this is also true of the final phase of development, old age, where people may decide to "become old" at quite variable ages.

Coupled to each phase of life and its associated activities is a set of assumptions about the sort of person who is going through it, and these assumptions provide clues about local conceptions of the self. At midlife, Shan expect people to be capable and productive, ambitious and energetic. They should be willing and able to take care of others and to direct the labor of these dependents toward household goals. It also falls to adults at midlife to make sound decisions (along with their spouse, if they have one) concerning how best to use the family's limited resources. Becoming a sponsor showcases all these traits and announces one's social maturity in a dramatic way that lends public recognition to one's accomplishments. It also signals one's commitment to making internal, personal changes that will be crucial during the next important phase of life—increased generosity, a tempered heart, self-discipline, and spiritual growth.

Thus, according to Shan views of the ideal course of human development, the cultivation of self-control and "domestication of the self" that began in childhood continues through midlife and on into old age. Just as sponsorship entailed a disciplining of the emotions and the courage to be selfless, so old age will require its own ethnopsychological project. And it is to that indigenous theory of mental health and well-being, a theory that underlies ideas about old age, that we now turn our attention.

Chapter 7

The Ethnopsychology of Aging and Overall Development

Fortunately [psycho]analysis is not the only way to resolve inner conflicts. Life itself still remains a very effective therapist.
KAREN HORNEY, *Our Inner Conflicts*

Although the literature about recovery from addiction and codependency borrows heavily from family systems theory and seems, at first, an offshoot of pop psychology, it's rooted most deeply in religion. . . . The ideology of recovery is the ideology of salvation by grace. More than they resemble group therapy, twelve-step groups are like revival meetings, carrying on the pietistic tradition.
WENDY KAMINER, *I'm Dysfunctional, You're Dysfunctional*

WE ARE SURROUNDED by free advice—people telling us how to live, what to eat, what to feel, how to behave, how to solve our problems, how to avoid having problems in the first place. And we are presented with a cornucopia of solutions—everything from psychoanalysis to self-help, pastoral care to yoga, medication to meditation. In many cultural traditions, including our own, we can find enduring affinities between prevailing religious teachings and the tacit assumptions that inform our everyday coping strategies. How are we to distinguish religion from psychology, therapy from spiritual growth, healing from salvation?

In Shan communities, too, I found an interweaving between the teachings of organized religion and indigenous psychology. There was, in particular, a strong connection between local ideas of mental health and the taking on of Buddhist ascetic practices. People who had suffered a major loss, for example, or a series of traumatic incidents, and who were finding it difficult to cope with the stress of everyday life (such as the young widower described in chapter 3), were often encouraged to become a Buddhist monk or nun, or in some cases simply a temple sleeper, to alleviate the symptoms. This solution was also recommended for people who were plagued by repeated spirit possession or who were trying to overcome an addiction to alcohol or opium (as we saw in the case of the healer, Uncle Pon, discussed in chapter 2).

Although these are extreme cases, they point to a method for safeguarding one's mental stability that applies equally to those whose behavior falls closer to the norm. This is evident in the general advice and psychological counseling people give each other and, most significantly, in the widespread efforts of older members of the community to learn new techniques of self-mastery based explicitly on Buddhist practice. As we will see, these techniques build upon conceptions of mental health that are more broadly available in the community but are practiced much more intensively and consistently by the old. The overall aim of this chapter, then, is to suggest that the goals and structure of "old age" in Baan Kaung Mu are best understood in the context of a larger set of values and practices concerning mental health—values and practices that are embedded in a discourse of self-control and spiritual growth.

The chapter is divided into three parts. In the first part, I offer a description of what might be called Shan popular psychology, that is, the folk theories and conventional wisdom commonly invoked in this community for how best to cope with everything from trivial, everyday stresses to life-shattering crises. Then, following this discussion of the general strategies that are urged upon all adults, the second part of the chapter describes the more specialized efforts that are enjoined for older people, along with a consideration of how this recognized life stage of "old person" affects the rest of Shan social organization. In the final section, I provide a summary analysis of some key points in Shan ethnopsychology, giving special attention to its theory of personhood and developmental processes.

A Shan Self-Help Primer

Shan frequently offer advice to each other, especially advice about how and when to control or modify one's behavior, thoughts, and feelings. Looking at advice is a good way to uncover clues about local ideas about the self, since (unlike some of the other aspects of people's folk theories about psychology) it is public—a kind of speech event, really—and, hence, available for scrutiny by anyone who happens to overhear it.

As speech events go, advice turns out to be a culturally loaded item of discourse, and there are many ways that one could unpack it. What I am most interested in unraveling are the sorts of assumptions and ideal images of persons that underlie the specific bits of advice people give each other. What are the advice givers assuming about the nature of the self? How do they imagine the mind works? What sorts of things can affect the mind? When should one attempt to exert control over these, and when is it pointless to try? By giving and receiving advice, Shan learn to comprehend themselves as particular sorts of persons, an effort that is revealed not only by the kinds of situations that seem to elicit advice but also, significantly, by those they choose to ignore.

Unlike much of the American self-help literature, for example, Shan popular psychology is not concerned with raising one's self-esteem, controlling one's intake of food, or helping one learn how to manage one's time. Nor does it have much to say about how to conduct romantic relationships or achieve financial independence. It does not assume that personal happiness or "self-fulfillment" are laudable or even attainable goals. This does not mean, of course, that Shan never worry about such things (many probably do), but it does mean that these are not the sort of concerns that are culturally recognized—much less given cultural elaboration or prominence—as important or common "problems." Instead, the psychological work that Shan advocate and find compelling seems to be directed primarily at achieving a certain peace of mind and, beyond that, a "quiet" mind. In fact, one of the most frequent problems I heard people complain about was that which they labeled "thinking continuously," or "thinking a lot."

In general, Shan say they try to avoid "thinking a lot," a state of mind that is associated with having a lot of problems to sort out. One "feels sorry" for someone like Nang Han, for example, a local woman whose son had recently been put in jail and who then confessed that she was "thinking all the time." In another incident, a young woman of dubious reputation was teased about "having to think a lot" because of her assignations with various men. I was also a target for their advice. If, for example, I happened to mention that I had not been able to fall asleep right away the night before because I was "thinking," I was always immediately told that this isn't good, that Shan people don't let themselves do it, and that I should try hard to stop the thinking.

In another example, a friend from a nearby village, Nang Laeng, complained about her scheming brother-in-law, who repeatedly contrived ways to avoid pooling his income with the rest of the family. She described him as one of those people who "think all the time." She added that this wasn't good and that she certainly didn't want to be like that. Sarcastically calling him "smart," she reported that he had forbidden his younger brother from marrying anyone who did not own some rice land. She went on to comment, in a tone that indicated utter disdain, that she did not believe he should be "thinking" like this all the time. Nang Laeng's sister (the brother-in-law's wife) usually sided with her husband in these quarrels, but Laeng did not hold her responsible for any of this "plotting" and, indeed, described her sister somewhat deprecatingly as someone who "doesn't think at all."

In this example, "thinking a lot" is clearly associated with being calculating or strategic, and one can detect a note of ambivalence in the accusation—rather like describing someone in American society as a perfectionist or a workaholic—where the accuser may be simultaneously impressed with and alarmed by the other's behavior. This ambivalence was amplified in other conversations about her family's finances, where Nang Laeng complained about other members of the household who "didn't think" *enough* and were sometimes oblivious to the needs of others and to the long-range financial goals of the household. As a result, she explained, she had been forced to become the household's reluctant strategist who had to "think all the time."

In spite of this ambivalence, there is a real and abiding fear that "thinking too much" will make a person *yaung,* "crazy." When I visited Nang Nu shortly after her father died, for example, she commented that she was spending a lot of time alone in the house each day, that she "thought all the time," and that it wasn't good. Later, while talking about how many of her own siblings had died as children, she observed, "After a couple of my siblings had died, my mother became sort of crazy. Sometimes that happens to people when someone dies." Recalling others from the village who had died since my previous visit, she commented, "With each one, I was sad. I'm the type of person who thinks a lot. When someone dies, I often become a bit crazy." Then, speaking of her own father's death again, she added, "Some people are already talking about where Grandfather is reborn, but I don't think he could be reborn as quickly as that. People say all sorts of things about where Grandfather is, but I don't believe any of it." Here, "thinking a lot" refers to a mental state that might be glossed as "obsessed" or "preoccupied." In these cases, one should try to avoid it, not because it is immoral or unethical, but because it may lead to some degree of mental instability and, ultimately, to one's own demise. Stories abound about people who were obsessed with one thing or another and who, when they died, were then forced to live out their obsession while in the form of a spirit—a Shan version, perhaps, of Sartre's *No Exit.*

Unlike the American folk theories with which I am familiar, in which thinking about and talking about a traumatic experience are considered therapeutic and even necessary for one to "heal" (and where failure to do so is given negative labels, such as "repression" and "denial"), villagers here advocate almost the opposite approach. In fact, the paradigmatic case for Shan where "thinking too much" about something is truly dangerous is the case of thinking about someone who has recently died. To help make sense of the underlying logic in their approach to dealing with grief, I will consider one particularly tragic case in some detail.

The case involves a young woman named Nang Laui, who committed suicide several months before I arrived in 1990. I had spent a lot of time with

Laui during an earlier field trip when she was just a girl, so the news came as a shock to me. In my absence, Laui had started working as a domestic helper in a house that was right across the street from the one where I lived in 1990. She eventually married one of the sons of that household—a boy she had known all her life—and had a baby with him. When her husband was killed in a freak accident, she reportedly could not stop thinking about him. And this obsession with her deceased husband, I was told repeatedly, was what eventually led to her own suicide some seven months later.

When I arrived about half a year after her death, the house she had lived in, which was quite upscale by local standards, stood empty, and it remained so when I left twelve months later. People were certain that it was haunted by the ghost of Nang Laui, and they walked quickly past it after dark. Young women who had been close friends of Laui's were especially careful, and many simply avoided the house altogether or, when that was impossible, insisted upon an escort. The reasoning behind these behaviors was that anyone who had an emotional tie to the deceased would be more likely to think about her a lot, and this, I was told, would prompt the ghost to call them—to literally call their name out loud as they walked by—and beckon them to join her in death. Strangers, on the other hand (who, presumably, would have no reason to think about the deceased at all), were in much less danger, and the house was, in fact, occasionally rented out to migrants and traders from the Shan States of Burma who needed a place to stay for a few nights.

When I tried to press one young woman on this point, she would not budge. What if two people were very good friends who really cared about each other, I asked, and one of them died—wouldn't the one who was left behind think about her friend? "No, she *can't*—it's too dangerous" was the reply. But surely she will miss her friend? "No, she *mustn't*," I was told. "She should tell herself, 'This person left no *wot* [karmic residue]—she's gone on now and exists no longer.'" In other words, my hypothetical mourner is supposed to comfort herself with the thought that her friend is not suffering in one of the hells or wandering about as a hungry ghost—the fate of those who do have *wot*. But, I continued to press the young woman, in Laui's case there *is* karmic residue, because she committed suicide [a serious "sin"], right? "Then you must tell yourself that you didn't do it, that you are not responsible for this problem," she explained. In other words, the friend should remind herself that there is nothing she can do about this, it is the deceased's problem, so the friend should not endanger herself by thinking about the deceased a lot.

Here, the Buddhist notion of karmic retribution is invoked as an underlying force to be acknowledged and reckoned with. Although Shan ethnopsychology cannot be reduced to Buddhist psychology, it clearly draws upon key Buddhist concepts to help explain why people do what they do. In a conversation I had with Laui's sister-in-law, for example, a woman named Nang Yaut, she talked about the strangeness of Laui's suicide, commenting, "If one hadn't already accumulated some bad karma, one wouldn't dare do such a thing." She went on to describe how oddly Laui had behaved after the accident that had killed her husband (Nang Yaut's younger brother)—how she had placed his photograph on an altar in their home, lit candles in front of it, put offerings of cigarettes and the locally popular Lipovitan tonic in front of it, and so on. "She went crazy," Nang Yaut concluded. Then, on the day Laui had chosen to commit suicide, "she dressed up in nice clothes, put powder on her face and red on her lips, and did her hair especially nicely. One would never have the nerve to do all that," she observed, "unless one was being driven by karmic forces."

But karma was not the sole explanation of Laui's behavior either. Nang Yaut reminisced for a while about the early days of Laui's relationship with her younger brother, speaking with both affection and amusement about their playful, sometimes almost childish interactions around the house, and then she offered this summary explanation of the suicide:

> Laui didn't know anything. She hadn't really ever experienced hard work. She finished school, came to work at our house washing clothes, got married, and had a child right away. She hadn't done much transplanting in the rice paddies or work in the forest. She hadn't learned yet about hardship and suffering. She didn't know anything, and when her husband died, she couldn't bear it.

Here, what caused Laui to be overwhelmed by life and unable to cope, according to Nang Yaut, was her lack of experience and, in particular, her naïveté about the "hardship and suffering" that Nang Yaut saw as an inevitable part of life.

From this and countless other examples, it is clear that Shan are very wary of what they consider excessive grieving, and they constantly advise each other to avoid it. Prolonged grieving is dangerous, according to Shan, because it is invariably interpreted as a strong desire to be with the departed loved one—a desire that just might be fulfilled by the mourner's own death, as it was in the case of Laui's suicide. Furthermore, what happened to Laui could also happen to her friends if they allowed themselves to think about her too much, hence their efforts to avoid both thoughts of her and even the physical site of her demise. Emotional attachment is a powerful causal force, by this account—not so much in the orthodox Buddhist sense (that is, that desire is what keeps one attached to the world and therefore continually frustrated and condemned to rebirth) but, rather, in the sense that people do (eventually) get what they want, so they had better be careful about what it is they want. For this reason, the bereaved are always in a psychologically precarious place and are continually counseled to "stop thinking" about the deceased and to "put it out of their mind."

We have already encountered, in chapter 3, another case where a similar logic was at work, the case of the young woman and child who were struck and killed by lightning. There, when distraught villagers could talk and think of nothing else, one man warned, "You just can't allow your heart to feel sorry for them constantly. One can't bear it. You must instead say to yourself, 'I, too, will die.'" These and other remarks were aimed at getting people to stop "thinking continuously" about the incident and at redirecting the public conversations in a manner that would help people "quiet" their thoughts. People were upset, but, as in the case of Laui's suicide, they were also frightened. The man's comments here reflect two themes that were also prominent in people's remarks about Laui's case and that, taken together, help form the foundation for Shan ethnopsychology: one is the strong presumption that people are ruled by their mental and emotional activity; the other is that one of the best ways to control this thinking-and-feeling activity is through a kind of reality check—in this case, a reminder that we are all mortal and will one day die too.

Although they were exceptionally prominent when dealing with death, especially a sudden or violent death, these same themes surfaced in many other contexts as well. The vulnerability of children, for example, is understood to be at least partly the result of their inability to control their minds, and, indeed, the entire maturation process is often portrayed as a lifelong effort to achieve this control. Sponsors of large-scale Buddhist merit-making ceremonies, as we saw in chapter 6, say explicitly that they are anxious to control their thoughts and emotions, especially any feelings of regret they might experience, however fleetingly, over the amount of money they are spending on the ceremony. They talk about it as a kind of psychological test or trial, the passing of which is crucial if they are to obtain any merit for the act of giving.

Physical illnesses as well as mental ones are often traced to unfulfilled desires of one sort or another, and, in fact, the people of Baan Kaung Mu recognize no hard-and-fast line between physical and mental distress. Strong emotions are thought to have long-lasting, even permanent consequences for one's health. Two local women, for example, who suffer from the syndrome known in Shan as *khi kwaang*,[1] an affliction that causes them to startle easily and engage in brief outbursts of inappropriate behavior (outside conscious awareness), attribute this condition to a combination of genetics (that the two women are sisters is pointed to as a relevant fact) and to the intense experiences with grief that they have both had. Another way that strong emotions can put one's body in physical danger, people say, is by making one more susceptible to soul loss and spirit invasion (which, as we have seen, can result in all sorts of physical ailments). If, expanding on this, we take the notion of being invaded by a malevolent spirit-being as a kind of local metaphor for not being fully in control of one's subjective experience of reality, then the line between one's mental and physical health gets even fuzzier.

A related bit of advice that one frequently hears in Baan Kaung Mu is the admonition not to cry. Crying is not good for a person—and is even dangerous—because it makes the blood "rise up" and the heart "boil." Therefore, I was told, crying should be suppressed or, if already begun, stopped as soon as possible. People had advice on how to do this; again, the main method or strategy is to direct one's thoughts toward the reality of the situation. One man put it this way:

> If you're crying due to grief, remind yourself that everybody dies and is reborn. It's just a fact of life. Think about that, and realize that the person you're grieving for may have already been reborn somewhere. You can also comfort yourself with the knowledge that you've made a lot of offerings and stored up a lot of merit, so you needn't fear death.

In a similar fashion, another woman advised, one can reason with oneself by saying, "So-and-so is dead now. Someday I, too, will die."

One of the things I find striking about this kind of advice is the implicit presumption that strong emotions indicate an "unrealistic" attitude, a distorted perspective on the human condition in the world. Conversely, cultivating insight into "reality" (as Shan perceive it) is the antidote to being "overly emotional." This fits nicely with Nang Yaut's position, stated earlier in conjunction with the case of Laui's suicide, that it is general life experience, especially the experience of hardship and suffering, that steels people for emotionally traumatic events and gives them the strength to cope without going crazy. While it may at first seem contradictory to be told, on the one hand, "Don't think about it too much" and, on the other, "Think hard about the true nature of reality," the contradiction is more apparent than real. The "it" that one is not supposed to dwell on is always local and specific (some particular event or incident), whereas the "reality" that one *is* supposed to ponder is always cosmological and general (the larger context in which all specific events occur).

Interestingly, this theme received further elaboration when people talked about the trajectory of their own lives, either spontaneously or in response to my request for life histories. Instead of highlighting the unique or idiosyncratic aspects of their lives or portraying themselves as the protagonist in

An old person who is a temple sleeper makes an offering at the start of temple services.

some yet-to-be-completed story, people exhibited a marked tendency to fit the various pieces of their own life into a kind of "master narrative" that was the same for everyone. According to this master narrative, any human life (my life, your life, anyone's life) is full of hardship and suffering *(dukkha),* and part of what happens over the course of a lifetime is that one slowly comes to this realization (unless, of course, one dies young, like Laui, and thus never has the opportunity to learn this). It is the realization and acceptance of this fact of life, Shan say, that gives one the equanimity and perspective to deal with life's troubles. And, I would add, far from making people depressed or disengaged with life, it is the presence or availability of this master narrative that allows people to create meaning in the face of tragedy, to find comfort in the face of painful or frightening circumstances, and to see repeated evidence for the poignancy of the human condition in the details of their own lives.

To this end, Shan engage in what might be called a "second socialization" in their later years, during which they are exposed, in a much more intense way than they have been before, to Buddhist teachings and practices aimed at helping them become specialists in the kind of self-control that is idealized in the personal advice described above. This is a period of heightened religiosity for them and the start of a new life phase, the period of life in which people become temple sleepers.

The Second Socialization

It was October 27, 1981, the end of my first field trip to Baan Kaung Mu. Roland and I were scheduled to leave the village the following morning and had been visiting with people all day long. Uncle Toen, also known locally as the Great Hunter (and Roland's self-appointed instructor in this art), was the last to leave our house that evening. He had come with a bottle of whiskey and some pheasant *(kai toen)* traps for Roland to take home with him, to remind him of all their hunting and fishing trips over the past two years. The talk of hunting (and the whiskey, perhaps) seemed to put Uncle Toen in a philosophical mood. "If you haven't known sorrow and evil, you can't really know happiness and virtue," he opined. "I've spent my entire life hunting and have been fairly successful at it. Lately, though, I've been getting omens that make me think I should quit hunting and start sleeping at the temple. I *am* getting older, you know."

He recounted two examples of the sort of omens he had in mind. Once, while hunting in the forest, he missed an animal at very close range. Since he is generally an excellent shot, he found this odd. On another occasion, he went fishing. He started out using a fishing pole but got nothing. He switched to a net but still caught nothing. Finally, he tried using his bare hands. (In this technique, one feels underwater for holes in the bank that would be likely to house a fish, then sticks one's hand quickly into the hole to grab it.) He did manage to get hold of one this way but then, inexplicably, was unable to pull his hand back out of the hole without first letting go of the fish. These incidents had roused him, made him think. And, he added, this is as it should be: "If you have no experience with the world, you'll never seek nirvana *(nik-pan)* with fervor—just as the Buddha himself was not motivated to do so until he saw sickness, old age, and death. The most devout and strict of the temple sleepers," he went on, "are those who have committed the most wrongs earlier in life."

He had just about talked himself into giving up hunting to seek enlightenment when he glanced back down at the pheasant traps. "But, you know," he added, smiling, "there are still a lot of things I haven't had a chance to teach Roland about the forest. I want him to know everything! So I'll just have to put off sleeping at the temple until you two return and I get a chance to teach him the rest. You'll have to hurry back, though, because I'm getting old and I can't wait forever, you know."

By the time I would return to the village ten years later, Uncle Toen and his protégé would both be dead, but I would be reminded of his words countless times as I listened to various people talk about "getting old" and their plans to become a temple sleeper. In Baan Kaung Mu, old age is associated most prominently with two different phenomena: decreased physical activity and increased religiosity. When it "occurs" is a highly individual matter, with people making claims to the status anytime from their mid-forties on. It usually begins with a reduction in one's physical labor. A man who is beginning to refer to himself as "old" will, for example, hire someone else to plow his fields in the spring rather than do it himself; a woman will send a daughter out to supervise the transplanting while she stays home to prepare the noon meal and "watch the house." Many self-described old people still engage in plenty of productive activities, but they choose tasks that are less physically demanding and that can be done at their own pace (versus tasks traditionally done by exchange labor, where there is some pressure to keep up with co-workers). They weave baskets and traditional hats, look after grandchildren, help prepare shingles for traditional-style roofs made of teak leaves, and prepare the traditional holiday foods and temple offerings. Many are ardent mushroom hunters and passionate gardeners. Eventually, these people will also become increasingly involved in temple activities and Buddhist ritual, and it is in this capacity that the social status of "old person," or "elder," truly inheres.

Some people are eager to begin this new stage. Others, like Uncle Toen, are ambivalent and hold off as long as possible. Women generally take it on at an earlier age than men. But everyone plans to become a temple sleeper eventually. As a result, the terms "old people" *(khon thao)* and "people who sleep at the temple" *(khon naun tsaung)* are used almost interchangeably in everyday conversation. The latter term refers to the practice of assuming eight restrictions, or precepts (rather than the usual five),[2] on *wan sin* (literally, precept day). Although it is not necessary to physically sleep at the temple in order to follow these restrictions, most people choose to do so because, they say, it is easier and more convenient to keep the precepts there; hence the term "temple sleepers." Furthermore, although one could, theoretically, practice these eight precepts on an irregular basis, treating them as a kind of occasional spiritual retreat (as, for example, pilgrimages to various holy places are treated) or as spiritual medicine for various ills (as, for example, the recitation of verses of Buddhist scripture are often treated), it is significant that Shan choose not to do so. Instead, they regard the assumption of these restrictions as a developmental stage—that is, as part of a larger behavioral pattern practiced continuously by people in a specific phase of life.

Once people decide to begin sleeping at the temple, they are, in effect, making a commitment to alter their lifestyle permanently.[3] They will now keep the eight precepts on each *wan sin* during *wa,* the rainy season retreat, and sometimes throughout the entire year.[4] In addition, they will no longer go hunting or fishing nor raise animals to be sold for slaughter. They will begin to turn over more and more of the day-to-day running of their farm to their adult children, and they will start to distance themselves from the mundane concern with money and material gain.[5] They will begin to attend more merit-making ceremonies and will do so in the role of religious participant rather than behind-the-scenes helper. And, perhaps most important, they become an additional "field of merit" (and, as such, an additional source of power) for the rest of the community.

This transformation begins with the simple act of staying at the temple on a *wan sin.* At the end of the morning temple service, the monk recites the five precepts that all Buddhists are supposed to keep, pausing as the congregation repeats each one. Then, as the other people return home, the "old people"—dressed in the characteristic style of temple sleepers that includes a towel or other cloth worn over the shoulder—stay behind and repeat the three additional precepts. At this point, the monk may recite an additional sermon, offer some group instruction on meditation techniques, or simply leave the people to meditate on their own. At 11:00, they eat the lunch they have brought with them, their last meal of the day. Afterwards, they may take a nap, bathe, and then spend the rest of the afternoon and evening engaged in any combination of meditation, listening to recorded sermons or other religious texts, or talking with the monks about religious topics before retiring early. In the morning, they return home.

Learning to meditate and doing it regularly is one of the central features of the temple-sleeping experience. Most temple sleepers know a variety of meditation techniques, learned over the years from different monks and religious adepts with whom they have come in contact, but almost everyone spends at least some time using a *mak nap,* or Buddhist "rosary"—a string of beads used to mark one's place as one repeats any of a number of mantra-like words or phrases. Perhaps the most common are those that employ some combination of the three Pali words *anicca* (impermanence), *dukkha* (suffering), and *anattā* (not-self), which, according to Buddhist teaching, refer to three aspects characteristic of all things found in this world.

For example, one woman described her use of the meditation beads this way: During the first three rounds, she says *"anicca"* to herself while fingering each bead, using a piece of popped rice as a marker at the end of each round. For the next five rounds, she says *"dukkha,"* again using the popped rice to keep track of her progress. Finally, she does seven rounds of saying *"anattā"* on each bead, again with popped rice as markers. The purpose of this, she said, is to take one's mind off everyday worries and interests. If one tried simply to sit quietly without the help of some technique like this, one would be distracted by a person walking by the temple or by sounds from the village. The people who sleep at the temple try to meditate as much as possible, she explained, but others may have their own method of using the beads. (Some, for example, simply say *"anicca, dukkha, anattā"* over and over, one bead per word.)

The goal the temple sleepers are striving toward with these activities is a disciplined and quiet mind, an absence of craving or desires of any sort, and the cultivation of tolerance and compassion toward all living things,[6] all key tenets of Buddhist teachings. Further, they aim to be constantly aware of the transience of life, of its inherent hardships, and of the wisdom, therefore, of not clinging to it but, rather, of preparing oneself for a better rebirth by cultivating self-control and making merit whenever possible. Old people are expected to exhibit these traits at all times (at least ideally), not just while staying at the temple. Since these values are shared more widely in the community, even by those who are not much practiced in them, their association with old people contributes in large measure to the respect that is accorded them. Conversely, if a temple sleeper is known to drink alcohol or be sexually active, is seen to lose his temper, or even simply kills a chicken to cook for supper, it is scandalous in a way that it would not be if a younger person committed these same acts.[7] Like monks (but not to the same degree), old people are held to a higher standard of morality than ordinary Buddhists.

These are the defining features of being a temple sleeper, but their public role is much larger than this. As a group, the category of "old people" constitutes a recognized component of village social structure. Twice a year—at the beginning of the New Year in the fifth month, and at the end of the rainy season retreat in the eleventh month—a person's status as someone belonging to the category "old people" is ritually marked and reinforced in a village-wide ceremony called Paying Respect *(kaentau)*. In this ritual, "young people" (again, a flexible category) visit the homes of temple sleepers on the appointed evening and formally pay respect. In a small Shan village, people would most likely visit the home of every old person. However, in a medium-sized or large village such as Baan Kaung Mu, where there were about fifty temple sleepers in 1990, young people do not attempt to visit every single one. They make sure they visit all those they count as relatives, as well as any others they may be close to (for example, neighbors and good friends of the family).[8]

While waiting for their visitors, the old people wear temple attire, a towel thrown over their shoulder, and often sit on a mat. The young people (who range in age from toddlers to adults in their thirties) arrive, dressed in their good clothes, and bring with them a silver bowl, or other suitable container, filled with flower bouquets and popped rice, along with a basket of gifts. The gifts are small bundles, secured with a rubber band, that typically include the sorts of things a temple sleeper might be able to use when preparing an offering, such as a package of candles, a package of incense sticks, a box of matches, and a store-bought sweet of some sort. Other gifts are also possible—fresh fruit or homemade sweets, sandals or temple paraphernalia for closer relatives, and so on.

Upon arriving at a house, the visitor puts a bouquet and some popped rice in the container provided (usually the large lacquered container, or *phaan*, that a person takes to the temple when sleeping there) and places one of the gift bundles in another container (usually a white basin or a basket), holding each briefly to the forehead before depositing them. Then the old person chants a blessing while the visitor sits respectfully, hands in a *waai*. The visitors do not necessarily pay close attention to this chanting—some chat, look around, and so on—but are always ready to raise their hands to their forehead at the very end of the blessing in a gesture of thanks and respect. There is little time for interaction between the visitors and the old people because other visitors are usually waiting their turn at the door, so as soon as the blessing is over, the visitor gets up and heads to another house.[9]

In addition to these biannual occasions for paying respect, the special status of old people is recognized throughout the year. Whenever anyone holds a merit-making ceremony of any sort—either in their home or in the temple—the "old people" are always invited and are treated to a meal or some liquid refreshments. When it is time for the sponsors of the ceremony to sit respectfully, hands in a *waai*, and formally receive their merit, the old people as well as the monks chant a blessing on their behalf. It is their regular keeping of the precepts that confers on them special powers, including the power to generate merit for those who approach them and ask their blessings, but also more general powers such as the power to heal, to drive out spirits, and to sanctify something with their blessings. The longer they have been in the role of temple sleeper, the more powerful they are thought to be, for it is at the temple that they accumulate the power that comes from meditation and other ascetic practices, as well as learn the powerful verses that can drive a spirit out of a crying baby, call the *khwan* of a startled child, and sanctify the union of a new bride and groom.

Thus, just at the moment when individuals are losing their ability to do hard physical labor, they gain new powers that allow them to be useful in a different, but highly valued, way. All village merit-making ceremonies benefit from the presence of temple sleepers, and some—such as weddings and the first-month bathing ceremony for newborns—simply cannot be performed without them. In both of these ceremonies, the ritual consists almost entirely in what the old people do, which is to tie white strings around the wrists of the bride and groom and the newborn, respectively, while uttering blessings for health and long life. There are no other ritual officiants of any sort.

Even young children seem to learn quite early both the special status of temple sleepers and their virtual identification with the category "old people." In an earlier fieldwork project (Eberhardt 1984), when I asked children to explain what they understood of the Buddhist concept of merit *(kuso)*, their answers (shown in italics below) were marked by clear age-specific associations:

FOUR-YEAR-OLD GIRL
What about *kuso* [merit]? Can you tell me anything about that?
That's when people raise their hands in a waai.
And if someone has a lot of merit?
Then they're old. Old people have a lot.

SEVEN-YEAR-OLD BOY
What can you tell me about merit?
It's at the temple.
Well, how does one get it?
You sleep at the temple.

EIGHT-YEAR-OLD GIRL
What is this "merit" you mentioned earlier?
It's words, Pali words.
How does one get it?
You become a nun. When you've learned the old people's book [of chants] already, when you've become old, then become a nun and chant the scriptures all the time. People will bring you offerings. [You chant for them] after they've brought you these, after they sit respectfully and waai *[i.e., you dispense merit in the form of Pali words at this time].*

ELEVEN-YEAR-OLD GIRL
When people go and make offerings, and they chant, that's merit.
How does one get it?
Make offerings, have a boy ordained as a novice.
If you have "good merit," what does that mean?
You don't get sick. If you [have been ordained as] a novice, you have a lot of money, you're wealthy and prosperous. Stuff like that.

THIRTEEN-YEAR-OLD GIRL
So how do you get the merit?

> *On the new and full moons, make offerings and feed the monks. You can also*
> *carry water for the old people who sleep at the temple, fill water jars, carry*
> *their clothes and other things to the temple for them, when they are going to*
> *sleep there. They sleep there on* wan sin.
>
> What does it mean, then, to have "good merit"?
>
> *It means you will be reborn as a good person. When you're reborn in another life,*
> *you won't be a bad person. You'll be a good person.*

Old people, then, are conceptually linked not only with temple sleeping but, through their involvement with merit making, are associated to a certain extent with "goodness" itself—an association that again recalls the moral dimension of this age phase. Further, since premature death is an indication of bad karma, the simple fact of achieving old age is, in itself, a sign of accumulated merit and good karma. All of these notions together help reinforce the high status of old people.

At the same time, the old people who become temple sleepers are themselves undergoing an extensive education process. During their stays at the temple on each *wan sin,* they are exposed to an extra dose of sermons and scriptural readings of various sorts. At the merit-making ceremonies that engage the services of a lay reader, they constitute the audience that sits and listens to scripture-inspired legends and stories[10] while younger people work under the house or in the kitchen, unable to hear but a fragment of the recited text. Often the reading of these texts will be followed by commentary of some sort by a monk or a lay reader, analyses that provide explanations for why various traditional rituals and practices are done the way they are. All of this exposure to texts and their exegesis constitutes something of a crash course in what amounts to a Buddhist "Great Books Program" for temple sleepers. Many of them express delight and awe at the new things they are learning, and they enjoy being able to explain various allusions in the text to the younger members of their households (as well as to visiting anthropologists).

Meanwhile, other members of the community contribute to creating the sense that old people have specialized knowledge, by claiming, for example, that they themselves "can't understand" the readings and that "only the old people" know the meaning of those texts. (At times, these claims approach a kind of willed ignorance on the part of those who advance them.) Old people thus take on an aura in which they come to personify tradition and "the old ways." They are respected for this and are deferred to in matters of ritual knowledge and proper behavior. Having been made into a repository of tradition and authority, they can then be invoked, perhaps strategically, when need be in order to justify a desired course of action as, for example, when a long-awaited wedding that was not scheduled to occur for several months was suddenly performed early at a more convenient time for the participants, with the explanation that "the old people said it didn't look good for these two to be engaged for so long and not be married."

As the foregoing examples suggest, having a parent or grandparent decide to "become old" (that is, to begin sleeping at the temple on *wan sin*) changes one's relationship with him or her in important ways. No longer supervising one's labor on a day-to-day basis, they become less authoritative in some respects and more authoritative in others, as they are gradually transformed into a more diffuse object of respect.[11] This change in social status has implications for how others in the village interact with them as well.

Since the periodic keeping of the eight precepts and the permanent changes in other aspects of one's lifestyle each constitute a kind of withdrawal from everyday social life, the pattern can be viewed as a symbolic anticipation of death. Indeed, much of the rhetoric that accompanies both the practices themselves and the explanations of why they are performed has death as a central theme. Old people are overtly concerned both with their immediate fate after death (which they hope will be to go directly to *moeng phi*, one of the Buddhist heavens) and with their eventual rebirth in *moeng khon*, the realm of humans (which they hope will be auspicious). Their enthusiasm for merit-making rituals of all kinds is explicitly directed at achieving these goals, as are their efforts at mind control. Many told me that it is important to direct one's thoughts "toward good things, toward the Buddha's teachings" right before one dies, as doing so ensures a good fate after death and a good rebirth. This meant that they also tried to avoid thinking about mundane, worldly matters like the day-to-day operation of their farms (although several confessed that this was hard to do). Old age is not a time to be ambitious or to strive to get ahead but a time to focus all one's energies on cultivating a quiet mind through the practice of meditation and the exercise of detachment and restraint. Everything else is a distraction from what is understood to be the true nature of reality, that is, an awareness of our mortality and the inevitable suffering that characterizes human lives.

At the same time, these practices also ease the transition from life to death for those who remain behind. As we have seen, Shan treat death as something dangerous, especially for those who have strong affective bonds with the deceased (such as the person's family, neighbors, and close friends), since the escaping life force does not necessarily sever its ties with the living immediately. Given this general view of death, the austerities and various forms of social withdrawal practiced by old people take on an added significance, namely, they help to neutralize, or render nondangerous, the old person's life force by virtually assuring that it will make a swift and trouble-free transformation from *khwan* (soul-stuff) to *phi* (spirit-being). Hence, the death of a temple sleeper is not (or should not be) frightening in the way that the death of a younger person usually is, although young children, who often display a spontaneous fear of all ghosts, sometimes have to be persuaded of this (see Eberhardt 1984, 1993).

Old people in Baan Kaung Mu, then, are involved in the most fundamental and radical sort of self-transformation, all the more remarkable in that it is expected to be performed by everyone, as a normal stage of life. Unlike many industrialized societies, including the United States, where it is generally assumed that most "development" occurs in a person's early years, Shan expect that one of the most dramatic stages of development and self-transformation occurs late in life and, further, that the changes that occur there are positive ones, providing a model for the rest of the community to emulate.

Aging as Moral Development

What do these accounts of popular psychology and old age suggest about the way Shan view persons and the process of development? There is a syllogism of sorts embedded in their discourse: Sanity requires insight, and insight comes from experience, knowledge, and self-control. These, in turn, are thought to come almost predictably with age. Old people, both because of their long years of experience in the world and because of their more focused efforts as temple sleepers, are expected to demonstrate at all times the same sort of control over their thoughts and emotions that is urged upon everyone in times of stress. According to this view, it is their recognition and acceptance of the "true" nature of reality that results in their characteristic patience, detachment, and relative immunity from spirit attacks. Younger people, because of their greater entanglement with social relationships and worldly matters, find it harder to achieve this level of self-control. Attracted to this, distracted by that, they struggle to satisfy the urgent demands of everyday life and to protect themselves from the unwanted attachments of nefarious others, human or spirit.

At the same time, there is a sense in which the younger people's greater involvement in the world enables the withdrawal from it that is practiced by their own parents and grandparents, just as it is the laity as a whole that provides material support for those who enter the Buddhist *sangha* as monks and novices. People told me, for example, that it was impossible for laypeople to follow the Buddhist precepts on a permanent basis. As one grows older, however, and has adult children or other junior relatives to look after one's physical needs and property, it becomes increasingly feasible to observe all the precepts for a short period of time (by sleeping at the temple) or to regularly keep one precept more strictly than one did before (by, for example, having one's children handle all slaughtering of livestock). To attempt such observance of the precepts earlier in life not only would inconvenience and burden others but also would make one delinquent in one's duties to one's children (who, while young, have a right to one's nurturing support) and to one's parents (who, having supported one earlier, now have the right to command one's energies toward their own spiritual pursuits).

Hence, the same logic that delays the direct pursuit of *nikpan,* or nirvana, until later rebirths (in favor of merit making directed at affecting the quality of the very next rebirth) allows the partial postponement of precept keeping until the achievement of old age. Just as one expects, in later rebirths, to eventually become a devoted monk, with one's material needs totally provided by the lay community and with the freedom to pursue enlightenment continuously, so one expects, in the course of a single lifetime, that the junior members of one's household and community will make it increasingly possible for one to ignore material concerns in favor of spiritual quests. Each individual life cycle is thus conceptualized as a microversion of the sort of development that is thought to occur across the extended cycle of many rebirths.

From the foregoing account in this and previous chapters, the outline of a distinct view of personhood and developmental processes begins to emerge. A person, in this view, is a being that acts and that bears the karmic consequences of past acts. It is also a seat of desire, thoughts, and affective bonds that may be more or less under the person's control and that serve to propel the person along its particular course of development. As such, each person one encounters is understood to be a unique manifestation of an accumulated history of willed acts, that is, of the sorts of acts that have moral consequences. Each person is also a potential site for other beings' activities, the point at which other beings' actions, desires, and attachments are focused. These other beings may be human or spirit, material or immaterial.

Indeed, a recurring theme in Shan talk about developmental processes is the fluidity of life-forms, the absence of a claim to radical "otherness" for humans (as opposed to, say, spirits or animals), and the contrary claim that at least some aspects of individuality are retained in the transformation from one life-form to the next.[12] That personhood can be attributed to beings in both the material and the immaterial world is an argument in favor of talking about the Shan life cycle and notions of development as processes that begin before birth and continue after death. In fact, "Shan theories of human development" might be better phrased "Shan theories of person development," since humanity is but one phase (albeit a recurring and privileged one) in a person's career—a career that spans many instances of human lives.

Consistent with this perspective, Shan views of individual development mirror their sense of historical progress to a certain extent, as revealed in life history statements and in less formal conversations with people about their individual lives and their collective past. Just as individuals are expected to develop from ignorant, *hai*, and vulnerable children into knowing, self-controlled, and more powerful adults, so the recent past is talked about as a progressive movement away from "wildness," from living at the mercy of the forest, and toward "civilization," where people imagine that they have more control over the forces that surround them.

Explaining Behavior, Explaining Lives

These are the broad outlines of a Shan theory of human development, of the forces and processes that many Shan assume are universally felt. How, then, are human differences explained? What happens in the course of any individual's development to make that person different from others? To what extent is development invoked to account for human behavior, and what sorts of learning theories do Shan subscribe to?

The people I spoke to recognized many different influences as having a causal effect on human behavior, at least some of which could be considered developmental in the sense that an event or action performed at point X in a person's development is invoked to explain later behaviors, actions, or personality characteristics at point Y in that person's life. Some of these causal influences stem from a person's previous lives, such as *kam* (karma) and *wot* (karmic retribution). Both of these notions attribute a causal relationship to events widely dispersed in time, but they tend to serve different functions in Shan behavior theory. While *kam* is used to explain the general stamp, or circumstances, of a person's life (the sort of household one is born into, one's physical characteristics, and one's overall station in life), specific events and actions are more often explained by reference to *wot*. In particular, if a person does something unusual or avoidable that leads to his or her injury or death—an action that, in retrospect, appears to have been unnecessary—this is often explained as being due to "stored-up *wot*," the karmic residue of some previously committed immoral act (in this or an earlier life).

A second influence on an individual's current state is personal experience. People recognize the effects of trial-and-error learning (saying, for example, of a child, "let her do it by herself, or she'll never learn how") and credit much to the experience of personal hardship, with physical labor, poverty, illness, and the loss of loved ones being mentioned most frequently. A person who has not yet experienced these things is said to not know anything *(am hu hang)*, to be less patient *(tsau yaao)* with others, and, in general, to have less emotional equilibrium in the face of life's troubles than a more experienced person who understands the "true nature" of human existence, namely, that it is full of suffering, disappointment, and frustration.[13]

A less negative aspect of experience often invoked to explain people's idiosyncratic habits, tastes, and preferences is *yaam*, or habituation, the process of getting used to something: if one starts taking naps in the afternoon, one will soon get used to doing so and will want to take them every day; a person who has not done much physical labor while growing up will find it difficult to do as an adult; people who are accustomed to eating soybean cakes and chilies enjoy them, but others do not; and so forth.

Other powers and forces that are invoked to explain differences in people's behavior but make less reference to developmental issues or processes include *tso* (one's luck or fate, based on the astrological forces and events coinciding with one's birth); *lom* (wind) and the other elements (earth, water, fire) that differentially constitute the bodies of people and leave them with somewhat different dispositions; eating mistakes *(kin phit)*, which can lead to illness or "craziness" *(pen yaung)*; spirit possession or spirit attack (the latter usually leading to *khwan* loss and illness); and, most important, other people—one's household members, close friends, and consociates—who are said to exert an influence on one's overall health and behavior for as long as one spends time with them.

Often more than one from the above list of possible causes are combined to explain someone's behavior in any given case. Laui's suicide, for example, was explained by reference both to karmic retribution *(wot)* and to her relative lack of experience with hardships and, hence, her inability to cope with the loss of her husband. In another case, a young boy's tantrums and general resistance to attending school in town were interpreted by his parents as due both to his "not yet being used to it" *(am pai yaam)* and to a spirit attack that left him without all of his *khwan*.

Although people often disagree about the details, there is a general sense that certain aspects of one's life are beyond one's current control (although one may nevertheless be held responsible for them ultimately). People take note of the unexpected twists and turns in their own and others' lives and strive to construct a plausible account of them, invoking and combining a wide range of causal factors in the process. The "default" case—a life that is of a consistent quality from birth to death—requires no special explanation; only those lives that change dramatically evoke interpretation.

As this last statement implies, the Shan I spoke with do not conceptualize the archetypical life as a unique odyssey of development, a dramatic narrative, a story with a plot, a "journey," or any of the other metaphors common to Western biographical discourse. Experience in the world can provide lessons for life, but the lesson is always the same. The role of experience in the developmental process is to provide us with insights into the nature of life and of human existence in general, not to serve as a vehicle for self-discovery, the cultivation of individual talents, unique perspectives, and so on.

The Shan take on human psychology that emerges from these and other examples is one that clearly draws upon many Buddhist concepts both for the language it employs and for the substance of its claims, and yet I think it would be a mistake to reduce Shan ethnopsychology to, say, Buddhist notions of conditioned genesis and the impermanence of the self. Even when indigenous notions can be translated into doctrinal ones (and they usually can be), we should be careful not to lose the broader connotations and nuances in the translation process. The local understanding of how emotional attachment and longing work, for example, and the way they can lead to a person's demise, could be assimilated into the Buddhist concept of *tanha* (thirst, desire, or craving) and the doctrinal teachings of its consequences. But doing so would risk losing the sense retained in the Shan notion of how people are physically and emotionally affected by those they associate with—a broader conception of persons as almost the terrestrial equivalent of astral bodies that have a kind of gravitational pull on one another.

Other aspects of Shan ethnopsychology point to an emphasis on the collective social life as the maintainer of health and well-being, and a concomitant de-emphasis on the individual as the appropriate unit of explanation. There is, for example, the notion that one's morale is associated with the presence of one's *khwan* and, further, that the mere presence of other *khwan* (without them having to do anything) is in itself both protective and a morale boost—a position reminiscent of similar beliefs found elsewhere in non-Buddhist Southeast Asia.[14] Along the same lines, in addition to the master narrative that paints all lives with the same broad brush, Shan ethnopsychology exhibits a very limited interest in the details of an individual's personal history and family life as an explanation for that person's current behavior. It would be hard to imagine Shan having much patience, for example, with the kind of one-on-one therapeutic counseling aimed at recovering information from childhood experience that is so popular in Europe and North America.

In this regard, a comparison with the discourse on self and the life course that is currently dominant in the United States is revealing. This is a view that, unlike the Shan approach I have tried to describe, relies heavily on notions of selves that are characterized as having "interiority" and "depth." Nancy Schnog offers this description of its distinctive features in her introduction to *Inventing the Psychological: Toward a Cultural History of Emotional Life in America*:

Although multifaceted and perennially rescripted, the mid- to late twentieth-century common language of selfhood [in the U.S.] can be said to rest on a foundation of accepted "truths" and practices that include the following: an arsenal of basic terms for the inner self and its dysfunctions (ego, unconscious, repression, Oedipus complex, neurosis); a structure of the mind imagined in terms of rational "conscious" processes and irrational "unconscious" desires; a developmental model of the self which posits the self's growth as a progressive movement through psychosocial stages; and a method of cure which depends on a patient's talks with a trained analyst, assumes the primary importance of a patient's family in the etiology of his or her symptoms, and presumes the possibility of a patient's self-improvement. (1997, 4)

This particular discourse of selfhood results in an inner/outer dichotomy when talking about individual persons. That is, Americans are culturally prepared for the outward appearance of a person to be deceptive, misleading, or unreliable. They are willing to assume that "you can't judge a book by its cover" and that there may be vast discrepancies between how a person acts or what they look like, on the one hand, and what they're "really" like.

The difference between this way of talking and thinking about a self and the Shan approach is striking. Instead of interiority, Shan stress exterior forms, the surface of things (including physical appearance, clothing, and so on), which are supposed to mirror not one's "inner state" but, rather, one's cosmological position. (Karma is not "in" you. You are "in" *it*.) One of the visual images of a person that Shan find most appealing and indicative of maturity—that of an individual displaying a calm, smooth, unperturbed (Buddha-like), even meditative demeanor—connotes not interior depth or complexity but insight, awareness, and transcendence.

The contrast for Shan is not between the psychologically "deep" individuals and those who are "shallow" but, rather, between the aware and the unaware, between the knowing and the ignorant, between those who have mastered and transcended the contradictions of life and those who are still struggling. The psychologically complex, even "neurotic" individuals so celebrated in twentieth-century American literature and popular culture (see Pfister 1997) would probably strike most Shan as belonging on the "still struggling" side of the continuum.

Hence, when Shan express a lack of interest in the "psychological interiors" of selves, it indicates that, for them, the causes of people's behavior do not generally lie inside them but, rather, in the world around them—in the events, forces, and social interactions (both mundane and cosmic) that they have encountered. Instead of seeing human development as a process of separating from an imagined state of wholeness with the mother and "achieving" uniqueness as a mark of maturity, Shan children are imagined as already unique and autonomous beings with their own karmic history. The process of "development" is therefore aimed at something else entirely.

Comparisons such as these, despite their necessarily sketchy nature, are useful, I think, because they help draw attention to important aspects of these ethnopsychologies that we might otherwise take for granted. Inevitably, they also raise other issues: What would give rise to such different interpretations of selfhood and human development? What are the larger structural forces that would help create and sustain any given ethnopsychology, as opposed to some other sort? Would we, for example, expect Shan ethnopsychology to bear a stronger family resemblance to that of urban Thais (with whom they share some basic cosmological-religious assumptions) or to that of other rural Southeast Asians (with whom they may share important social, political, and economic circumstances but who may participate in very different religious and cultural traditions)? The way one answers these and similar questions will depend on how one theorizes the nature of indigenous psychologies and their relationship to the social and material organization of people's lives. An extended treatment of this topic would be well beyond the scope of this book, but I discuss briefly, in the next and final chapter, what I consider to be the most promising paths of inquiry for those readers who may be interested in exploring this territory further.

Chapter 8

Imagined Lives

We do become what we practice being.
MARILYN FRYE, *The Politics of Reality*

MY TEN-YEAR-OLD SON makes frequent reference to "teenagers," a group he seems to regard with the studied curiosity of a professional ethnographer. Sometimes he informs me of their habits; other times he questions me about them. He wonders aloud (with an unmistakable ambivalence) what it will feel like to actually be a teenager. Our conversations on this topic remind me of similar ones I've had with Shan boys the same age who were also thinking ahead—in this case, imagining what it would feel like to become a novice Buddhist monk. Consider these notes from my first field trip to Baan Kaung Mu, during which I was working primarily with children:

MARCH 23, 1981: I am chatting with Tsit, a ten-year-old boy, who has come to visit. Since it is the school break, many children have been stopping by the last few days. I ask Tsit if he misses school. "Yes. I'm bored with hanging around and going visiting." He is interested to hear that I had attended a novice ordination festival in another village yesterday and asks me all about it. Me: "Would you like to be ordained as a novice?" Tsit: "I will be. You have to." Me: "Do you think it will be fun?" Tsit: "N— er, yes, it will be." Me: "Not sure, huh?" Tsit: "Well, I couldn't come and visit anymore." Me: "That's OK. I'll come and visit you at the temple."

Minutes later, Tsit's friend Weng shows up. He had also gone to the festival yesterday but had missed the actual ordination part of the ceremony, having left with the early truck that dropped people off to shop in town before coming back for the rest of us. Weng is enthusiastic about the possibility of becoming a novice, though, and wants very much to do it. In contrast to Tsit, he can hardly contain his excitement when he talks about it. He chatters on happily for some time, then asks me, "If we do a novice ordination festival here, will you take lots of pictures?" "Sure," I say. Tsit has remained quiet during all of this, then comments pensively to his friend: "She said she'd come and visit us at the temple."

Further conversations with these boys made it clear that they had widely divergent feelings about the prospect of becoming a novice. Tsit was worried about being lonely and sleeping away from home. Weng was focusing almost exclusively on the festival part of the ordination and looking forward to the party. Both were concerned about not being able to eat after noon. Nevertheless, together with my son, they all have something in common. In their conversations with others and perhaps in more private musings, each of these boys is anticipating a transformation of self that has been culturally organized and over which they have very little control. And this act of anticipation is itself significant.

When each of us surveys the landscape of imaginable life trajectories and looks toward the horizon, what we see not only helps prepare us for the future but also shapes our experience of the present. Our perceived "lifescape," as one might call it, affects our routine, day-to-day understanding of who we are. Regardless of whether he is dreading it or looking forward to it, a boy who knows that he will someday become a Buddhist novice and a boy who knows he will someday become an American teenager are going to understand themselves differently, imagine different possibilities for themselves, and perhaps begin to develop different sets of sensibilities. Put another way, the cultural constructions of "selves" and "lives" are inextricably intertwined.

Throughout this book, I have argued that people's understandings of themselves and others are linked to local assumptions and beliefs about the life course, and that a person cannot properly study one without studying the other. Studying people's ideas about human development and the life course adds, in effect, a "time dimension" to our analyses of concepts of self. It helps free us from overly static models of personhood by forcing us to attend to the temporal aspects of any given depiction of selfhood. The preceding chapters have described some of the ways this works out in the Shan case. For example, I have tried to show how the centrality of emotional attachment in Shan constructions of personhood, and the view of the self as a contested site where these emotional pulls are played out, are linked to (and informed by) a related view of human development in which "emotionally driven" children are expected to become emotionally controlled adults and, eventually, emotionally detached old people. Similarly, to the extent that a Shan self is defined by perceived moral status in a hierarchy of social positions, I have tried to show how these concerns are linked to local understandings of broader cosmological processes that include (but are not limited to) the transformation of lives over time.

Inevitably, this process of tacking back and forth between particular ideas about the self and related ideas about the life course has required some accommodation. In particular, I have tried to highlight what I see as the on-going dialectic between cultural forms and personal interpretations. As a result, this book has been shaped by dual goals that have sometimes been in tension with each other. On the one hand, in keeping with the warnings of those writers who have repeatedly (and wisely) emphasized the need to avoid creating homogenized portraits of the communities we study, I have tried to situate my description of Baan Kaung Mu in the context of concrete incidents, events, and people. When I wanted to invoke the significance of a ritual or customary practice, I chose to describe historically particular events rather than generic, timeless ones. I have tried to highlight the ways in which different segments of the community make strategic use of the cultural frameworks they have inherited, and I have showcased specific individuals in the act of interpreting and engaging in talk about the self.

On the other hand, I have felt equally compelled to draw attention to the structural and systemic—one might say "relentless"—aspects of local discourses on self and development. These are the aspects of conceptual frameworks that carry sufficient cultural capital or prestige to dominate people's consciousness or, less dramatically, to be simply taken for granted. People may choose to resist these to some extent and with varying degrees of success, but they continue to live their lives "in tension with them" (Frye 1983). Any adequate ethnographic account, it seems to me, cannot neglect to describe these culturally salient and pervasive systems of thought and practice that continually intrude on people's subjective experience of themselves. It is with this in mind that I have sometimes found it necessary (at the risk of appearing to essentialize the people of Baan Kaung Mu) to talk about "Shan" conceptions of self and "Shan" ideas about human development. The boys Tsit and Weng, for example, had virtually opposite personal reactions to the idea of becoming a novice, yet both lived with the culturally nurtured conviction that it was inevitable. Similar things could be said about Uncle Toen's ambivalence (described in chapter 7) toward becoming a temple sleeper, or the anticipation of the young women working in the fields (described in chapter 6) who "played" at being ordination sponsors while transplanting rice. These same cultural forms, when used with a backward glance, can also help people make sense of their past. Here, even unanticipated events (such as Uncle Pon's becoming a healer or Laui's tragic suicide) come to be understood as part of a life plan previously undiscerned. One might even say that it is only when they are embedded in such a conceptual framework or cultural discourse that such events become comprehensible.

My approach has therefore been to listen to Shan's talk about selves and lives with an ear both to its recurrent and to its improvisational moments. That is, I have sought to demonstrate that Shan views of self and human

development have both a logical coherence (they are not random compila-
tions of ideas or ad hoc lists of rules) and areas of inconsistency and ambiguity that require ongoing interpretation by those who would use them, areas
that also open up possibilities for resistance and innovation.

At the same time, I am acutely aware that the portrait of Shan thinking
and practice that I have attempted to capture in the preceding chapters is a
historical one; it is sustained by a particular configuration of social, economic, and ideological factors that is not ancient and that, even as I write, is
undergoing further changes and development. Some of these changes have
to do with the villagers' increasing reliance on cash and their expanding involvement in the Thai market economy. Others have to do with the influx of
novel ideas and images via the news media and popular culture (especially
print media, films, and, most recently, television). Will these changes result
in radically different understandings of personhood and the life course? Or
will the Shan ethnopsychology that I have described in the preceding chapters persist in some recognizable form under greatly altered circumstances?

How one approaches these questions depends upon how one theorizes
the relationship between ethnopsychological beliefs and their broader social
and cultural context. Here I am persuaded that the approach taken by those
who have studied the emergence of modern views of the self in Europe and
North America (summarized in chapter 1) provides one promising model
that is worth exploring. According to this body of research, the key developments to watch are changes in the division of labor and in family organization. The work of Zaretsky (1976) and Demos (1978 [1997]) has been
particularly influential in showing how the separation of work from home
and the creation of the child-centered family in the rapidly industrializing
cities of late nineteenth- and early twentieth-century America led to a host of
other changes that ultimately gave rise to new and unprecedented ways of
thinking and talking about people and their expected course of life.

Although I can only speculate about the historical trajectory of the views
I have outlined in this book, I suspect it would be a useful exercise to com-
pare the Shan social context as I encountered it in 1990–1991 with what
these and other writers suggest were the conditions that spawned the overtly
psychological view of self and the life course that is currently dominant in
the United States. For example, if (as this body of research suggests) the new
social arrangements that accompanied the process of industrialization functioned as preconditions for people's new understanding of themselves as psychological creatures, then it is not surprising that Shan and many other
nonindustrial societies described in the ethnographic literature do not share
this particular discourse of self and human development. As I have tried to
show in the preceding chapters, Shan social life as I encountered it in 1990–

1991 was not characterized by the sharp distinction that developed in industrializing America between work (as a site of "rational" labor) and home (as the new site of nurturance and emotional repair), nor was there a gender ideology dedicated to maintaining sharply separate spheres of civic and domestic duties for men and women.

This does not mean, of course, that villagers' views of the self and the life course were immune from influence by external factors and a changing economy. As mentioned in chapter 7, several people told me that they wanted to postpone becoming a temple sleeper until "after the house is built" or "after my last child finishes school," or until other such activities that required significant expenditures of cash had been completed. In the coming years, as the perceived need for cash increases (for newly available consumer items, for school fees and uniforms, for new-style houses, for more elaborate rituals, and so on), the period of adult life devoted to productive work may well be extended, while old age (in the form of temple sleeping and semi-retirement from household labor) may be further postponed.

Meanwhile, as discussed in chapter 6 (in the context of its effects on novice ordinations), village children are spending an increasing number of years in formal schooling, both because the Thai state continues to increase the minimum number of years all children are obligated to complete, and because parents perceive the increased social status and economic opportunities that formal schooling confers. This, in turn, affects other segments of the life course as children's agricultural labor is lost and must be replaced, and as the schooling itself must be paid for, requiring adults to spend yet more time participating in the cash economy and providing an added incentive to postpone "old age."

These changes are significant, but they do not, in themselves, indicate that children, adults, or old people are being regarded in a fundamentally new way, nor have they been accompanied by a major reorganization of the household division of labor (though such changes may well be around the corner). Indeed, the Shan household in 1990 was still primarily a pragmatically oriented economic unit firmly integrated into the larger village community, not a private sentimental one that was set apart from (and in opposition to) society. Shan children's growth and development were assumed to proceed normally without much in the way of specialized techniques or knowledge. There were no recognized "child experts" (in fact, there was considerable diversity of opinion among caregivers), and child rearing was, on the whole, treated as unproblematic by Shan parents. Responsibility for socializing children was shared with nonparents (teachers, monks, grandparents, and so on) and any unusual qualities found in a youth were as likely to be explained by referring to karma as by blaming (or crediting) a parent. In short, the particular constellation of social arrangements that have been identified as a precondition for the development of the "modern psychological self" (Pfister and Schnog 1997) was largely absent in Baan Kaung Mu at the time of my fieldwork.

Inevitably, this will change, and depending on the sorts of changes that occur, Shan understandings of themselves and of what constitutes a "normal" life trajectory could shift rather dramatically in the coming years. An increase, for example, in the number of young people who migrate to urban areas in search of wage work (this group constituted a small percentage of village youth in 1991 but was definitely on the rise) would have a significant structural impact on village household organization and division of labor, precisely the sort of factors that earlier studies suggest should result in a changed consciousness and self-understanding. This is indeed what Mary Beth Mills (1999) found in her insightful ethnography of urban migrants from a community in northeastern Thailand where the migration process was extensive and long established.

While considerations such as these provide a framework for contemplating future changes in Baan Kaung Mu and suggest the sorts of structural factors that are likely to have a significant impact on any society's cultural discourse on self and human development, what happens in any particular case will always be complicated by local exigencies and by people's creative and largely unpredictable responses to the changes they confront. For, as we have seen with the children whose comments began this chapter, it is in the space "between" the cultural forms and our anticipation of them that our subjective sense of self adheres.

As I bring this book to a close, I am reminded that Shan are well practiced at eluding categorization—as their ethnographers from Leach (1954) to Tannenbaum (1995) have repeatedly pointed out—and I suspect that my attempt to describe Shan views of self and human development has missed as much as it has captured. I offer it nonetheless because, first, I find much to admire and appreciate in the particular inventions of selves and lives that they have fashioned—acts of cultural imagination that, in my view, accord dignity and value to the course of a human life and that, even when I am living away from Baan Kaung Mu, continue to inform and enrich the way I live. It is a view of persons and personal development that I think deserves a wider audience.

Finally, beyond the merits of the Shan case in particular, I am convinced that it is only through immersion in the details of another way of thinking about the course of a human life that we can begin to see the outlines of our own formulations and, equally important, begin to imagine alternatives. This is worth doing because—to return to the theme with which I began this book—each of us is guided in innumerable and surprisingly intimate ways by our often unexamined assumptions about the process of human development. If there is nothing "natural" or inevitable about the particular cultural discourse that dominates our consciousness and organizes our daily life, then it is surely worth the effort to try to discern its structure and origins. Ethnographic examples, however flawed and partial, provide a resource for the imagination. As we ponder the possibilities and strive to create ever more humane options for ourselves and our children, we could do worse than to recall the Shan image of human hearts in motion, orbiting and exerting an emotional pull on each other in sometimes problematic but always significant ways.

Notes

1. Introduction

1. Collins (1998), for example, has suggested that Buddhist ideology is meant to put everyday life into question as much as to provide ideals or norms for it. Similarly, Laidlaw (1995) offers an extended discussion of how a community of Jains in northwestern India manages to thrive while embracing a religion that prescribes impossible ideals and values. I thank Steve Collins for bringing these similarities to my attention.

2. In the discussion that follows, my goal is not to assess the success of these endeavors so much as to simply reveal the sources of influence on this project. Obviously, much more could be (and has been) said about this literature (see, for example, Kondo 1990, 33–43, or Lamb 2000, 37–41). Nor is the discussion I provide here by any means a comprehensive review of recent research in psychological anthropology. Other branches developed almost simultaneously with those I mention, some involving several of the same researchers, so my casting of this body of work as a school constitutes my own reading of its logic and legacy. Shweder, for example, has distinguished an approach he calls "cultural psychology" from both psychological anthropology and ethnopsychology, though he adds (somewhat mischievously) that "many ethnopsychologists today are in fact doing cultural psychology" (Shweder 1990, 17).

3. I do not mean to suggest that psychoanalytically informed research was abandoned by psychological anthropologists. On the contrary, it remains a vibrant subsection of the discipline (see, for example, Obeyesekere 1990 or Heald and Deluz 1994). My aim here, once again, is simply to outline the intellectual history of those particular schools of thought that have most directly influenced this book.

4. See Harkness 1992 for a helpful review of the history of anthropological interest in human development, and Harkness and Super 1996 for a collection of case studies of parental ethnotheories, described from multiple disciplinary perspectives.

5. Symonds' recent book, *Calling in the Soul: Gender and the Cycle of Life in a Hmong Village* (2004), is a welcome exception.

6. According to Collins (1982), some of these alternative formulations would be well within the range of acceptable canonical interpretations of Buddhist doctrine.

7. While this is true for the aspects of family life that relate to concepts of self, major changes in other aspects of the family are not necessarily tied to industrialization. Recent scholarship has disputed, for example, the notion that nuclear families and some form of family limitation occurred only after industrialization (see Hareven 2000, 321ff).

8. "Shan" is a Burmese word for this group of people that was adopted by English speakers during the time of British colonial rule in Burma. Speakers of Central Thai (the version of Thai spoken in Bangkok and the central plains) refer to them as Thai Yai. The Shan call themselves Tai (with an unaspirated *t*), however, and recognize numerous subcategories within this ethnic designation (e.g., Tai Nue, Tai Lao, and Tai Hkamti). The Shan of Mae Hong Son Province are predominantly Tai Long.

9. Two main branches of Buddhism have survived among contemporary populations, Theravāda Buddhism (also sometimes referred to as Hīnayāna Buddhism, but not by its adherents) and Mahāyāna Buddhism. Theravāda Buddhism is the variety of Buddhism found predominantly in the countries of Southeast Asia (including Sri Lanka, Burma, Thailand, Laos, and Cambodia), whereas Mahāyāna Buddhism is more common in the countries of South Asia and East Asia (including India, Tibet, China, Korea, and Japan).

10. Shan and Thai are related but mutually distinct languages, akin to the relationship between, say, Spanish and Italian. When I began working in Baan Kaung Mu in 1979, few but the schoolteachers were fluent in Thai, though many adults had at least some minimal speaking competence in the language and many could read it. Since then, fluency in Thai has increased along with the increased access to Thai media (described later in the text).

11. Depending on the time of year, there may be religious services on each of these days, or only on the full moon and new moon days. On these days the devout commit themselves to strict observance of a group of Buddhist commandments, or precepts. See chapter 7 for more on *wan sin*.

12. In some Shan villages, "dry" (nonirrigated) rice has also been planted on hillside swiddens as a supplementary rice supply. No household in Baan Kaung Mu is currently planting dry rice, although some have in the past. For a detailed discussion of Shan agriculture, see Tannenbaum 1982 and Durrenberger and Tannenbaum 1983.

2. Spirits, Souls, and Selves

1. Uncle Pon died in 1999.

2. All Shan villages have a designated guardian spirit drawn from a "pool" of thirty-two such beings whose headquarters are said to be in Chiang Dao cave (in Chiang Mai Province). For more on the *tsao moeng* in Baan Kaung Mu, see chapter 5. For descriptions of analogous but rather differently conceived systems among the Burmese and the Northern Thai, see Spiro 1967 and Tambiah 1970, respectively.

3. I have met several Shan men who have been successful in their efforts to stop drinking with this method.

4. Neither of these is a static, clearly bounded category. What counts as "traditional" in Baan Kaung Mu today is not what passed as such twenty years ago. The same is true for practices that are currently labeled *farang* ("Western").

5. A *waai* is a gesture of respect, made by placing the palms of the hands together in a prayerlike fashion and inclining the head slightly. The word *waai* can be used as a noun (referring to the gesture) or as a verb (referring to the act of making such a gesture). For an example of the gesture, see the photo on page 155.

6. "Nang" is a polite term of address and reference used in conjunction with women's names, regardless of marital status.

7. *Khwan* (which is sometimes pronounced *"kwan"*) has been variously translated as "souls," "life force," "vital essence," and the like. I use all of these when they seem appropriate, but since none of them adequately conveys the meaning of the term and since each carries problematic connotations in English, I often rely on the Shan word itself. Although described as plural in number, these "units" are never differentiated. (They do not, for example, scatter in different directions or require multiple and differing things to return.) Instead, they are spoken of as a collective unit, rather like the use of the word "wits" in the English phrase "to have one's wits about one." Consequently, in the exposition that follows, I sometimes translate the term as a singular noun, when that seems most appropriate.

8. A more drastic method of evicting the offending spirit, called *tat phi* (cutting off the spirit), is used for chronic and particularly troublesome illnesses that do not respond to the *pat phi* treatment. It is more expensive. Uncle Pon's fee for the *tat phi* treatment was "over 700 baht."

9. My impression is that Shan apply this conceptualization of "curing as contest" to their encounters with Western as well as traditional medicine, although my evidence for this is less systematic.

3. Souls into Spirits

1. Nang Nu used the term *pei tsau*, which means to beat, or triumph over, [one's] heart.

2. In urban centers and towns, including the provincial capital of Mae Hong Son, monks follow the traditional practice of going out each morning to collect donations of food. The lay donors wait for the monks along the side of the road and place food offerings in the monks' alms bowls. Many rural communities in Thailand, however, have adopted the practice of delivering the food offerings directly to the temple each morning, eliminating the need for the monks to leave the monastery.

3. See Gombrich 1971, 71–73, for a similar interpretation of these concepts by Sri Lankan Buddhists. For more on the Buddhist doctrines of "not-self" *(anattā)* and "conditioned genesis" *(paṭicca-samuppāda),* see Collins 1982 and 1994, and Rahula 1974, 51–66.

4. See also Mulder 1979, 21–55, for the Thai, and Tannenbaum 1987, 1989, 1990, and 1995 for the Shan. Tannenbaum in particular writes extensively and persuasively in these works about the importance of the notion of power in the Shan worldview.

5. On less formal occasions, the gift giver simply sits respectfully with hands held in a *waai* while the recipient chants the blessing.

6. My translation. In the more poetic Thai version, the last word of each line rhymes with the first word of the subsequent line: *pai mai klap, lap mai tuun, fuun mai mii, nii mai phon.*

7. Although, to my knowledge, there is no formal rule against it, Shan do not ask boys who have never been ordained before to undergo the ceremony in honor of a deceased relative, choosing instead to call upon those who are already familiar

with its requirements. A boy's first ordination ceremony is an elaborately celebrated affair, described in chapter 6.

8. After natural deaths of old and respected people, it is traditional to "play" with the coffin on the way to the cemetery, pulling it back and forth along the road in tug-of-war fashion in order to call attention to and celebrate the person who died. During my 1979–1981 field trip, such funeral displays were popular for old and esteemed members of the community. Grandfather would have been a good candidate for a full-blown version of this rite, but concern for the fragility of the fancy (and expensive) coffin cover caused people to check their enthusiasm and observe the custom in a restrained form.

9. Although the explanatory rhetoric is somewhat different in each case, a distinction of some sort between "good" and "bad" deaths is common throughout Southeast Asia, even among highland groups that are not followers of Theravāda Buddhism. For an example of such a distinction among the Hmong of northern Thailand, see Symonds 2004, 152–156.

10. I and at least one other local woman who wanted to attend the cremation were strongly advised not to go (presumably out of concern that our *khwan* could not handle it), and, indeed, no women from Baan Kaung Mu ended up going. However, the following morning I learned that some women from a nearby village did attend.

11. "Mae Kham" is a title of respect that Aunt Ying has earned by having sponsored several novice and monk ordinations.

12. *Asak syeng yao*, literally, age spent already.

13. Weeks later, I heard people tease him on occasion about having been crazy, but this was only after he had clearly weathered the worst of his grief and was able to smile at their suggestion.

14. See chapter 5 for a description of this ritual.

15. Other styles are also popular, including some commercial versions that are available for purchase in Mae Hong Son town.

16. If the reading occurs in the evening, a simple snack is served to the guests, and the meal for the monks, along with the rest of the rite, takes place the following morning.

17. This particular arrangement of five items—one each in the four corners of a (real or imagined) square and the fifth in the center—is a common configuration that occurs in many sorts of Shan rituals. With its implicit reference to the four cardinal directions radiating out from a central point, it functions as a kind of mandala, a condensed symbol for "the world," such that anything done to it is simultaneously done "to the world."

4. Domesticating the Self

1. Note that this is a somewhat different task from attempting to provide an exhaustive account of Shan child-rearing techniques. Here my focus will be on ideas about the developmental process. Parenting techniques will be mentioned only insofar as they help to illustrate these. The acquisition of this body of knowledge (and other culturally constructed domains) by children is, similarly, an important topic

about which I have written elsewhere (Eberhardt 1984, 1993). Here I restrict myself to adult understandings of the process of human development.

2. Interestingly, in every rebirth story I heard, the gender of the person said to be reborn remained the same. This was so even though, when speaking in the abstract about their own future rebirth, many people, especially women, anticipated a possible change in gender in their next life. Tannenbaum (pers. comm.), commenting on her experience elsewhere in the province, recalled one incident in which a man was said to be reborn as an infant girl, but otherwise Tannenbaum concurred that rebirth stories generally retained the same gender for the transformed person. I think this indicates the strength of gender identity in Shan constructions of the self, a strength that would make it hard to recognize a reborn person as "the same person" if the gender differed.

3. As we saw in chapter 2, the continuity between the two is clearly recognized, but *khwan*, unlike *phi*, is a life force that is properly attached to a material body, even though parts of *khwan* may be temporarily separated from it, to the detriment of the body.

4. In each process—birth and death—a being is undergoing a change of state that entails crossing the line between material and immaterial life-forms. Although one's karmic history places constraints on where one can end up when making such a transition, it is not wholly determinative. There is still some room for other forces to contribute to the outcome, and, of these, a person's thoughts and desires are considered especially powerful. Since, in the case of the infant, these have not yet developed, the thoughts and desires of the mother predominate.

5. At the time of this particular birth, most women delivered their children in the village with the help of midwives. Hence, a delivery in town was unusual. Now the situation is reversed, with most babies being born in the town hospital.

6. Because of this association, people with chronic problems of some sort (usually health related) will sometimes "change their identity" by changing their name, a procedure that is considered effective at any point in the life course. Similarly, any ritual done to improve one's health or one's luck (e.g., having one's *khwan* called, lighting a specially made candle, or making offerings at a temple or pagoda) is thought to be most effective if performed on the same day of the week as one's birthday. For more on this topic, see chapter 5.

7. Indeed, recalling the rebirth stories in which spirit-beings choose where they will be reborn, one could even say that this autonomous will exists in a person's "prehuman" state.

8. That Shan seem to refer only to young children as "so-and-so reborn" and never to adults in this manner is surely significant and probably indicates the "presocial" character of children in Shan thinking. That is, with no recognized social identity of their own yet, they can be "given" one, whereas this is more difficult with adults.

9. Obviously, it has never been the only view. Competing explanations, such as an appeal to genetic differences, have often been invoked to explain a child's temperament, talents, and so on. Nevertheless, the dominant American folk theory remains

one in which children are seen as susceptible to considerable influence by external factors such as parenting style, the home environment, and the quality of the schooling the child receives. Even Kusserow's research (1999), which provides fascinating information on how class differences are reflected in American parents' conceptions of the child's self, nevertheless suggests that American parents of all class backgrounds see their child's success as crucially linked to effective parenting, though they differ on what style of parenting they regard as effective. For more on the historical ascendance of the tabula rasa view in the United States, see Lowry 1997.

10. In the United States, it resulted in what some have called the "cult of motherhood," in which the role of mothering is both elevated and intensified and is culturally available as a form of identity. That is, while an American woman might be able to identify herself as "a mom" or even "a full-time mom," I think it safe to say that, at this historical moment, no Shan woman in Baan Kaung Mu would ever do so.

11. Interestingly, children are never coaxed to respond with the Shan equivalent, *yindii nam nam*.

12. We have already encountered it, for example, in the discourse that accompanies soul-calling rituals, where people speculate about what the soul wants (chapter 2); in discussions about the role of emotional attachment in defining what counts as dangerous and safe deaths (chapter 3); and, in this chapter, in references to "unfulfilled desires" in people's explanations of who has been reborn as whom. In chapter 7, it will appear again in ideas about the causes and cures of mental illness.

13. When asked to describe "a good child," for example, mothers often offered some variant of "A good child is one who is industrious *(kai hetkaan)*, not lazy."

14. Traditionally, adolescent boys received elaborate tattoos that nearly covered their bodies from neck to knees. This "armor" was meant to provide protection in dangerous situations, such as hunting or fighting, as well as make the boys more attractive to young women. Today only the oldest men in the village sport such tattoos. Most boys now opt for a few strategically placed tattoos on the forearms, chest, and back. For more on the history and significance of Shan tattooing practices, see Tannenbaum 1987.

15. Ironically, divorce sometimes does. As one young woman who had recently divorced her husband and returned to her natal household put it, "When you're a *saao*, people are always ordering you about, telling you what to do. But now that I'm divorced, nobody tells me what to do."

16. As in many mainland Southeast Asian groups, Shan women observe a confinement period after giving birth, called lying by the hearth *(yu phai)*. Childbirth is thought to leave a woman's internal organs in need of "drying out," which is accomplished by "roasting" beside a fire of aromatic woods, on which are placed boiling pots of herbal water that produce a health-inducing steam. Although traditionally this confinement period lasted thirty days, it is now much shorter, usually about two weeks. For a description of this custom as it was practiced among the Central Thai, see *Maternity and Its Rituals in Bang Chan*, by Jane Hanks (1963).

17. Many sermons by local monks and popular texts recited by Shan lay readers at *thaum lik* include such stories, some of which appear to be based on or inspired by

the Sigalovada Sutta (Rhys Davids 1965, 168–184), a Buddhist text that offers detailed advice on how to conduct oneself in relation to one's parents, teachers, spouse, children, friends, and servants.

18. The philosopher Tachibana makes a similar point in an early work on Buddhist ethics (1926, 221), where he contrasts Buddhist and Hindu attitudes. "Filial duty as it is taught in Buddhism," he notes, "is not founded upon authority on the part of the parents, as is the case of Brahmanism; but upon gratitude on the part of children for the affection, benevolence, &c., of parents."

19. The money a Shan groom gives to his bride's parents is also said to be given to "pay back the mother's milk."

20. Examples include the relationship between a Buddhist novice monk and his ritual sponsor, which is patterned after the parent-child relationship; the relationship of monks, healers, craftspeople, and performers of all kinds with their apprentices, which is patterned after the teacher-student relationship; and the relationship between local village residents of the same generation, which is patterned after the sibling relationship.

21. The second one born is understood to have been the first one "in" and, hence, is considered the older sibling of the other.

22. I provide additional examples of this sort of tactical deployment of the rhetoric of inequality in chapter 6.

5. Maintaining Health and Well-Being

1. The original Shan script—which uses a modified version of the Burmese alphabet, even though it is in the Tai language family—was written without tone markings. "New Shan," a revised and more explicit rendering of the language that adds tone markings to the old script, is a product of Shan nationalists from the Shan States in Burma (Myanmar). Although it has been introduced to the area by immigrants from the Shan States for some time now, many older people, especially ritual specialists, continue to read and write in what is now called "old Shan." The vast majority of villagers, however, are literate in neither version, having been taught only Central Thai in the state schools.

2. As we saw in chapter 3, such miniature pagodas of sand are made whenever people want to generate a bonus of merit.

3. Many other Shan rituals also use this number. It is considered an auspicious number throughout all Indian and Indian-influenced societies.

4. For example, some pagodas make use of this configuration, being built in an octagon with each side associated with one of the eight days of the week. When people visit such a pagoda, they may pause at the side that represents their birth day and light a candle, say a prayer, leave an offering, and so on.

5. Uncle Samaun explained that it would *"pei wot pei ihang nau to"* (win out over any negative karma she had accumulated and/or anything else [bad] in her body).

6. This notion is similar to the Northern Thai concept of the *lak moeng.* See Lehman 1981.

7. In at least some instances, these beings can be construed as the spirits of the

virtuous dead who are not yet reborn but who are "in a good place," that is, not hungry and wandering the earth.

8. This is a fairly typical place to put it, but some Shan communities have the village guardian spirit shrine inside the village, rather than on the outskirts.

9. When asked about this, women said they didn't like to go, because of the drinking that always accompanies the offerings to the guardian spirit. In some other Shan communities, however, especially where the village guardian spirit shrine is inside the village proper (and the drinking is thus, presumably, more under control), men and women participate more equally.

10. The spirits consume the "essence" of the food, leaving the rest for human consumption. These "leftovers" are considered especially good for people to eat, rather like a tonic, and men often take a portion home for their wives and children.

11. In other years, I have also seen men fire a few shots from their hunting rifles at this point, both as a signal to the village and, they said, "because the guardian spirit likes it."

12. Benevolent spirits are thought to be attracted to sweet-smelling things, and mediums are often said to have fragrant hair.

13. The thirty-two ruling spirits are said to be headquartered in Chiang Dao cave, a site that is east of Mae Hong Son and north of Chiang Mai—approximately equidistant from both cities—where a thirty-third spirit, Pha In (Indra), resides as overlord. This scheme is a reference to the Mount Meru conception of Hindu-Buddhist cosmology (popular throughout Southeast Asia) in which thirty-three gods guard the top of the mountain at the center of the world. In the Shan version of this cosmology, these gods become guardian spirits who are dispatched from their headquarters by Pha In to rule over all the various regions where there are Shan villages. Every Shan village is assigned one of these lords, who provides protection and promotes prosperity in return for respect and deference from his subjects.

14. This conversation was reported in chapter 3.

15. The Shan version of this condition closely resembles the syndrome known as *latah* in Malaysia and Indonesia, where it has been observed and studied most extensively. There is some debate among its researchers as to whether it is strictly a culture-bound syndrome or, rather, a local variant of a more universal human startle reflex. For extended descriptions of the phenomenon and a balanced and helpful discussion of the literature on this topic, see Winzeler 1995 and Simons 1996.

16. Although I will return to the topic of how people deal with stress later, here I would like the reader simply to note how, in this case, the medium managed first to create (or at least elevate) an anxiety and then proposed to be able to alleviate it—for a fee, of course.

6. Marking Maturity

1. From a 1990 brochure for Holiday Inn Mae Hong Son.

2. There is some evidence that this is beginning to change, at least for the local elites. In 1991 a small group of the more well-to-do young couples discreetly gathered for an invitation-only New Year's Eve party, a heretofore unheard-of event.

Later that year, two of the wealthier households threw a joint birthday party for their two children, dressing up the youngsters to look like Thai classical dancers, complete with makeup, and offering a meal and treats to the invited guests.

3. For descriptions of the ordination ceremony in other Buddhist communities, see Keyes 1986; Spiro 1970; Tambiah 1970; and Tannenbaum 1995.

4. The more the better, but there is no rule about a minimum or maximum number. I have never seen a *paui sang long* performed for only one boy, although it is occasionally performed for two (especially in smaller villages). Ordaining ten boys would be considered a big festival. Most probably fall in the range of four to six ordinations. Often, a young man who has previously been ordained as a novice will be recruited by one of the sponsors to ordain again as a monk, thus adding to the number of people involved and increasing the amount of merit earned by the sponsor.

5. In a regular *paui sang long* that is formally planned and publicly announced, the boys' bodyguards are hired with food and drink to protect the ordination candidates against the possibility of kidnapping. The main sponsors of this 1981 ordination, in which the boys were kidnapped already anyway, could not afford to hire such a guard. The group who ended up taking the boys around from house to house could be viewed either as volunteer bodyguards or as proof of what happens (kidnapping) when you fail to hire any. In either case, the net effect is the same.

6. This section of the chapter owes much to Llewelyn-Davies' brilliant analysis (1981) of women's involvement in *moran* rituals among the Maasai. A modified version of this portion of the chapter was presented at the fiftieth annual meeting of the Association of Asian Studies (1998) as part of the panel "In Honor of Jane Richardson Hanks in Her 90th Year: Culture, Gender, and History in Mainland Southeast Asia." The subtitle of this section is a reference to Jane Hanks' well-known monograph, *Maternity and Its Rituals in Bang Chan* (1963), in which Hanks was one of the first to point out that ordination rituals and local conceptions of motherhood were somehow connected. More recently, Barbara Watson Andaya (2002) has suggested that the successful spread of Theravāda Buddhism throughout Southeast Asia during the twelfth and thirteenth centuries may well have been due to its appeal to women, given the prominent place of maternal metaphors in Buddhist texts and the many opportunities it provided for women to engage in merit-making activities, especially the ordination of their sons. For relevant comparisons with the ideology of motherhood in non-Buddhist communities of Southeast Asia, see Hayami (1998) on the Karen of northern Thailand, and Blackwood (1995) on the Minangkabau of Indonesia.

7. The mother is archetypically the boy's sponsor because the boy is, in some sense, more "hers" to give. However, that relationship is primarily due not to a biological connection between mother and son but, rather, to the mother's (presumed) preeminent gift of nurturance. A father or an adoptive parent of either gender could also, theoretically, be in this position.

8. Recently, a few Thai women have been ordained as female monks *(bhikkhuni)*, but such ordinations are still quite controversial. It will no doubt be many years before they are fully accepted and become commonplace, especially in the countryside.

9. Spiro (1970, 235, 239) describes an "ear-boring ceremony" *(natwin)* for the Burmese, in which the sister of the initiate is given an important, if secondary, role in the ordination rites. Shan, however, have no ritual comparable to this for girls.

10. Although it would be something of a sidetrack to go into it here, there is a real sense in which this kind of village-wide labor for the ordination ceremony—which is on a scale much greater than that for any other merit-making ritual that Shan perform—can be said to "reproduce" the village itself by, among other things, creating, maintaining, and reinforcing the underlying social relationships that distinguish a group of people with a shared identity—that is, a genuine community—from a group of households that simply happen to be in geographical proximity to one another. That women are key players in this reproduction of village social relations is significant.

11. In the ordinations I witnessed in Mae Hong Son Province, the intended audience was still predominantly local, although the occasional tourist also attended casually. If this were to change, one wonders whether women would be allowed to remain in charge of the event or whether it would be taken over by men.

12. Comparisons could be made with the Latin American system of religious cargoes, where one gains prestige and stature in the community by having the resources to sponsor a major religious feast and by doing it well.

13. For another study of the nonsymmetrical connotations of titles that include *mae* and *pau* (*phau* in Central Thai), see James Ockey's fascinating study of criminal bosses in Thailand, "God Mothers, Good Mothers, Good Lovers, Godmothers: Gender Images in Thailand" (1999).

14. In Baan Kaung Mu, this is the point at which parents frequently pull their children out of the village school system and begin sending them to school in Mae Hong Son town (Eberhardt 1991). Thus, the ordinations are timed to coincide, roughly, with the end of a boy's time in a strictly village setting.

15. Parents can also "cash in" on their investments in daughters, but this is done in a different way, most commonly in asking for old-age care and assistance.

16. In this, it is similar to many rituals in other societies that accord women/mothers a key role in the passage of their sons/daughters into adulthood, e.g., bar mitzvahs and wedding ceremonies in the United States and *moran* rituals among the Maasai (Llewelyn-Davies 1981).

7. The Ethnopsychology of Aging and Overall Development

1. See chapter 5, note 15, for more on this condition.

2. The five precepts that all Buddhists are supposed to practice are to refrain from killing, from stealing, from sexual misconduct, from lying, and from becoming intoxicated. The eight precepts add three more to this list: to refrain from eating solid food after noon, from entertainments and bodily adornments, and from sleeping on a high bed or mattress.

3. In this sense, it is a much more serious commitment than becoming a monk or a novice, even though one takes on fewer restrictions than do individuals who enter the *sangha*.

4. Sometimes a woman will elect to keep the eight precepts on a daily basis, not

just on *wan sin,* in which case she takes up residence in the monastery compound, shaves her head, and wears white robes. These female ascetics, often referred to as Buddhist nuns, are called *mae khaao,* or "women in white" in Shan (*mae chi* in Thai).

5. This is one reason that some people delay becoming a temple sleeper. People have told me, for example, that they plan to become a temple sleeper "after the house is built" or "after my last child finishes school," both being the sorts of achievements that require extensive outlays of capital and, therefore, considerable energy and commitment from the person who will be financing it.

6. The classic example that people give when describing this third aim is that when a mosquito lands on a temple sleeper's arm during services or while meditating, he or she does not swat it but simply brushes it away.

7. Interestingly, when conducting an earlier research project on Shan children's moral reasoning, I found that children consistently claimed that it was "more wrong" to lie, steal, or commit any other act of wrongdoing when it was directed at an old person (Eberhardt 1984), indicating that the behavior of others (non-elders) is also supposed to be morally more circumspect when they are in the presence of temple sleepers.

8. The average number of houses visited in 1990 was between fifteen and twenty.

9. Besides temple sleepers, there are a few other categories of people who may be paid respect on this night: one's ritual sponsor (*mae kham* or *pau kham*) if one has been ordained, and the village men who hold political office or are otherwise perceived as locally powerful.

10. These are similar to midrashim in the Jewish tradition, that is, texts that elaborate on some element of the scriptures, sometimes in a fanciful or highly creative way.

11. One can imagine that this transformation might also facilitate the transfer of decision-making power in the household from one generation to the next, as the person taking on the status of "old" finds it increasingly unseemly to be actively involved in the more blatantly commercial aspects of running a farm. At the same time, new tensions may be introduced by the older person's increasing desire to spend household funds on merit-making rituals, which may sometimes conflict with the plans of other family members.

12. Southeast Asian specialists and students of religion may find it useful here to recall the idea discussed in chapter 4 of spirits as having a contingent otherness vis-à-vis humans. Several features of Shan beliefs and claims about spirits make it reasonable to extend personhood to these beings, including the following points: (a) Spirits have agency; they perform actions, helpful and unhelpful, that impinge upon the human realm. (b) Spirits have idiosyncratic tastes and preferences (for certain types of food, jewelry, weapons, clothing, and so forth) that cannot be known without prior communication from them; hence, when making offerings to spirits whose tastes and preferences are unknown, one offers many different kinds of things ("the things that we [humans] like") in order to cover all possibilities. (c) Spirits have gender and age, and these attributes are thought to influence the sorts of things they want from the human realm. In the case of the young woman struck by lightning (discussed in chap-

ter 3), for example, multiple explanations of this tragic event were given, but among these was the important "fact" that, at the spot of her death, there was the ghost of a young man who had died before marrying and who was still looking for a wife. (d) At least some spirits are capable of development that entails a change in their tastes and preferences, so that one's offerings to them must be adjusted accordingly. For example, during the time that has elapsed since I first began research in Baan Kaung Mu, the village guardian spirit *(tsao moeng)* has aged and has entered the life stage of "old person." This development was accompanied by several announcements, communicated via spirit mediums, that he no longer wanted offerings of meat and liquor, so that the annual ceremony performed in his honor looks quite different today from that in 1980. To retain an aspect of the ritual that many found highly enjoyable, a bit of sophistry was employed, to the effect that although the *tsao moeng* himself would no longer be partaking of meat and liquor, his less-enlightened entourage of rowdier spirits would still accept such offerings to be placed at their side altars during the ritual.

13. This same "life is suffering" theme sometimes emerges in stereotypical depictions of the life course in which life in the womb is described as cramped, uncomfortable, and smelly; birth is traumatic and painful; infancy is marked by constant frustration of one's desires to eat and sleep; childhood involves continual disciplining and spanking by one's parents; years of hard physical labor "in the sun and the rain" follow childhood; and so on.

14. See, for example, Shelly Errington's description of Bugis-Makassarese notions of soul-stuff in her article "Embodied Sumange' in Luwu" (1983).

Glossary of Shan Words and Phrases

The glossary below provides brief definitions for those Shan words and phrases that are used repeatedly throughout the book. If a word or phrase is used only once, it is defined at that spot in the text and thus does not appear here. I have also included a few Thai and Pali words that have become commonplace "loan words" in Shan speech. Pali is the language of the Theravāda Buddhist scriptures, so most of the words borrowed from this language refer to religious concepts.

Note: The letters *k* and *kh* appear to be in free variation as an initial consonant in contemporary spoken Shan for words that have close cognates with an aspirated *k* in Central Thai. So, for example, the word for "person" in Baan Kaung Mu is often pronounced *khon* (as in Central Thai) rather than *kon* (as in traditional Shan). Similarly, for words that have more than one pronunciation, such as *khwan* and *kwan*, I have listed them below according to the pronunciation I heard most frequently.

akuso demerit, evil deeds (from the Pali *akusala*). See also *kam* and *kuso*.

anattā not-self, the doctrine that human beings have no unchanging, essential self or soul (a Pali word).

anicca impermanence (a Pali word).

ap loen a bathing ritual for newborns performed by village elders approximately one month after a child is born. It is intended to strengthen and provide protection for the infant.

dukkha suffering (a Pali word). See also *tukkha*.

hai bad, naughty (when said of children), troublesome, disruptive, wild, uncontrolled.

haung khwan calling the soul(s). This rite is an important component of many larger Shan ceremonies, including healing rituals and rites of passage.

kaentau a village-wide ceremony in which people "pay respect" *(kaentau)* to the temple sleepers, or village elders. In other contexts, it means "Excuse me" or "I beg your pardon."

kai productively energetic, industrious.

kam volitional actions (from the Pali *kamma;* Sanskrit *karma*). Refers to the overall standing of a person with respect to his or her accumulated merit *(kuso)* and demerit *(akuso),* as well as its implied effects on circumstances in this life and in one's future rebirths.

kamnan   the head of a cluster of villages constituting one "administrative unit" (Thai *tambon*); a regional headman (a Thai word).

kau yau   grown-up (literally, big person).

khamun   sweets, treats (Thai *khanom*).

khi kwaang   a locally recognized startle reflex that closely resembles the syndrome known as *latah* in Malaysia and Indonesia.

khon   a person.

khon long   an adult.

khon naun tsaung   people who sleep at the temple, or temple sleepers; people (usually older) who choose to remain at the temple after services in order to engage in various ascetic practices and who usually opt to spend the night there, returning home the following morning.

khon thao   old people.

khwan   variously translated as "souls," "life force," "vital essence," or "soul-stuff"; sometimes pronounced *"kwan."* See chapter 2, note 7, for more on the meaning of this word.

kotsaa   a merit-making ceremony performed in the eleventh lunar month for those who have died in the previous year.

kuso   merit, goodness (from the Pali *kusala*). Refers to any good deed that affects one's karmic status and overall chances for rebirth. See also *akuso* and *kam*.

lai wot   to get one's due, to suffer karmic retribution. See also *wot*.

lak sang long   to "steal" or "capture" the *sang long;* a version of the ordination festival that entails a mock kidnapping of the boys to be ordained.

latah   See *khi kwaang*.

liang   to take care of, to nurture and provide for; to treat or pay for; to provide a meal for, to feast; to be responsible for and in charge of.

luk aun   a child or children.

luk kham   one's child (son) by ordination. Refers to a boy or young man whom one has sponsored for ordination into the Buddhist *sangha*.

mae khaao   women in white (*mae chi* in Thai); female ascetics, often referred to as Buddhist nuns, who elect to keep the eight Buddhist precepts on a daily basis. They generally take up residence in the monastery compound, shave their heads, and wear white robes.

mae kham   mother-sponsor; a woman who provides the financial and logistical support for the ordination of a boy or young man into the Buddhist *sangha;* a title used to address a woman who has served in this capacity. See also *pau kham*.

mei waan   repairing the village; an annual rite of renewal.

naung   a younger sibling (male or female).

nikpan   enlightenment, ultimate reality (Pali *nibbāna*, Sanskrit *nirvāna*).

pat phi   a healing ritual; literally, to sweep [away] the spirits.

paui sang long   a novice ordination festival. See also *sang long*.

pau kham   father-sponsor; a man who sponsors a boy or young man for ordination into the Buddhist *sangha*. See *mae kham*.

phi   an invisible being, a spirit, a spirit-being.

pi   an older sibling (male or female).

sangha   the community of Buddhist monks and novice monks; the Buddhist monastery.

sang long   boys dressed in elaborate princely costumes as part of an ordination festival *(paui sang long)*.

saraa   a learned person, someone with specialized knowledge (related to
the Pali *ācariya* and the Central Thai *acaan*). Most often used now to
refer to a traditional healer; can also be used as an honorific title in
front of a person's name, much like the English word "doctor."

song phi   to send the spirits away. This rite is an important component in
several larger Shan ceremonies, including healing rituals, certain types
of funerals, and an annual community ritual.

tambon   See *kamman*.

tam khaun   a funeral offering specifically intended to generate merit
(kuso) for the deceased.

thaum lik   a ritual reading of a text (usually quite lengthy) based on Buddhist scriptures.

tok su   a ritual demand for payment; the custom of visiting the home of the
sponsor of a recently completed merit-making ceremony in order to request additional compensation for services rendered during the course of
the ceremony.

tsalei   reader; a layperson skilled in the reading of the Shan script who is
asked to read various sorts of religious manuscripts at merit-making ceremonies, healing sessions, funerals, and so on.

tsao moeng   the village guardian spirit, or "lord of the realm"; a localized
deity associated with a particular village or villages.

tsao paui   the patron or sponsor of a ritual, especially a large one.

tsau waan   "heart of the village"; a simple wooden structure near the center of a Shan village on which offerings are placed.

tukkha   most often used as an exclamation that means "Such suffering!" or
"How miserable!" (from the Pali *dukkha*, suffering); also occurs as part
of a mantra used in meditation practices, along with *anicca* and *anattā*.

wa   the rainy season retreat (Thai *phansaa*), during which Buddhist monks
do not travel but stay continuously in their home monasteries; a period

of heightened religiosity for villagers; sometimes known in English as Buddhist Lent.

waai   a gesture of respect, made by placing the palms of the hands together in a prayerlike fashion and inclining the head slightly. The word can be used as a noun (referring to the gesture) or as a verb (referring to the act of making such a gesture).

wan sin   the Buddhist "Sabbath" days that occur approximately four times a month (on the full moon, the new moon, and the two half-moons in between them); literally, precept day, in reference to the Buddhist duties, or precepts *(sin)*, that one should follow especially closely on that day.

wot   karmic residue; usually refers to a negative situation or event that is understood to be linked to a wrongdoing in the past (possibly derived from the Pali *vipāka,* result or consequence). See also *lai wot.*

yaat nam   a brief rite performed at the conclusion of any act of merit making. It entails pouring a small container of water onto the ground (or into a bowl that will later be emptied onto the ground). The ground acts as "witness" to one's merit making (in memory of a similar incident in the Buddha's life) and to the traditional declaration of one's intention to share the earned merit "with all sentient beings."

yaun   to beg or ask for, to demand.

yaung   mentally disturbed, "crazy."

yu li kin waan   to be healthy and thrive/prosper (literally, to be well and eat with good appetite); a general state of well-being. It is the most frequently offered reason for performing any given rite.

References

Andaya, Barbara Watson. 2002. Localising the universal: Women, motherhood, and the appeal of early Theravāda Buddhism. *Journal of Southeast Asian Studies* 33:1–30.

Ariès, Philippe. 1962. *Centuries of childhood: A social history of family life.* New York: Alfred A. Knopf.

Blackwood, Evelyn. 1995. Senior women, model mothers, and dutiful wives: Managing gender contradictions in a Minangkabau village. In *Bewitching women, pious men: Gender and body politics in Southeast Asia,* ed. Aihwa Ong and Michael Peletz, 124–158. Berkeley and Los Angeles: University of California Press.

Broch, Harald Beyer. 1990. *Growing up agreeably: Bonerate childhood observed.* Honolulu: University of Hawai'i Press.

Collins, Steven. 1982. *Selfless persons: Imagery and thought in Theravāda Buddhism.* Cambridge: Cambridge University Press.

——. 1994. What are Buddhists *doing* when they deny the self? In *Religion and practical reason: New essays in the comparative philosophy of religions,* ed. Frank Reynolds and David Tracy, vol. 4/5 of SUNY Series, Towards a Comparative Philosophy of Religions, 59–86. Albany: State University of New York Press.

——. 1998. *Nirvana and other Buddhist felicities.* Cambridge Studies in Religious Traditions 12. Cambridge: Cambridge University Press.

Cushing, J. N. [1914] 1971. *A Shan and English dictionary.* Westmead, Farnborough, Hants., England: Gregg International.

Davis, Richard B. 1984. *Muang metaphysics: A study of northern Thai myth and ritual.* Bangkok: Pandora.

Demos, John. [1978] 1997. Oedipus and America: Historical perspectives on the reception of psychoanalysis in the United States. In *Inventing the psychological: Toward a cultural history of emotional life in America,* ed. Joel Pfister and Nancy Schnog, 63–78. New Haven, CT: Yale University Press.

Durrenberger, E. Paul, and Nicola Tannenbaum. 1983. A diachronic analysis of Shan cropping systems. *Ethnos* 48:177–194.

Eberhardt, Nancy. 1984. Knowledge, belief, and reasoning: Moral development and culture acquisition in a Shan village of northwest Thailand. PhD diss., University of Illinois at Urbana–Champaign.

——. 1988. Siren song: Negotiating gender images in a rural Shan village. In *Gender, power, and the construction of the moral order,* ed. Nancy Eberhardt, 73–90. Madison: Center for Southeast Asian Studies, University of Wisconsin.

——. 1991. Minorities, education, and social mobility in northern Thailand. Paper presented at the 40th annual meeting of the Midwest Conference on Asian Affairs in Iowa City.

——. 1993. The cultural context of moral reasoning: Lessons from the Shan of northern Thailand. *Crossroads: An Interdisciplinary Journal of Southeast Asian Studies* 8:1–25.

Errington, Shelly. 1983. Embodied *sumange'* in Luwu. *Journal of Asian Studies* 42:545–570.

Freud, Sigmund. [1930] 1961. *Civilization and its discontents.* Trans. and ed. James Strachey. New York: W. W. Norton and Co.

Frye, Marilyn. 1983. *The politics of reality.* Trumansburg, NY: The Crossing Press.

Geertz, Clifford. 1973. Person, time, and conduct in Bali. In *The interpretation of cultures,* 360–411. New York: Basic Books.

——. [1974] 1984. "From the native's point of view": On the nature of anthropological understanding. In *Culture theory: Essays on mind, self, and emotion,* ed. Richard A. Shweder and Robert A. LeVine, 123–136. Cambridge: Cambridge University Press.

Geertz, Hildred. 1959. The vocabulary of emotion: A study of Javanese socialization processes. *Psychiatry* 22:225–237.

Gombrich, Richard. 1971. *Precept and practice: Traditional Buddhism in the rural highlands of Ceylon.* London: Oxford University Press.

Hanks, Jane. 1963. *Maternity and its rituals in Bang Chan.* Data Paper 51. Ithaca, NY: Cornell University Southeast Asia Program.

Hanks, Lucien. 1962. Merit and power in the Thai social order. *American Anthropologist* 64:1247–1261.

Haraway, Donna. 1990. *Simians, cyborgs, and women: The reinvention of nature.* London: Free Association Books.

Hareven, Tamara K. 2000. *Families, history, and social change: Life-course and cross-cultural perspectives.* Boulder, CO: Westview Press.

Harkness, Sara. 1992. Human development in psychological anthropology. In *New directions in psychological anthropology,* ed. Theodore Schwartz, Geoffrey M. White, and Catherine A. Lutz, 102–122. Cambridge: Cambridge University Press.

Harkness, Sara, and Charles M. Super, eds. 1996. *Parents' cultural belief systems: Their origins, expressions, and consequences.* New York: Guilford Press.

Hayami, Yoko. 1998. Motherhood redefined: Women's choices on family rituals and reproduction in the peripheries of Thailand. *Sojourn* 13:242–262.

Heald, Suzette, and Ariane Deluz, eds. 1994. *Anthropology and psychoanalysis: An encounter through culture.* London: Routledge.

Hollan, Douglas W., and Jane C. Wellenkamp. 1996. *The thread of life: Toraja reflections on the life cycle.* Honolulu: University of Hawai'i Press.

Holland, Dorothy, William Lachicotte Jr., Debra Skinner, and Carole Cain. 1998. *Identity and agency in cultural worlds.* Cambridge, MA: Harvard University Press.

Horney, Karen. 1945. *Our inner conflicts: A constructive theory of neurosis.* New York: W. W. Norton.

James, William. [1902] 1985. *The varieties of religious experience.* Cambridge, MA: Harvard University Press.

Kaminer, Wendy. 1992. *I'm dysfunctional, you're dysfunctional: The recovery movement and other self-help fashions.* Reading, MA: Addison-Wesley.

Keeler, Ward. 1983. Shame and stagefright in Java. *Ethos* 11:152–165.

——. 1987. *Javanese shadow plays, Javanese selves.* Princeton, NJ: Princeton University Press.

Kerns, Virginia, and Judith K. Brown. 1992. *In her prime: New views of middle-aged women.* 2nd ed. Urbana: University of Illinois Press.

Keyes, Charles. 1984. Mother or mistress but never a monk: Buddhist notions of female gender in rural Thailand. *American Ethnologist* 11:223–241.

——. 1986. Ambiguous gender: Male initiation in a northern Thai Buddhist society. In *Gender and religion: On the complexity of symbols,* ed. Caroline Bynum, Stevan Harrell, and Paula Richman, 66–96. Boston: Beacon Press.

——. 1987. *Thailand: Buddhist kingdom as modern nation-state.* Boulder, CO: Westview Press.

Kirsch, A. Thomas. 1982. Buddhism, sex roles, and the Thai economy. In *Women of Southeast Asia,* ed. Penny Van Esterik, 16–44. DeKalb: Center for Southeast Asian Studies, Northern Illinois University.

——. 1985. Text and context: Buddhist sex roles/culture of gender revisited. *American Ethnologist* 12:302–320.

Kondo, Dorinne K. 1990. *Crafting selves: Power, gender, and discourses of identity in a Japanese workplace.* Chicago: University of Chicago Press.

Kusserow, Adrie S. 1999. De-homogenizing American individualism: Socializing hard and soft individualism in Manhattan and Queens. *Ethos* 27:210–234.

Laidlaw, James. 1995. *Riches and renunciation: Religion, economy, and society among the Jains.* Oxford: Clarendon Press.

Lamb, Sarah. 2000. *White saris and sweet mangoes: Aging, gender, and body in north India.* Berkeley and Los Angeles: University of California Press.

Leach, Edmund R. 1954. *Political systems of highland Burma.* Boston: Beacon Press.

Lehman, F. K. 1972. Doctrine, practice, and belief in Theravāda Buddhism. *Journal of Asian Studies* 31:373–380.

——. 1981. On the vocabulary and semantics of "field" in Theravāda Buddhist society. In *Essays on Burma,* ed. J. P. Ferguson. Leiden: E. J. Brill.

Llewelyn-Davies, Melissa. 1981. Women, warriors, and patriarchs. In *Sexual meanings: The cultural construction of gender and sexuality,* ed. Sherry B. Ortner and Harriet Whitehead, 330–358. Cambridge: Cambridge University Press.

Lowry, Richard. 1997. Domestic interiors: Boyhood nostalgia and affective labor in the Gilded Age. In *Inventing the psychological: Toward a cultural history of emotional life in America,* ed. Joel Pfister and Nancy Schnog, 110–130. New Haven, CT: Yale University Press.

Lubin, David. 1997. Modern psychological selfhood in the art of Thomas Eakins. In *In-*

venting the psychological: Toward a cultural history of emotional life in America, ed. Joel Pfister and Nancy Schnog, 133–166. New Haven, CT: Yale University Press.

Lutz, Catherine A. 1985. Ethnopsychology compared to what? Explaining behavior and consciousness among the Ifaluk. In *Person, self, and experience: Exploring Pacific ethnopsychologies*, ed. Geoffrey M. White and John Kirkpatrick, 35–79. Berkeley and Los Angeles: University of California Press.

———. 1988. *Unnatural emotions: Everyday sentiments on a Micronesian atoll and their challenge to Western theory*. Chicago: University of Chicago Press.

Lutz, Catherine A., and Lila Abu-Lughod, eds. 1990. *Language and the politics of emotion*. Cambridge: Cambridge University Press.

Mageo, Jeannette Marie. 1998. *Theorizing self in Samoa: Emotions, genders, and sexualities*. Ann Arbor: University of Michigan Press.

Mills, Mary Beth. 1999. *Thai women in the global labor force: Consuming desires, contested selves*. New Brunswick, NJ: Rutgers University Press.

Mulder, Niels. 1979. *Everyday life in Thailand: An interpretation*. Bangkok: Editions Duang Kamol.

Murray, D. W. 1993. What is the Western concept of the self? On forgetting David Hume. *Ethos* 21:3–23.

Obeyesekere, Gananath. 1968. Theodicy, sin, and salvation in a sociology of Buddhism. In *Dialectic in practical religion*, ed. E. R. Leach, 7–40. Cambridge: Cambridge University Press.

———. 1990. *The work of culture: Symbolic transformations in psychoanalysis and anthropology*. Chicago: University of Chicago Press.

Ockey, James. 1999. God mothers, good mothers, good lovers, godmothers: Gender images in Thailand. *Journal of Asian Studies* 58:1033–1058.

O'Connor, Richard A. 1990. Siamese Tai in Tai context: The impact of a ruling center. *Crossroads: An Interdisciplinary Journal of Southeast Asian Studies* 5:1–21.

Pfister, Joel. 1997. Glamorizing the psychological: The politics of the performances of modern psychological identities. In *Inventing the psychological: Toward a cultural history of emotional life in America*, ed. Joel Pfister and Nancy Schnog, 167–213. New Haven, CT: Yale University Press.

Pfister, Joel, and Nancy Schnog, eds. 1997. *Inventing the psychological: Toward a cultural history of emotional life in America*. New Haven, CT: Yale University Press.

Plath, David W. 1980. *Long engagements: Maturity in modern Japan*. Stanford, CA: Stanford University Press.

Rahula, Walpola. 1974. *What the Buddha taught*. Rev. ed. New York: Grove Press.

Reynolds, Frank. 1978. The holy emerald jewel: Some aspects of Buddhist symbolism and political legitimation in Thailand and Laos. In *Religion and legitimation of power in Thailand, Laos, and Burma*, ed. Bardwell Smith, 175–193. Chambersburg, PA: Anima Press.

Rhys Davids, T. W., ed. 1965. *Sacred books of the Buddhists*. Vol. 4, *Dialogues of the Buddha, Part 3*. London: Pali Text Society.

Rosaldo, Michelle. 1980. *Knowledge and passion: Ilongot notions of self and social life*. Cambridge: Cambridge University Press.

Sartre, Jean-Paul. [1945] 1989. *No Exit and three other plays.* New York: Vintage International.

Schnog, Nancy. 1997. On inventing the psychological. In *Inventing the psychological: Toward a cultural history of emotional life in America,* ed. Joel Pfister and Nancy Schnog, 3–16. New Haven, CT: Yale University Press.

Shweder, Richard A. 1990. Cultural psychology—What is it? In *Cultural psychology: Essays on comparative human development,* ed. James W. Stigler, Richard A. Shweder, and Gilbert Herdt, 1–43. Cambridge: Cambridge University Press.

———, ed. 1998. *Welcome to middle age! (and other cultural fictions).* Chicago: University of Chicago Press.

Shweder, Richard A., and Edmund J. Bourne. 1984. Does the concept of the person vary cross-culturally? In *Culture theory: Essays on mind, self, and emotion,* ed. Richard A. Shweder and Robert A. LeVine, 158–199. Cambridge: Cambridge University Press.

Shweder, Richard A., and Robert A. LeVine, eds. 1984. *Culture theory: Essays on mind, self, and emotion.* Cambridge: Cambridge University Press.

Simons, Ronald C. 1996. *Boo! Culture, experience, and the startle reflex.* New York: Oxford University Press.

Spiro, Melford E. 1967. *Burmese supernaturalism: A study in the explanation and reduction of suffering.* Englewood Cliffs, NJ: Prentice-Hall.

———. 1970. *Buddhism and society: A great tradition and its Burmese vicissitudes.* New York: Harper and Row.

———. 1986. Cultural relativism and the future of anthropology. *Cultural Anthropology* 1:259–286.

Symonds, Patricia V. 2004. *Calling in the soul: Gender and the cycle of life in a Hmong village.* Seattle: University of Washington Press.

Tachibana, S. 1926. *The ethics of Buddhism.* London: Oxford University Press.

Tambiah, Stanley. 1970. *Buddhism and the spirit cults in north-east Thailand.* Cambridge: Cambridge University Press.

———. 1976. *World conqueror, world renouncer: A study of Buddhism and polity in Thailand against a historical background.* Cambridge: Cambridge University Press.

Tannenbaum, Nicola. 1982. Agricultural decision making among the Shan of Maehongson Province, northwestern Thailand. PhD diss., University of Iowa.

———. 1987. Tattoos: Invulnerability and power in Shan cosmology. *American Ethnologist* 14:693–711.

———. 1989. Power and its Shan transformation. In *Ritual, power, and economy: Upland-lowland contrasts in mainland Southeast Asia,* ed. Susan Russell, 67–88. Center for Southeast Asian Studies Occasional Paper Series, no. 14. DeKalb: Northern Illinois University Press.

———. 1990. The heart of the village: Constituent structures of Shan communities. *Crossroads: An Interdisciplinary Journal of Southeast Asian Studies* 5:23–41.

———. 1995. *Who can compete against the world? Power-protection and Buddhism in Shan worldview.* Ann Arbor, MI: Association for Asian Studies.

Taylor, Charles. 1989. *Sources of the self.* Cambridge, MA: Harvard University Press.

Tufte, Virginia, and Barbara Myerhoff, eds. 1979. *Changing images of the family.* New Haven, CT: Yale University Press.

Turkle, Sherry. 1984. *The second self: Computers and the human spirit.* New York: Simon and Schuster.

Van Esterik, Penny, ed. 1982. *Women of Southeast Asia.* DeKalb: Center for Southeast Asian Studies, Northern Illinois University.

———. 1996. Nurturance and reciprocity in Thai studies. In *State power and culture in Thailand,* ed. E. Paul Durrenberger, 22–46. New Haven, CT: Yale University Southeast Asia Studies.

Weisner, Thomas S., and Lucinda P. Bernheimer. 1998. Children of the 1960s at midlife: Generational identity and the family adaptive project. In *Welcome to middle age! (and other cultural fictions),* ed. Richard A. Shweder, 211–257. Chicago: University of Chicago Press.

White, Geoffrey M. 1992. Ethnopsychology. In *New directions in psychological anthropology,* ed. Theodore Schwartz, Geoffrey M. White, and Catherine A. Lutz, 21–46. Cambridge: Cambridge University Press.

White, Geoffrey M., and John Kirkpatrick, eds. 1985. *Person, self, and experience: Exploring Pacific ethnopsychologies.* Berkeley and Los Angeles: University of California Press.

Wijeyewardene, Gehan. 1986. *Place and emotion in northern Thai ritual behaviour.* Bangkok: Pandora.

Wikan, Unni. 1991. *Managing turbulent hearts: A Balinese formula for living.* Chicago: University of Chicago Press.

Winzeler, Robert. 1995. *Latah in Southeast Asia: The history and ethnography of a culture-bound syndrome.* Cambridge: Cambridge University Press.

Zaretsky, Eli. 1976. *Capitalism, the family, and personal life.* New York: Harper Colophon.

Index

Page numbers in **boldface** refer to maps, photographs, and illustrations.

About the Author

NANCY EBERHARDT received her Ph.D. in anthropology from the University of Illinois at Urbana-Champaign and is currently professor of anthropology at Knox College. Her research interests include religion, psychological anthropology, subjectivity and modernity, and social inequality.

Production Notes for Eberhardt/*Imagining the Course of Life*

Cover design by Santos Barbasa Jr.

Text design by University of Hawai'i Press production staff
in Cordelia with display in Marigold and Stone Sans.

Composition by inari information services.

Printing and binding by The Maple-Vail Book Manufacturing Group.

Printed on 60 lb. Text White Opaque, 426 ppi.